Linda's deep desire to b for all who believe that the Lord is looking for a person to stand in the gap, Linda and Mike, and their team of intercessors, are a corporate voice asking for mercy. Theirs is a remarkable journey.

—Francis Frangipane
Pastor and author

[We] believe this book will truly be a tool in the hands of Iowa intercessors, showing us how and what to pray for our state. Linda has left spiritual footprints by which the intercessor can walk (in prayer) county by county, calling forth the blessings and purposes of God. This is a true gift to Iowa intercessors. Thank you Linda, every state needs a book like this."

—Teri and Jim Kohl
Heartland House of Prayer
Council Bluffs, Iowa

While living in such an urgent hour in the Kingdom of God, it's imperative that strategically led journeys occur all across our nation. It's not that the Lord has withheld His will for our states and cities, a Divine permission described in Colossians 1:9-10. But few are listening for the leadership of the Lord beyond the scope of their own needs. Even fewer dare take action in kingdom adventures, and from those, only a rare commodity of voices will decree a thing so it will be established. Linda has followed our savior through many journeys. She challenges the body of Christ to move beyond the basic revelatory elements and launch into fantastic and challenging adventures with our Lord and Savior. May your Kingdom come and your will be done, Lord.

—Ric Lumbard
Senior Pastor
WFM Missions Base
Marion, IA

It's been said that the highest expression of worship is obedience. Linda and Mike Schreurs are worshippers extraordinaire! I have been witness to their selfless and sacrificial obedience to the Word of the Lord. They are true spiritual parents with apostolic authority in our state of Iowa. Linda's words carry the breath of the Spirit of God. I want readers of this book to know the words contained in these pages have been written with the pen of the Lord. The ink is the oil of the Spirit mixed with Linda's prayerful tears and first hand experiences which carry the authority of Heaven. This book should be read prayerfully allowing the Holy Spirit to instruct the reader at will. Thank you, Linda, for so faithfully watching over the Word of the Lord to Iowa. Thank you for obeying the command to go to every county and decree. Thank you for your worshipful act of obedience that is shifting the spiritual environment over our state. May the Kingdom of God break in and King Jesus be enthroned!

—Randy Bixby
Director
Kingdom House of Prayer
Des Moines, IA

WORDS
APTLY
SPOKEN

A Prophetic Prayer Journey
to Iowa's 99 County Courthouses.

Discover your divine destiny.

Linda Schreurs

Cover design/Photography: Patrick John Green
Manuscript preparation: Patrick John Green

"IOWA" Photograph, pg. 27: Sarah Green
Photograph on back cover: Ilze Kalnins

All other photographs: Linda and Michael Schreurs

First Edition

08 09 10 11 12 — 987654321

www.xulonpress.com

dedication

This book is lovingly dedicated to all those
who have gone before, alongside and behind us,
in intercession.

*"So then neither the one who plants nor the one who
waters is anything, but God who causes the growth."*

—1 Corinthians 3:7

contents

Alphabetical Listing of Counties by Page xi

Prologue 1

1 Divine travels. Holy tracks! 5

2 What does God have to say? (prophecies) 13

3 Launching of the Prophetic Prayer Journey to
  Iowa's 99 County Court Houses 29

4 Plymouth, Sioux, Lyon, Osceola, Dickinson, Clay 39

5 Humboldt, Palo Alto, Pocahontas, Emmet, Kossuth,
  Calhoun, Webster 55

6 Carroll, Sac, Buena Vista, Cherokee, O'Brien, Ida 77

7 Shelby, Crawford, Monona, Woodbury, Harrison 97

8 Hamilton, Wright, Hancock, Winnebago, Worth 113

9 Cerro Gordo, Franklin, Hardin, Story 129

10 Floyd, Chickasaw, Allamakee, Howard, Mitchell,
   Winneshiek 141

11 Boone, Greene 155

12 Marshall, Grundy, Butler 161

13 Jasper, Tama, Benton, Iowa, Poweshiek 169

14 Dallas, Audubon, Guthrie 185

15 Black Hawk, Bremer, Fayette, Clayton, Buchanan,
   Delaware 195

16 Mahaska, Keokuk, Washington, Johnson 211

17 Linn, Jones, Dubuque, Jackson, Clinton, Cedar 225

18 Scott, Muscatine, Louisa, Des Moines, Lee, Henry 243

19 Davis, Van Buren, Jefferson, Appanoose, Monroe,
    Wapello 259

20 Marion, Lucas, Wayne, Decatur, Clarke, Warren 273

21 Madison, Adair, Union, Adams, Taylor, Ringgold 295

22 Pottawattamie, Cass, Mills, Fremont, Page,
    Montgomery 313

23 Polk County and the State Capitol 335

24 Iowa Supreme Court 349

counties by alphabet, county seat

Adair, Greenfield 299
Adams, Corning 305
Allamakee, Waukon 151
Appanoose, Centerville 267
Audubon, Audubon 191
Benton, Vinton 175
Black Hawk, Waterloo 196
Boone, Boone 156
Bremer, Waverly 198
Buchanan, Independence 207
Buena Vista, Storm Lake 85
Butler, Allison 167
Calhoun, Rockwell City 73
Carroll, Carroll 79
Cass, Atlantic 329
Cedar, Tipton 240
Cerro Gordo, Mason City 130
Cherokee, Cherokee 88
Chickasaw, New Hampton 153
Clarke, Osceola 287
Clay, Spencer 53
Clayton, Elkader 202
Clinton, Clinton 238
Crawford, Denison 100
Dallas, Adel 186
Davis, Bloomfield 264
Decatur, Leon 285
Delaware, Manchester 205
Des Moines, Burlington 251
Dickinson, Spirit Lake 51
Dubuque, Dubuque 233
Emmet, Estherville 67
Fayette, West Union 200

Floyd, Charles City 142
Franklin, Hampton 133
Fremont, Sidney 320
Greene, Jefferson 159
Grundy, Grundy Center 165
Guthrie, Guthrie Center 189
Hamilton, Webster City 113
Hancock, Garner 120
Hardin, Eldora 135
Harrison, Logan 109
Henry, Mt. Pleasant 256
Howard, Cresco 145
Humboldt, Dakota City 59
Ida, Ida Grove 93
Iowa, Marengo 177
Jackson, Maquoketa 236
Jasper, Newton 171
Jefferson, Fairfield 260
Johnson, Iowa City 220
Jones, Anamosa 230
Keokuk, Sigourney 215
Kossuth, Algona 62
Lee, Ft. Madison 254
Linn, Cedar Rapids 228
Louisa, Wapello 249
Lucas, Chariton 277
Lyon, Rock Rapids 46
Madison, Winterset 296
Mahaska, Oskaloosa 212
Marion, Knoxville 274
Marshall, Marshalltown 162
Mills, Glenwood 317
Mitchell, Osage 144
Monona, Onawa 103
Monroe, Albia 268
Montgomery, Red Oak 327

Muscatine, Muscatine 246
O'Brien, Primghar 91
Osceola, Sibley 49
Page, Clarinda 324
Palo Alto, Emmetsburg 65
Plymouth, Le Mars 42
Pocahontas, Pocahontas 70
Polk, Des Moines 335
Pottawattamie, Council Bluffs 314
Poweshiek, Montezuma 180
Ringgold, Mount Ayr 309
Sac, Sac City 81
Scott, Davenport 244
Shelby, Harlan 98
Sioux, Orange City 44
Story, Nevada 137
Tama, Toledo 173
Taylor, Bedford 306
Union, Creston 302
Van Buren, Keosauqua 262
Wapello, Ottumwa 270
Warren, Indianola 290
Washington, Washington 218
Wayne, Corydon 281
Webster, Ft. Dodge 56
Winnebago, Forest City 122
Winneshiek, Decorah 148
Woodbury, Sioux City 106
Worth, Northwood 125
Wright, Clarion 117

prologue

Words weigh in with the heart like honey or bitter herbs. They form our world with light or darkness, with joy, or unspeakable pain. By any language, words can heal or destroy. Spoken phrases pierce one's soul for better or worse. A profound one is penned in Proverbs 25:11, *"A word aptly spoken is like apples of gold in settings of silver."* Priceless!

The longing of every human heart is for their destiny to be fulfilled. It's found in *God's Word*, the Holy Scriptures. Human dignity and salvation are born out of knowing the Lord Jesus Christ, the Word made flesh (John 1). He dwelt amongst us, died for us, rose from the dead and is coming again!

We've entered a time where the weight of words must be calculated cautiously, especially to such venues as today's internet communications. Death and life are in the power of the tongue according to Proverbs 18:21. It creates destiny!

Taking a cue from such great men of God as Chuck Pierce and Dutch Sheets, we felt the call of God to follow their path of *decreeing words* by the power of the Holy Spirit, to bring forth healing, deliverance, restoration and transformation to our area. They published a book after their 50 state prophetic prayer tour called: *Releasing the Prophetic Destiny of a Nation*, (Published by Destiny Image). Based on a similar concept, we embarked on a prophetic prayer journey to Iowa's 99 county courthouses. These are places of governmental decrees on many issues such as land

1

settlements, divorces, child custody cases, criminal justice, etc. They are strategic areas to declare righteousness, justice and mercy. It's the perfect place to decree God's laws to prevail where many times men's laws fail to bring forth these godly values.

Uncertainty and corruption can seep into these governmental entities causing much heartache in people's lives. Weighty decisions flow from the courthouse into neighboring towns and communities within that county.

In these places of earthly government, God seeks to establish His divine government that His kingdom would prevail in truth, righteousness, power and purity of purpose. Divine destiny!

SEED

Iowa is a SEED state, both in the physical and in the spiritual realm. It's one of the top producers of grain, corn, soybean and other farm products. It has been called the 'Bread Basket' of the nation. If its farmers are blessed, the nation is also blessed.

Likewise, with its first in the nation Caucus status, it is also a *gate* for the journey to the highest office in the land, that of President of the United States of America. Iowa is extremely strategic. It's also recognized for its energy renewable fuels and major insurance and financial services. It's noteworthy that the two aforementioned prophets of God have prophesied that this state's prayers would affect Iraq. Within several months of that prophecy, Saddam Hussein was captured. That's far reaching!

Iowa's position in the heartland of America denotes the heartbeat, the pulse if you will, of this nation as to the life and prosperity of its people. What generates here economically, politically, and spiritually, flows out into every state and nearly every nation. It is crucial that Iowa has a firm foundation in the truths of the Lord that affect our lives "under God, indivisible, with liberty and justice for all." Let us retain these sacred and holy truths so this country can once again be all God has called it to be.

PASS THE BATON

Declarations made in honor of the Most High God are having a rippling effect not only in Iowa but other states and beyond. This work is the catalyst for other states to pick up the baton. Let them pass it on, until God's truth, righteousness, justice and mercy fall upon the land like sweet, refreshing rain drenching a dry and weary land.

This book is not just about Iowa. It's about *all* the states of America. Every state is a jewel in the Lord's eyes and He is waiting to release their divine destiny (Zech. 9:16)! It's about individual states picking up this prophetic prayer mantle, declaring the authority of God to rule in their midst. This book is about restoring all our religious freedoms which have been fast slipping away. This book is about bringing forth, in every part of this country, an epic revival of unprecedented measure!

The Lord told us to "spread the Bread of His Presence." We cannot afford to see Amos 8:11 come into this beautiful land of America: *"Behold, days are coming declares the Lord God, when I will send a famine on the land, not a famine of bread or a thirst for water. But rather for hearing the words of the Lord."* Let us be on alert! Let the people hear the word of the Lord! May all the states begin making prayerful, prophetic proclamations! It will forever change the spiritual landscape of America for our generation and those who follow.

Our prophetic prayer journey across Iowa wonderfully highlighted Proverbs 25:11....

"A word aptly spoken is like apples of gold in settings of silver."

Let us begin to frame our destiny with words aptly spoken by powerful prophetic declarations that will change history!

❦ one ❦

DIVINE TRAVELS. HOLY TRACKS!

"Arise and walk about the land through its length and breadth; for I will give it to you." —Genesis 13:17

oly Tracks! I didn't feel like Superman! But I knew the task God was assigning was bigger than anything I'd previously done. At the time, I didn't feel anything special other than I knew I was being sent out on a journey where holy tracks would remain by the grace of God. This wasn't about "tracts" where people drop off leaflets. That would have been far easier. This one involved physically traveling to every county courthouse in the state of Iowa, all 99 of them! The Lord wonderfully termed it *"divine travels"* where the power of His Presence would leave, as it were, a spiritual foot print - *holy tracks!* Like designs on freshly fallen snow, the Most High God would manifest His power in fresh, vibrant ways. I felt like Joshua. *"Every place on which the sole of your foot treads, I have given it to you, just as I spoke to Moses."* (Josh. 1:3).

The Lord never ceases to amaze me with His creativity in speaking to us. On July 8th, 2005 while in prayer, my gaze fell on a tiny and rather insignificant Hallmark gift box that was lying near my desk. It's in the shape of an envelope like one you'd send in the mail. Suddenly, it held prophetic meaning! As I held it in my hand, I heard the Lord speaking to my heart. He told me I was

5

being *sent* to the places where man's government and decrees are made at the county courthouses. I was to make certain declarations, proclamations and decrees according to His Word, by the power and authority of His Name. It was an Esther call to intercede for people right in my own corner of the world. Precious ones, the mission field is closer than we think.

A profound statement

Holding that little ceramic box, I knew 1 Corinthians 15:46 had been initiated. It's a profound statement. Have you ever pondered it? It says, *"However, the spiritual is not first, but the natural; then the spiritual."* Look around you. Stop. Listen. Observe. Ponder. Pray. God may be showing you in the natural what your next steps are toward your divine destiny. How wonderful can that be?!

The unusual assignment God gave me to travel to all 99 Iowa county courthouses, making prophetic declarations in His Name, was a physical one which held enormous spiritual impact. He uniquely designed it as a precursor for spiritual destinies to be called forth and His perfect will to be unfolded. But we must realize God has a great destiny for each one of us. Do you know yours?

I have often felt like a toddler when taking my first spiritual steps into a divine directive given by Abba Father. I hear His voice urging me onward, "You can do all things through Christ who strengthens you. I will be with you to the very ends of the earth." Sometimes I may sway back and forth wondering if I've heard correctly because of the huge step of faith required. But we all need to remind ourselves that if the assignment is bigger than our own capabilities, it must be of God, otherwise we wouldn't need Him! Let us learn not to waver in our obedience to Him. How glorious it is when we catch the wave of the Holy Spirit ascending higher than we ever imagined.

Again!

The Lord again spoke to me regarding this divine assignment a few months later in 2005 on September 24th giving me 2 Chronicles 16:9-10:

> "And they taught in Judah, having the book of the law of the Lord with them; and they went throughout all the cities of Judah and taught among the people. Now the dread of the Lord was on all the kingdoms of the lands which were around Judah, so that they did not make war against Jehoshaphat."

The very next day, on September 25th, He again reiterates the calling of those "divine travels and holy tracks," this time taking me to 2 Chronicles 30: 9-12:

> "For if you return to the Lord, your brothers and your sons will find compassion before those who led them captive, and will return to this land. For the Lord your God is gracious and compassionate, and will not turn His face away from you if you return to Him. So the couriers passed from city to city through the country of Ephraim and Manasseh, and as far as Zebulun, but they laughed them to scorn, and mocked them. Nevertheless some men of Asher, Manasseh and Zebulun humbled themselves and came to Jerusalem. The hand of God

7

was also on Judah to give them one heart to do what the king and the princes commanded by the word of the Lord."

Still, I hesitated, because I had not shared any of this with my husband for fear of what he might think. I continued to pray about it asking for more confirmations. Oh you of little faith, Linda! "I believe, Lord, just help my unbelief!" (Paraphrased from Mark 9:24).

Sail into your divine destiny!

When the Lord has a plan, He develops the man or woman He's going to use to accomplish His purposes. He develops their faith, obedience and trust in Him into ever deepening levels. The servant or messenger whom the Lord chooses becomes quite willing to surrender to God's desires and to His strange and oftentimes, peculiar ways that may take them out of their comfort zone. These blessed servants of the Most High God sail into their divine destinies out of deep love and intimacy with their Beloved Savior, Jesus. These are the ones who are brimming with holy confidence knowing that He who began a good work in them will be faithful to complete it (Phil. 1:6). They become unshakeable and fearless in the face of any and all obstacles. Are you and I like that? Can we submit enough of ourselves to God that He might be able to use us in ways we never dreamed? This is the hour we must now do so.

As I continued to ask the Lord for more confirmations for this prayer journey through the state of Iowa, He began to inundate me. I couldn't share them all for there are too many. However, some are worth incorporating here that your faith may be built up and to know whomever the Lord calls, He equips. Think of the directives He's given you. He is now blessing you for that very calling!

Fields

On October 18th, 2005, while sitting at my computer working on one of our monthly Intimacy With God (IWG) Journals, I felt the Presence of the Lord so strong that I simply had to stop and *listen.* This happens to me quite often where I will be in the middle of something and suddenly *He will come!* It's as though He takes my breath away and there's a humbling, a holy wonder that sweeps over my soul. I'm simply awestruck by the power and glory of His Presence. It's all-consuming! What splendor! Do you know Him this way? I pray that you do.

On that beautiful, warm autumn day in October as I listened intently, the Lord told me to turn my computer off, grab my camera, and go outside of town to take pictures of the fields of harvest. I quickly gathered a few things and was out the door, finding myself pondering a scripture He'd given me 10 years earlier on the first day of my first 40 day fast, 2 Samuel 12:16-17a: *"Even now take your stand and see this great thing which the Lord will do before your eyes. Is it not the wheat harvest today?"* I didn't have much grid for that particular verse at the time, but kept it hidden in my heart. It's become much clearer since then.

Autumn Harvest Fields in Iowa

It surely doesn't take a rocket scientist to see the Lord wanted me to physically document the fields being white unto harvest

(John 4:34-38). Again, it's the natural coming before the spiritual. Many souls are about to come into the kingdom of God. The 500,000 new souls for this area the Lord showed me on August 4th, 1996 during a dramatic vision and encounter with Him, has become a consuming fire of desire in my life. He confirmed this from Joel 3:14, *"Multitudes, multitudes in the valley of decision. For the day of the Lord is near in the valley of decision."* It will happen! But it will not be by man's feeble efforts, but by the power of the Holy Spirit not unlike a fresh Pentecost.

Other assignments

The Lord has a marvelous way of putting arrows in front of us pointing the way forward. I believe our spiritual walk, or spiritual "tracks" are gloriously exciting. I see this in my own life through many prayer assignments that have led up to the Prophetic Prayer Journey to Iowa's 99 Counties.

One of those assignments was when a group of us meeting in our home, prayed through the entire residential listing of names in the phone book one year. Likewise we were also called to begin a *Prayer Patrol* in the inner city of Des Moines where each Saturday, rain, shine, cold or snow, we were praying with people we met on the streets. Time and time again we saw the power of God as His Presence would overtake us. Busy street corners became strangely calm as we prayed. He blanketed us with such a powerful anointing that perfect strangers would weep as we prayed with them.

We've held *Baby Showers for the Lord* where we prayed for "new babes or new births" in Christ, but also taking baby gifts with scriptures attached, wrapped in love, and taken to those in need in our city. *Bridal Showers for the Lord* were also held according to the mandate of scripture "to prepare the way of the Lord," making way for the return of our heavenly Bridegroom. We entered into repentance as well as praying for Israel where Jesus' feet will once again touch this earth. We prayed over the prophecies given for our area and concluded with intimate Holy Communion. Many people also came dressed in white. What fun!

We have hosted events such as our Statewide Worship War Rooms, where all quadrants of the state come together in strategic intercession and high praises of worship and adoration of King Jesus! Our Roar of War Conference with Jill Austin and Stacey Campbell certainly shifted the spiritual atmosphere over this state along with our Eye of God Conference with Shampa Rice.

I remember the spring day in May of 2002 when I left for another town in eastern Iowa where I was to spend 24 hours on a prayer hermitage. I usually go on these kinds of retreats several times a year. However, little did I know the Lord had other plans. I'd no sooner arrived, when fifteen minutes later the Lord told me to go back home! Astounded, I asked, "Why?" He said He'd had taken me there that I might turn around, and on my way back I was to pray at each Rest Stop along the interstate. I was to anoint those places of rest. It took me many more hours to return home! But it was a joy ride with the Lord! He showed me Living Waters from His Throne Room flowing north, south, east and west like a mighty rushing river and that weary travelers on the road of life would come to the state of Iowa to be refreshed. I was to declare Isaiah 35:8; Isaiah 40:3; Isaiah 57:14; Isaiah 62:10. All of this aligned with the words in Luke 14:23: *"Go out into the highways and along the hedges and compel them to come in, that my house may be filled."* We were already doing that on Prayer Patrol. Yet, somehow I knew that portion of our ministry would expand. It did —to all 99 Iowa counties.

Finally

All these and more prepared us for the assignment of the Prophetic Prayer Journey across the state of Iowa.

Look into your own life. What precursor events have been preparing you for "a time such as this?" The Lord wants each one to pick up the spiritual baton He's passed them and run the race with respect, dignity, holiness, honor and power to advance His kingdom.

So what is *your* divine destiny? Is it to write heavenly anointed songs? Is it to open up a new business walking in the anointing of Joseph? Is it to make inspiring and wholesome movies in Hollywood? Is it to pray and serve in some foreign bush country, or make prophetic proclamations in Washington, D.C.? Whatever it is, go! But remember the words of Moses, *"If Thy Presence does not go with us, do not lead us up from here"* (Exod. 33:15). Go under the anointing of God and under His power not your own.

We weren't the first to go across this state praying for each county or each quadrant. Women's Aglow and the USGAPN group have gone before us and I'm sure others will follow. The important thing is, let's pray! Let's take our Promised Land! We are more than conquerors through Christ Jesus. (Heb. 11 and 12; Rom.8:37).

✤ two ✤

WHAT DOES GOD HAVE TO SAY?

"Surely the Lord God does nothing unless He reveals
His secret counsel to His servants the prophets. A lion
has roared! Who will not fear? The Lord has spoken!
Who can but prophesy?" —Amos 3:7-8

One thing for sure, God is into multiplication and addition. Remember how He multiplied the loaves and fishes and fed thousands (Matt. 14 & 15)? He still wants to multiply His blessings. So when He told us to spread the Bread of His Presence across the state of Iowa, this included the power of His prophetic words spoken through surrendered saints.

There here has been such an **abundance** and **overflow** of His prophecies over Iowa, I need to acknowledge being unable to include them all. Some have been given in years past, some very recent. Suffice it to say, the Lord has already begun to release His fresh Living Waters over Iowa because of *words aptly spoken*, through much intercession, along with the fragrance of praise and worship through Houses of Prayer being raised up. We want to drink it in as deeply as we can!

Pray it through!

We are encouraged in 1 Corinthians 14:1, to pursue love and yet to earnestly desire spiritual gifts, but especially that we may prophesy. Destiny lies within the prophecies spoken. Consider

Paul's words to Timothy, *"Do not neglect the spiritual gift within you, which was bestowed upon you through prophetic utterance with the laying on of hands by the presbytery. Take pains with these things; be absorbed in them, so that your progress may be evident to all."* Each county we visited is now called to pray through the prophecies, the seeds if you will, that were declared and planted by virtue of this Prophetic Prayer Journey (Luke 8:4-18). This task must be taken seriously if these counties are ever to come into all God has for them. It's time to embrace that mantle!

Chuck Pierce (Glory of Zion Int'l Ministries, Denton, Texas. VP of Global Harvest Ministries) and Dutch Sheets (Sr. Pastor of Springs Harvest Fellowship, Colorado Springs, Colorado)

We will begin with these two renowned prophets of God who were called to all 50 states in 2002 and 2003 making declarations for divine destinies to come forth. See their book: *Releasing the Prophetic Destiny of a Nation* published by Destiny Image, for a complete look into what was given.

Interestingly, while Michael and I were on one of our journeys to the counties late one November day, we saw a farmer and his wife carrying bags at their sides gleaning a harvested field. We've lived in Iowa all our lives, but we had never seen anything like that before! Suddenly we remembered what these two gentlemen had prophesied when they were in Iowa. One prophecy given was: *"I'm going to begin to break down that circle of darkness that dwells in the center of this state. I call you like Ruth at this time, and I would say, if you would go to the corners and begin to glean... if you'll glean in the corners, then the center will have to respond."* Then Chuck goes on to say, "Now I believe these words have a **literal meaning;** you won't be able to see transformation in

14

the center without starting at the corners." Then he began to prophesy by the Spirit of the Lord regarding the southwest, northwest, southeast and northeast corners.

We were fulfilling that very prophecy and hadn't even realized it! Literally, the natural precedes the spiritual exactly as it says in 1 Corinthians 15:46. We must never forget that God is looking to fulfill His Word according to Isaiah 55:11. How is it that we are surprised when He does? Let faith arise in our souls.

Valentine's Day vision

While on a Solitude Retreat in 2005, I had a vision of Iowa as if it were a photograph negative, like the ones that have to be dipped in a solution in order for it to appear. I saw Iowa being dipped in God's Presence, as bread is dipped in oil at a dinner table. I saw Iowa being "developed" by God for something great. The Lord told me that He was *developing* a heavenly corridor over our state.

Another word He'd given me was about a hairline crack over Iowa. Praise and worship would widen that crack, providing an open heaven. Thank God for all the Houses of Prayer being raised up in Iowa. Do you have one? If not, start one!

Likewise He revealed: *"There is a place of no walls. But there is a door! Dreams are sign posts. Watch them closely. A field of dreams means a vast amount of dreams and visions. Watch what I show you. Do what I show you."* Many in this state will begin to dream big dreams. They will be given divine destinies as a result. It's not ironic that the movie, *Field of Dreams* was filmed in Dyserville, Iowa! Lou Engle has a special place in his heart for this particular movie. This came as a result of a conference in Council Bluffs in August of 2005 where he was speaking. A prophetic word was given by Chris Bergland during that conference regarding, I - I - O - W - A. This was interpreted as **Iowa's Intercession Over White House Affairs**. Certainly this state is strategic in its political position of being the first in the nation presidential caucuses. This prophecy is being fulfilled!

No wonder the Lord had me take pictures of the "fields" of Iowa on that autumn day in October 2005. Another key phrase given to me on that retreat was: *"Stockpile the grain. Spread the Bread. Spread the Bread of My Presence."* This speaks of a Joseph anointing for this state which was given many times as we toured the 99 counties. It became even more evident as we concluded at the center of the state in Polk County where it was once again decreed–right next to the Farmer's Market!

During one of our last tours of the 99 counties, one of our prayer warriors saw a vision of the "Field of Dreams." She saw a grand ball game that's coming to Iowa. New mantles are falling (i.e., Mickey "Mantle"). Each person has a part to play in this game and each one is hitting their pitch. Then she declared, "Lord, let the games begin! Let your plan and purpose begin. Let people be struck with awe so they will say, 'Is this heaven? No, it's Iowa! Lord, kiss Iowa!' I truly believe this prayer went up as sweet incense into the Lord's nostrils, for it was offered in the same area where He'd given me the vision for 500,000 new souls.

How wonderful that God is always weaving the prophetic pieces together for His glory. Here are several more.

Beth Alries (Intercessor International at an Aglow Retreat in Des Moines. 3/1/93)

"Because of hurts and wounds spoken over and over, because of My people who are called by My Name who have humbled themselves and prayed, I will hear from heaven and heal their land. You have had a dependency on the government for the sake of money. I will turn it around if you seek it for My sake. As you have prayed and sought, so I have heard. As people were bound, so they will be set free. As you have prayed and repented, the Indians have been set free. This is a new generation, a new day. Verbalize the positive not the negative. My hand is upon Iowa. Ballistic missiles of prayer will go to other states and nations. I will bring Iowa to the forefront of what I am going to do. God has so much He wants to do in and for Iowa."

An inmate at the Newton Prison facility (5/06)

This gentleman had a dream. In the dream, he was looking down on a table where there was a map of Iowa. He saw little pieces of paper on the map and they were about 2 or 3 inches wide and seemed to represent 2 or 3 counties. There appeared to be a hand holding a pen that was drawing a line from north to south and then back and forth sideways, east to west across the map. Several men were drawing the lines closer together…perhaps connecting different areas of the state. In the dream, he said it appeared that each area where these pieces of paper were falling, there had been much brokenness. But now it would become a place of supernatural power and healing!

This dream was given a month *before* we'd begun our Prophetic Prayer Journey to Iowa's 99 County Courthouses, but it was sent a month *later.* Our hearts were warmed as we received this confirmation for this divine assignment. How wonderful our God is not confined to a space or a place in time, but that He is omnipresent, omniscient and omnipotent! He can speak to anyone, anywhere, anytime. He can use any one of us. Are we listening?

Chuck Pierce again

In February of 2006, Chuck gave this word of prophecy over Iowa:

"You come here and let me hand you this...." (Those in this national meeting from Iowa were given a tent peg to drive into the ground to start a new season). "...Iowa has some things that we want to see that get nailed to the ground, that there be new processes....I decree that right now new processes are beginning in Iowa. I decree that there will be a supernatural alignment of marketplace processes and spiritual processes. Father, it will be a model, Lord. I say that certain wrong religious structures will dry up, Lord. I say that there will be a supernatural alignment going on in Iowa this year. Lord, I say in the cornfields, we will actually see new fuel for our future released. Lord, I say there will be alignments, there will be victories, there will be understandings. Lord, we say come down and connect into Iowa this year in Jesus Name, Amen."

Cindy Jacobs in Texas, January of 2006 (Generals International, Dallas, Texas)

"Oh Iowa, Iowa, Iowa, is anybody here from Iowa?! The Lord says, get ready for the move of God there in Iowa. I am coming to release a new wind anointing upon that state, and the Lord says corn and cattle…there's a market place anointing (both the corn and cattle industries). God is going to bring the excellency. Are you understanding the excellency there? The marketplace movement has been in infancy, but God says by 2007, there will be 'establishing.' But the Lord says by 2010, it's going to sweep the nations of the earth. Many businesses will turn to Christ."

The year before, in July of 2005, Cindy also had a word about those along the corridor of I-35. This interstate runs right through the state of Iowa! A few years later she initiated a prayer focus for this interstate that goes the length of the United States. This correlates exactly to what the Lord had me proclaiming in May of 2005 as I anointed and prayed over the Rest Stops and the two connecting interstates in Iowa. Interstate 80 is the other one. Take note of this portion of Cindy's prophecy at that time:

"…I am calling unity to come to this nation and there will be no unity unless the Highway of Holiness (Isa. 35) draws from both directions to the middle. The core of this nation is its midland….the heartland is the middle of this land. The heart for the land will come as you traverse north to south. The expanse of My Glory will go east and west as you go north and south. As the rubber meets the road, the **heavenly tracks** will be seen in the spirit world…." (See chapter 1).

It was also noted that Prophet Bob Jones has spoken of I-35 for many years!

Cindy Jacobs while in Iowa on December 14, 2007 (Iowa Arise Conference, Des Moines)

Iowa is acronym for Intercessors on World Affairs, Iowa intercessors are called to change world affairs. Iowa is a tipping point state. This is a tipping point time where God wants to throw this state into a massive move of God. Iowa is on the verge of birth pains of revival. This state is about to deliver. The German pious people settled in the Amanas of Iowa. God wants to light a great fire of reformation. Iowa is an Issachar state. (Chuck Pierce from Texas, is the only other to receive a prophetic word about Iowa having the Issachar anointing in the last 25 years.) There is a link in spirit between Iowa and Texas. Large numbers of people will move into Iowa. There are new companies coming in, new cities being built. It will not hurt the farming. God is bringing an influx of people into this state. Many people have been transplanted to Iowa. In the next few years the population will double. The flight in Iowa will be reversed.

There is coming a day in Iowa where you will have a historic move of God that is going to sweep from North to South and East to West. The Holy Spirit is going to move in a remarkable way greater than you can imagine. It is going to happen. God is going to move in a very special way.

Iowa was the 29th state admitted to the Union. Iowa is an Issachar state. What is the connection between people transplanted to Iowa and Iowa being the 29th state? To all those carried away captive to Iowa, observe Jeremiah 29:4-5. People called and carried to Iowa are to: Build houses and dwell in them; plant gardens and eat their fruit. Take wives and beget sons and daughters; and take wives for your sons and give your daughters to husbands, so that they may bear sons and daughters - that you may be increased there, and not diminished. And seek the peace of the city where I have caused you to be carried away captive, and pray to the Lord for it; for in its peace you will have peace. (Cindy actually stayed on the 29th floor when in Iowa.)

The Lord will be bringing more people to Iowa for revival to be touched by Holy Spirit. **"Iowa will be a state of visitation." Iowa shall come into a state of visitation**. Not only have you been visited by politicians, the Lord says you are going to be visited by Me, you're going to be visited by My power says God. Iowa will be a state of miracles. I'm going to pour out signs and wonders upon this state says the Holy Spirit and I am going to do wonders - not only am I going to do physical manifestations in bodies, but wonders in the heavens and creative miracles. I am the God of creation, I never stopped being the God of creation, says the Lord. I'm going to begin to kiss and bless the land here like the Garden of Eden. You're going to see award winning vegetables. I'm going to bless your produce, I'm going to give the increase. The curse has been broken off the land in Iowa.

The Lord says in the North, fire in the North! I'm going to pour down FIRE from the North. The Lord says I'm going to visit the frozen places with my fire. I'm going to begin to heat up this state says God. I'm going to visit the Lutheran Churches. Look and see. The Fire of Reformation will once again burn in my German people says the Lord. Fire of Holy Spirit is going to come and light up this place with my Northern lights. I'm going to begin to release my glory says God.

FIRE ON THE ALTAR!!! Iowa is an altar unto Me says the Lord and I'm going to cause 24/7 prayer houses to spring up. Look to the **University of Iowa** says God, for I am coming for a GREAT VISITATION. I am going to shift it from the left to the right. I am coming in a major shift for this is a TIPPING POINT TIME says God. I'm getting ready to tip it, says the Lord. You've only seen the tip of the iceberg of what I'm getting ready to do.

And the Lord says come and let us go unto the Mountain of the Lord. I'm getting ready to release the nations to flow into Iowa. God says there will be new airports, expect airport expansions. See new things. Population will double.... Buy land! Buy land! Buy land before the prices shoot up. Buy in Iowa, says God. Buy in these places everybody moved out of because I'm getting ready to move in says the Lord.

Identity of Iowa: (1 Chron. 12:32) Iowa has understanding of the times, to know what the nations ought to do. Iowa is a major key. You are a strategic tribe. You are of tribe of Issachar. This state is a COMMAND POST for understanding prophetic intelligence that will change the nations of the earth. A command post to shift and change national policies.... There is a weightiness about what you pray, a small but mighty tribe here in Iowa. You're going to be great and mighty in the nations of earth. There's going to be increase in harvest, buy property and land. This is a time of increase.... New things.

Sanctify yourself, Joshua 3:5 set yourself apart...holiness... doctrine of sanctification, important that you do this. You have to be more than a subset of the world in order to see change and to shift. You have to be set apart in your attitude and what you watch. Many Christians have critical sarcastic spirits...not fashionable in God's Kingdom. We need be kind, holy, radically different–either a Nazarite or Nazi nation. Sometimes God requires a counter-culture shift to change situations. Do we carry the fragrance of Christ?

Issachar anointing knows the signs of the time. Iowa is a prophetic and discerning state. You'll be seers. You'll be able to know and see when to shift. That means that Satan wants to blind you. There will be a whole movement that will teach against the prophetic, a whole movement that says God doesn't speak today. You can probably see these two different camps. There is a generation of young seers arising that are like nothing we have ever known. The children and youth of this state are seers. Don't shut them down. Make a place for this gift.

Issachar knew when it was time for Saul's Kingdom to be over and David's Kingdom to begin. There is a transfer of Kingdoms taking place. Satan has held his sway for a long time. Issachar knew when religious spirits would not change and they had to make a shift...hard thing. Go where God says go. Don't you become old wine...be ready to shift when God says shift.

Iowa is a Daniel and Joseph state...governmental, but Joseph anointing. There will be a national poll taken and the number of entrepreneurs and new business start-ups coming from Iowa will exceed all other states. Is there faith in the house? The word did not profit not being mixed with faith. The word works for those who work the word.

Think forward for the next generation. Be John the Baptist, a forerunner for Iowa. Be Issachar...fast and pray. Genesis 49:14-15 prophecy given by Jacob over Issachar. Satan will try to build strongholds to try and undermine your destiny. Issachar strong donkey (strong fire), but his love of comfort could also cause him to settle down for an easy way out. Jacob said, "Issachar strong fighter," but love of comfort could settle for an easy way out.

Mt. Tabor was in Issachar district, where Deborah and Barrak fought. Marauding tribes were attracted to their land because their land was so rich agriculturally. Like Issachar, Iowa has rich land

and would attract Eastern religions and strange beliefs...we have to keep marauding tribes out of our land.

Issachar to call out blessings - Deuteronomy 27:12, different tribes to call out blessings and curses... we (Iowa intercessors) are called to speak out blessings and prophetic blessings to the world. God will show us how to have a life style of wealth in 2008 "work less and make more". One of the curses of the garden is to work the soil by the sweat of the brow.

Numbers 34:12-29 - Issachar tribe was one of the tribes assigned to help divided up the land of Canaan among the children of Israel. Very fertile land belonged to the Issachar tribe. Iowans will understand land issues...know how to sanctify land. When land is cursed, the land will vomit out its inhabitants. Leviticus 18:25

It is time for Iowa to wake-up! High time to wake out of sleep, it is high time to wake out of sleep...let us cast off works of darkness and put on the armor of light. Roman13:11. Satan will send diversions, so we need to learn divine perseverance and knowing the time to wake out of sleep! To see His Kingdom come and His will be done on earth as it is in heaven...proclaim and decree! Matthew 6:10. Let your dominion come and let it be done on earth as it is in heaven.

There are people who have a Cyrus anointing and some of you... God is going to show you where petroleum reserves are hidden in this state, something to do with Northeast part of state. We call in these petroleum reserves that have been kept for the end times. There will also be new bank start ups that will be Christian banks or Issachar banks. There will be women starting new business. Issachar was the tribe that knew how to move into the new. They were a tribe that understood times and seasons (End of Cindy's Words).

I will close with a portion of Chuck Pierce's word from the August 28, 2007 Elijah List: "We however, must learn to respond to the Lord within time. We are called to represent Him as ambassadors in our generation. The decisions and actions we take now affect three generations ahead. Therefore, when we know how the Lord wants us to respond and we do so, His glory infiltrates the earth and we see Him change our atmosphere and environment. Because of God's position relative to time, He can--and often does--seem to answer our prayers before they have been uttered! God has chosen us as the necessary link to bring His will from Heaven to earth. He wants us to commune with Him, listen carefully to His voice, gain prophetic revelation, and decree that revelation into the earth. This will unlock miracles and release His blessings. Once we hear God, we can intercede. We can also prophesy. Prophecy is declaring His mind and His heart. When we receive prophetic revelation, we need to decree the prophetic revelation and then the atmosphere into which we decree goes on 'Heavens time' instead of 'earth time'."

Stacey Campbell, a speaker at our Roar of War Conference, 12/05 (Revival Now Ministries/Be A Hero, Kelowna, BC Canada)

A few months after our conference, in February 2006, Stacey emailed us one day saying:

"While I was in Redding, California about a month ago, I clearly heard a word for the state of Iowa. I saw a small fire beginning and knew that it was the fire of revival. I felt the Lord's eyes are turned toward the state of Iowa because of the longing for a move of God by a remnant. He said that if leaders would fan this small flame, which has already begun, it would turn into the fire of revival. There is a spiritual grace on Iowa right now and it is incredibly strategic that the House of Prayer is starting at this time. I believe that if the fire is blown on, what begins in Iowa will spread out to many other states.

I don't know if I can articulate all the feelings I had when I saw this small fire–the potential in it is HUGE, but it was like Iowa was "hanging in the balances" whether the fire would grow bigger or just stay small. The Lord told me to ask at the Redding Conference if anyone from Iowa was there, especially leaders, because it's crucial to blow on the fire to see God's purposes fulfilled. "The Lord looked for a man..." kind of feeling. I feel His grace over your state and just encourage you to BLOW, BLOW, BLOW with the wind of prayer to take what has begun to the next level. The size of the wind will affect the size of the fire.

I was so happy to hear about the [Kingdom] House of Prayer near Des Moines," she continues. "I really know that God has raised it up to release what He wants to do in Iowa and beyond. I encourage many to get behind this and provide leadership so that it goes to the level that God wants it to. Co-labor with Him!"

Jill Austin, a speaker at our Roar of War Conference, 12/05 (Master Potter Ministries, Laguna Hills, California)

"Watch and see that out of the heartland there will be a mighty move of God, a mighty revival...that here in the cornfields, this will be known as a state that will be a supplier. It will be a refuge state. This is a state that's going to feed the other states. This is a state that has a Joseph anointing on it. It has an anointing like

26

Joseph… like Joseph who went to Pharaoh and was one that came up with strategies for supplies for the earth. I tell you IOWA, IOWA, IOWA, you are going to be known as a state not only of corn but a state that brings supply and provision! You are a refuge state! You're a state that when the nations on the east and west coast go through great catastrophe, that many will come to you. You are a state that's going to release fuel, you're going to release strategies and inventions. You're a state that's going to move into entrepreneurial and finances, says the Lord! So let's give the Lord a clap offering!"

Shampa Rice, a speaker at our Eye of God Conference, 1/07 (Jacob Generation Ministries International, California and India)

She emailed us awhile later saying that she'd had a vision of Iowa as she lifted off the ground in the airplane carrying her back home. She saw "fireworks" going off all over the state. She said it was as

if heaven has been dropping bombs on places that embrace His strange moves. Amazing! A few months later, as our grown children were home for an "Iowa vacation," they wrote out the word: "Iowa" with *sparklers* in our backyard, capturing it through a camera lens (see Photo). Shampa's very prophecy had been illumined!   Once again, keep in mind the natural precedes the spiritual. (1 Cor. 15:46)

It's also quite amazing the year I prayed over the highways and byways at the Rest Stops, I'd also seen by way of the Holy Spirit a "firestorm" that hit Iowa. It was like a downpour of rain and wind blowing upward, but also sideways. Quite strange, but powerful!

While on our tour

While we were in Story County on Veteran's Day, 11/11/06, the Lord gave a personal "word" to Mike and I: "Because you are doing this assignment, I am going to bring IOWA into pre-eminence."

Prepare the way of the Lord. Iowa get ready! United States of America, get ready!

◆ three ◆

LAUNCHING OF THE PROPHETIC PRAYER JOURNEY TO IOWA'S 99 COUNTY COURTHOUSES

"Now after this, the Lord appointed seventy others and sent them out two by two ahead of Him to every city and place where He Himself was going to come." —Luke 10:1

This trek across the state of Iowa did not go as planned! You'd think we would know that. But isn't it human nature to try to plot our own course? We knew that in our hearts, but needed to learn it anew. It became most evident that we had to follow our heavenly Commander in Chief. He knew the way. We did not. So He continually attuned our listening skills on which way to go, where, when and how.

I'd thought from the beginning that there would most likely be just two of us traveling to all these counties, myself and a close friend. This was because we thought the trips would be taken during the week, freeing up weekends for other things. She and I were even planning on using her RV for part of the travels.

But as my husband came along the first day to help launch this amazing journey, the Lord made it clear to him that he was to go to every county with me. Michael had felt such a powerful anointing on that first day, he did not want to miss one minute of these ordained travels! So, the whole prophetic journey took place only on weekends so he could participate. As it turned out, my friend was only able to go once, and our plan gave way to the Divine way.

Map Quest

Nothing quite like this had been done before. Map Quest could not plot this course. It was divinely orchestrated by the King of glory. It was orchestrated by Him to make prophetic decrees in every courthouse in this state, the very places where earthly decrees are made. These are places where doors are opened or shut governmentally on earth. However, it's God's purpose to ordain them as avenues of His government, His holy authority of righteousness, justice and mercy. We came to declare these areas to be portals, open heavens where Living Waters of God's love would flow into each county creating a spiritual tsunami of awakening and revival!

There were two things we felt the Lord wanted us to do at each and every county without fail. One, we were to anoint the front door declaring the coming in and going out would be ordained of God. Secondly, we left a little stone with Isaiah 28:16-17 written on it to make a physical announcement that the Lord is laying a new foundation of His holiness, justice and righteousness. It reads:

> "Behold, I am laying in Zion a stone, a tested stone, a costly cornerstone for the foundation, firmly placed. He who believes in it will not be disturbed. And I will make justice the measuring line, and righteousness the level; then hail shall sweep away the refuge of lies, and the waters shall overflow the secret place."

Amazingly, we accomplished this task in every single county without coming under suspicion by the public, being questioned or stopped. God

always enables whom He sends. Glory!

Be alert

As already mentioned earlier, we recognize the natural precedes the spiritual according to 1 Corinthians 15:46. It is after all, God's Word and its Truth. The Bride of Christ, the Church, must learn to be on high alert to her surroundings so she is not slumbering when the final trumpet blows and Jesus comes!

Prophecy is a gift of the Holy Spirit. He teaches us to perceive earthly things to help us discern what's behind the thin veil separating the realms of the natural and spiritual. We must embrace and understand Luke 12:54-56 when the Lord says,

> "When you see a cloud rising in the west, immediately you say, 'A shower is coming,' and so it turns out. And when you see a south wind blowing, you say, 'It will be a hot day,' and it turns out that way. You hypocrites! You know how to analyze the appearance of the earth and the sky, but why do you not analyze this present time?"

Let's not be hypocrites. Let us learn to discern the days in which we live. These are precarious days and we need to be wide awake!

Again the Lord Jesus brings clarity to this issue in Matthew 24:32-33,

"Now learn from the fig tree: when it's branch has already become tender, and puts forth it's leaves, you know that summer is near; even so you too, when you see all these things, recognize that He is near, right at the door."

Saints, do you hear the "knock knock"?

Finally, let us take heed of Romans 8:19 where it says that all of creation is anxiously longing and eagerly awaits the revealing of the sons of God. Therefore, discerning and declaring prophetic utterances is vital to our lives, both in the natural and spiritual realms. We must not be oblivious to these things. Our lives depend on it!

Headliners

God communicates with His people first and foremost through His written Word, the Bible. Do you long to know His will for your life? Then start there. It's laid out for the whole world to see. Then again, He can use a sermon, a song, a conference or a book that will speak volumes to us. Understandably, our Creator God also loves to use creative ways in which to communicate His message. There's a lot of "writing on the wall" so to speak, just within our daily newspapers! Take for instance the following headlines as time and time again, the Lord confirmed that He was indeed calling us to take the leap and go to all 99 Iowa counties (Taken from the Des Moines Register).

"Iowa's Mighty Winds." May 5, 2005. It was a story about a utility in our state, along with a renewed state tax credit, pledged to help farmers and other rural residents harness Iowa's wind. Note the date: 5th month, 5th day, 2005. Five means *favor* and there were three of them! Prophetically, we saw this as Holy Spirit revival winds being released across this state.

"Serious Rider." September 20, 2005. This was a story of a man attempting to ride a horse to all the contiguous states, visiting each capital. It showed a picture of him after leaving the Iowa Capital in Des Moines with a fenced cornfield in the background. He was going to governmental places, the capitals, and the autumn cornfield spoke of harvest time! Surely, if he could go by horseback, we could go by car!

"'Saints' March Through Iowa On Four Lanes." May 25, 2006. Part of the opening lines read: "The Avenue of the Saints four-lane highway has completed its march through Iowa at a cost of $541 million–two decades after Iowa community leaders began lobbying for the massive construction project." Another portion of the story told how it was the biggest road project in Iowa history.

Needless to say, what first catches your attention is the word: *Saints*. The Lord was making this assignment very clear! The story said this was the biggest road project in this state and the costliest. Our assignment seemed huge to us knowing it would take many weekend trips over many miles. There was, of course, a *cost* involved. There was the element of *time* as well as vehicle and food expenses that go along with a road trip. But we gave those concerns to the Lord. Thus by virtue of the joy of obedience to the assignment, we felt the cost was minimal.

We must learn in our walk with God to not count the cost. We need to embrace the example of Mary in John 12:3 who lovingly and graciously poured very costly perfume on the Lord's precious feet. Cost is not the issue. The heart is. Love does not count the cost. Lovers are givers.

This was now only four weeks before our Launch Day. *"O my soul, march on with strength."* (Judg. 5:21).

"Interstates' 50th Year Marked With Caravan." June 24th, 2006. Our Launch Day. Could the Lord have made it any clearer? We felt *Jubilee* in our calling! As our little caravan set out across the highways, we knew the Lord was preparing to restore Iowa (Lev. 25:10)! The newspaper article had begun with the following: "State officials and members of a national caravan stopped in Urbandale on Friday afternoon to celebrate Iowa's interstate highways and to commemorate the 50th anniversary of the ubiquitous transportation network." Our task of the Prophetic Prayer journey to all 99 county courthouses in Iowa began to spiritually link the entire state together for its divine destiny. The Lord ordained this to be a holy networking!

This story went on to say that there had been an event, dubbed "Rock'n Roads" which drew 500 people to *Living History Farms*. Prophetically, it is quite clear to see the Lord's desire to bring forth life by declaring Iowa's ordained history. We felt like spiritual farmers going across the land of Iowa planting the Word of the Lord. Not only that, but every courthouse we visited, we left a ROCK with Isaiah 28:16-17 written on it. It doesn't take a rocket scientist to see that things in the natural realm reflects and trumpets spiritual activity. Learn to discern!

As if this headline wasn't enough the day of our launch, four days later the Lord again confirms our divine assignment with the following headline.

"TOUR DE IOWA!" June 28, 2006. Yes we were! We had just set out days earlier on the first leg of our Prophetic Prayer Tour of Iowa. This headline in the morning paper was in larger than normal bold print on the cover page. It was "confirmation" of Lance Armstrong's participation in RAGBRAI and Iowa was excited! (Register's Annual Great Bike Ride Across Iowa). Lance of course, is the seven time conqueror of the Tour de France. Seven is God's prophetic number of completion and perfection. Over and over again, the Lord made it clear that our "tour" was perfectly aligned with His will.

The last two headlines are from 2007 just as we had been nearing our half way mark across the state of Iowa. We were surprised we were actually going to finish this divine assignment well ahead of our original estimation. Our plans of traveling once or twice each month, turned into almost every weekend, even during Iowa's precarious winter months. We couldn't help ourselves! This assignment became bigger than anything we'd imagined and it was fun! It became quite exhilarating as we traveled county to county, feeling the strong presence and power of the Lord. Additionally, we witnessed our state up close and personal. We saw firsthand, this land called: *BEAUTIFUL!* Even though Mike and I were born and raised here, we fell in love with Iowa all over again and with her people.

"Culver Speech: An 'Era Of Greatness.'" January 12, 2007. A subtitle read: "Incoming governor represents a shift of generations." This attested to many of the prophetic proclamations we made by the power of the Holy Spirit for a healing of generational issues in the counties across Iowa. Indeed, we felt the Lord's declarations were releasing an era of greatness of this strategic Midwestern state.

"Iowans, This Is Our time." January 13, 2007. Indeed it is! The new governor may not have been aware that his words held so much prophetic meaning. It's clear the *timing* of God's divine assignment for this county tour was perfect. I recall a dream I had during these travels. In the dream, I was in an aircraft and I was looking down over the entire United States. Then I heard a voice, as if it was the pilot making an announcement. But it was God's voice! He was peering down with me at all the landscape below. His eyes were going back and forth from "sea to shining sea" looking at all the different states. Suddenly, with great excitement and joy He made a grand announcement! He declared loudly: "And now...(drum roll)...I choose...IOWA!"

So Iowa, this is your time! What happens here will affect the nation! Come to the Lord now!

Conclusion

A few days after the above January 13th headline, once again the newspaper had a "tidbit" on the new governor's swearing in ceremony. It was in the section called: IOWA EAR. The governor had raised the wrong hand. He'd raised his left hand and placed the other one on the Bible. Traditionally, one raises the right hand and puts the left one on the Bible. Prophetically speaking, could this "switch" of the hands reflect what is about to transpire not only in this state, but across this nation? Could this represent the changing of the times where many of our Judeo-Christian foundational truths will be challenged, not only in the spiritual realm, but also in the courts of this state and across this nation?

Iowa needs to lend an EAR to what God is saying and DO those things to SEE her divine destiny fulfilled. Matthew 13:9 says, *"He who has ears, let him hear."* These same words are given repeatedly in the opening chapters of the final book of the Bible - Revelation. Hearing is strategic!

Are *you* listening?

Is Iowa listening?

Is the United States listening?

● four ●

PLYMOUTH, SIOUX, LYON, OSCEOLA, DICKINSON, CLAY

"...And Moses recorded their starting places according to their journeys by the command of the Lord, and these are their journeys according to their starting places...the sons of Israel started out boldly in the sight of the Egyptians." —Numbers 33:2,3b

"You will also decree a thing, and it will be established for you; a light will shine on your ways." —Job 22:28

On our virgin journey, we didn't know what to expect. It was all so new to us. We were just following the mandate of the Lord. We kept learning more as we went along. Consequently, we were much more prepared in subsequent journeys on what to bring and not bring, as we'd set out each time. One thing for sure however, we prayed most all the way, all the day. We always took worship CDs in order to maintain an atmosphere of revelation from the Holy Spirit. Many times, even as we crossed the county line, revelation would begin to flow spontaneously.

I (Linda) lost several pens that first day, so we weren't able to write many things down much to my chagrin. We also didn't have much paper with us on which to write. You would have thought! Nonetheless, powerful prayers went forth under the divine unction of the Holy Spirit, for it was He who directed this anointed campaign across Iowa. Those things which were prayed and prophesied on this first journey, God is watching over it like a mother hen! Jeremiah 1:12 says, *"You have seen well, for I am watching over My Word to perform it."*

I have since felt that perhaps the reason the Lord allowed not much to be written on those first counties, is because they were the *pictorial* prophetic beginnings of what God wants to do in those places. At least, we got pictures and there's a saying: "A picture is worth a thousand words."

In other words, it's as if these particular first counties represented a "clean slate" for God to rewrite divine strategies and destinies for this entire state. So do not lament that *your* county may not have a lot recorded from this Prophetic Prayer Journey. The exciting thing is–godly history is now being written and lived out even as you read this!

Starting position

Our 6,608 mile journey to all the county courthouses began on June 24th, 2006. It was the day before my birthday and I was excited to say the least. Mike and I left the house bright and early at 6:05 AM under cloudy skies. Mary Ellen Earles, Iowa's Women's Aglow Prayer Chairman at the time, would meet us later. We may have been few in numbers, but isn't that the way it is sometimes? I'm reminded often, that even ONE man or woman can affect a whole nation! Esther, Samson, Elijah, John the Baptist, Joan of Arc, Abraham Lincoln, Martin Luther King, Billy Graham are just some examples.

The temperature that summer morning was 66 degrees. And with the date of 6/06, I turned the two sets of sixes, upside down making it 99. Ninety-nine counties to go! We prayed this journey would turn this state upside down for God's glory!

That first morning on the road, I'd taken a newspaper clipping with us, dated about 7 weeks earlier. It was a story of two captured German engineers in Iraq and how they'd been set free after 99 days of captivity. This article reminded me of Chuck Pierce and Dutch Sheet's prophesy that Iowa's prayers would touch Iraq. Within a short time of that declaration, Saddam Hussein was captured. I felt this story was a prophetic link that our prayer journey to Iowa's 99 counties, gave credence to God's plan to bind the enemy and set *captives free*!

Our starting position would be in the northwestern most part of the state. If Iowa were a clock, this position would be the 11:00 o'clock hour. Eleven is a transitional number. After the Ascension of Jesus into heaven, there were only eleven apostles and everything was in transition and change. After seeking the Lord as to who should replace Judas, Matthias was chosen. Then - Pentecost! All signs seem to point to the fact that we are in the 11th hour of humanity leading up to a grand finale of an unprecedented Pentecost that will outshine the first! Haggai 2:9 affirms the latter glory will be greater. Everything is about to shift into transition ushering in the Last Days. Let us fulfill our divine destinies now!

First sightings

As the four hour trip unfolded to the northwestern section of the state, we had already driven through clouds, rain, fog and a little bit of sunshine. As the day progressed, we encountered ever changing atmospheric conditions. Mostly it was sunshine, but there were times of churning, billowy, fluffy white clouds. Conversely, we ran into dark, foreboding and threatening ones. Certainly we were stirring up the mid-heavens. The fight was on! Spiritual warfare had begun!

Making our way along the scheduled route, we drove past Sioux City in Woodbury County where we'd visit another day. As we drove by we saw a dark, smoky cloud hanging in the air. Mike suspected it had something to do with the meat packing plant located there. It smelled terrible! Mike remembered that once when he was in that city, he could actually *feel* a substance fall on his skin. Yuck! This would be a county that we would have to spend a good amount of time in and the Lord was already alerting us. We'll give you more on that in another chapter.

Our plans were to make our first stop in the farthest northwest county of Lyon. However, our divine Commander in Chief took us on a "detour" that first morning on the road. Whistling down the interstate making good time towards our goal, Mike said, "We're driving through Plymouth County, why don't we stop there first?" I agreed. As we drove into the little town of Le Mars, Iowa, we were filled with anticipation. What would the Lord show us?

PLYMOUTH COUNTY
Le Mars

So much of the Prophetic Prayer Journey was significant beyond what was evident in the natural as with our beginning at Plymouth County. We knew the Pilgrims came to the land of

42

spiritual freedom and the Rock known as Plymouth. *"The Rock! His work is perfect, for all His ways are just; a God of faithfulness and without injustice, righteous and upright is He"* (Deut. 32:4). Likewise, our tour had a governmental purpose and declaration of freedom and thanksgiving. All the attributes we celebrate at Thanksgiving is about God's bounty, freedom and His desire to bring people

Plymouth County Courthouse

together under His Name. He delights in blessing His children.

This place, known for its ice cream and dairy delights, prompted us to pray the spirit of joyous, delightful celebration in relationship with Him.

Majestic Pillars!

So on this lush summer day, we declared this county to be one of thanksgiving and unity. A spirit of freedom and delight is coming here. The Lord purposes to awaken the people that they may taste of Him and see that He is good. *"O taste and see that the Lord is good; how blessed is the man who takes refuge in Him! O fear the Lord, you His saints; for to those who fear Him, there is no want"* (Ps. 34:8-9). We proclaim an invasion of the Holy Spirit into this county.

The town of Le Mars was named by using the initialed first letters of the **Christian** names of the ladies who visited the new town site with a railroad official. We prayed, "Lord, let the **influence** of Your children, those who are called by Your Name, be **influential** in this county. May they be called to lead others into righteousness for Your Name's sake."

Martial law was declared here in 1929 because of an organization calling itself the "Farmers Holiday Group," who were upset with a certain judge. This group kept their products off the market waiting for a higher price. They had dragged the judge from the courtroom threatening to hang him on the courthouse grounds. He was freed but the governor had to call out the National Guard. We decreed the Lord's rule and reign in this place that justice, mercy and righteousness will come forth. (James 2:25).

SIOUX COUNTY
Orange City

Our next unscheduled stop was in Sioux County. As we drove

Sioux County Courthouse Tower

into town, I felt more like a newspaper reporter. I knew I had been called to *report* what God is doing, not only in this county, but all across the state of Iowa. Little did I know at the time I'd be writing this book! My thoughts and feelings were confirmed later that day when our oldest daughter called and asked if the media was there?! She was quite sure they'd be following us with TV cameras reporting this great adventure God had given us. Bless her heart!

We sensed a gate for Iowa in this place. A gate of inventions, ideas and innovations. It's a big gate through which a natural, spiritual abundance will flow. Prayers have opened up the gate to the blessings the Lord wants to pour out upon His people.

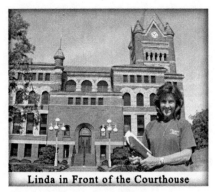

Linda in Front of the Courthouse

That which is not yet seen will be seen in Sioux County.

The county is named in honor of the Sioux Native American tribe, which once was prosperous in this area. But the name means, "snakes" or "little snakes." We rebuke Satan and his cohorts. We rebuke craftiness and deception according to Genesis 3. Sioux County, you must claim this passage from Luke 11:11-13:

> "Now suppose one of you fathers is asked by his son for a fish; he will not give him a snake instead of a fish, will he? Or if he is asked for an egg, he will not give him a scorpion, will he? If you the, being evil, know how to give good gifts to your children, how much more shall your heavenly Father give the Holy Spirit to those who ask Him ?"

We declared that gates would be opened here according to Psalm 24 and that the King of glory will come in. We decreed a reversal of generational curses of past generations. Wash and cleanse the land and all the sins associated with warring with

Native Americans. Cleanse families of generational sins. *"They will come and will declare His righteousness to a people who will be born, that He has performed it."* (Ps. 22:31).

Lighting struck the courthouse tower in 1907 which knocked off four feet of the pinnacle. A ten foot bronze statue of "Lady Justice" replaced it. Holy Spirit, strike this county with Your justice, mercy and righteousness!

LYON COUNTY
Rock Rapids

We finally made it to our first scheduled stop of the day, Lyon County. Mary Ellen Earles, pictured with me in the photograph below, had an interesting experience while driving from her hometown of Independence, Iowa to meet up with us. This was

Linda with Mary Ellen Earles

about a six hour drive for her. Bless her heart! Along the way, she saw a truck carrying about 12-15 canoes. She said she felt like the Lord showed her this Launch Day of this Prophetic Prayer Journey was a "launching of the new" as we go into the highways and byways. Canoes go back and forth into places larger boats cannot navigate. They are sleek and smooth, and represent "refreshing and rest." She went on to say that God wants us to move into a new, restful mode, relying on the current (water flow) that He prepares. He will send His representatives to the uttermost parts of the land to tell about Jesus. We prayed into the *new* and into the *current* to flow in Iowa–the Holy Spirit current!

46

Also while traveling towards her destination to meet us Mary Ellen saw the back of a semi that read: "Proud Member of the Dream Team." She thought that was who we are. We are the Godly dream team who envision the places where Jesus is lifted high there will be a harvest of souls breaking forth. We want to be carriers of God's dreams for His people. She also saw a brand new John Deere "seed planter." It was very wide and is able to plant wide rows of seeds. Mary Ellen declared that we are planting seeds at every courthouse across Iowa, seeds of the Word of God, and declarations of His grace and goodness. These declarations, prayers and scriptures that are proclaimed, will bear fruit and a harvest for the kingdom of God.

I'd felt that Lyon County was where the first day's tour would begin. It was indeed one of the first three. I saw in the spirit, the Lord wanted to use this strategic corner county to make a ROAR like the **Lion of Judah** across this entire state in all directions. His authority will reign. It was in part, to set a tone for the entire tour! *The young lions do lack and suffer hunger; but they who*

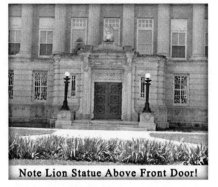
Note Lion Statue Above Front Door!

seek the Lord shall not be in want of any good thing. Come, you children, listen to me; I will teach you the fear of the Lord." (Ps. 34:10-11). Imagine our delight in seeing a huge lion statue above the front door of the courthouse! This lion symbol speaks to this county of boldness in battle, boldness in seeking the Lord's favor, protection, provision and grace.

Mary Ellen noted the four large spotlights on the courthouse lawn. We proclaimed this prophetically as the light of God shining forth in this county. The wind was blowing the flag around in several different directions and we prayed the Holy Spirit would blow everywhere across this county. We declared that any religious spirits be removed and that freedom, integrity and righteousness would blow into Iowa.

It was here and in many other counties in this region of the state, where we sensed a *blessing* for the women. Women of valor will come from here warring for their children and families. We saw them as a "Joan of Arc" who went to Lyon, France to prepare the way for the king's victory. We saw Deborahs arising. (Judg. 4 and 5).

This beautiful building had 10 majestic pillars on its front. We decreed those to represent the 10 Commandments of the Lord and that the foundational principles of God would come forth. We proclaimed lawful and righteous decrees to proceed from this place.

This is a corner or gateway county for God's movement to enter into this entire state. It's a "wakeup gateway" for Iowa.

We prayed for spiritual blindness to be removed so that people might see Jesus. We decreed in His Name, the veil to be lifted off their eyes.

Mary Ellen noted that an Aglow chapter was begun in Rock Rapids a few years ago. She felt the Lord saying that Aglow had plowed some spiritual ground there and that it's now time to reap!

OSCEOLA COUNTY
Sibley

Next we arrived at Sibley. Our records told us this was one of the highest geographical areas in Iowa. May the Most High God reign in this place! We prayed for the higher purposes, the better things of God's plan would be made evident here and across this state. *"'For My thoughts are not your thoughts, neither are your ways My ways,' declares the*

Osceola County Courthouse

Lord. 'For as the heavens are higher than the earth, so are My ways higher than your ways, and My thoughts than your thoughts'" (Isa. 55:8-9). May this entire chapter of Isaiah speak to Osceola County.

As we walked around the beautiful monuments to veterans from all the wars, we began praying for our troops. We also prayed for chaplains in the war zones.

We declared salvations will come forth from Osceola County.

Mike's Bible on a Rock

As we picnicked on the lawn in front of the courthouse, and with the Bible lying on the large rock, it seemed significant to declare God's Word would go forth from all the pulpits, not only in this county, but also the whole state. We decreed the Word to arise and God's kingdom to come.

49

It was a beautiful day with a comfortable breeze as we broke bread under God's lovely sky.

Mike Beside Veteran's Monument

This place is really peaceful, unassuming, off the beaten path and yet our paths intersected with a special man named Dale. This gentleman pulled up into the convenience store parking lot where we had made a quick stop. He approached Mike and said, "You must be a pastor." Mike couldn't imagine why he said that but didn't deny it. He simply asked him, "How can I pray for you?" Dale was an older, retired man and he requested prayer for his wife, Florence, who had been ill.

About this time, Mary Ellen and I came out of the convenience store and joined the two men in prayer. There, in the middle of the afternoon sun, in the parking lot, we joined hands in agreement as the Lord stilled the atmosphere and we prayed for healing and full

Mike Anoints the Front Door

life on this couple. A divine intersection had just occurred for the glory of God and for the whole world to see. May healings become a spiritual *high water* mark in this county (John 5 and 9)!

We knew we had entered into a time of going higher and deeper in the Lord with our proclamations over Osceola County and Iowa.

DICKINSON COUNTY
Spirit Lake

This was an interesting stop along our prayer journey that first day. We didn't expect to find construction sites. However, these things speak prophetically of change and how the Lord is ready to reconstruct people's lives according to His will if they will allow Him to do so. He wants to do major makeovers in many

New Courthouse Under Construction

hearts. The Lord spoke to us about tearing down the old and building the new. He spoke about the need for the Him to build the house! *"Unless the Lord builds the house, they labor in vain who build it; unless the Lord guards the city, the watchman keeps awake in vain"* (Ps. 127:1). We proclaim a new move of the Holy Spirit to infect this place and all of Iowa. We proclaim a bending and bowing of many knees to the Lord's purposes and plans in this county. We decreed Jesus is Lord here. May divine destinies come forth by the power of His Name.

Front of New Courthouse

This area is known for the Spirit Lake Massacre of 1856-1857 in which some Native Americans attacked settlers around the lake, killing many. We declared a cleansing in the natural and spiritual realms. May all the people become covenant keepers with the King of Kings (Ps. 111; Ps. 25:10). Let healing and restoration be establish this area.

The Lord's desire is to pour new spiritual wine into new wineskins (Matt. 9:17). Make way!

As we searched for a good place to pray when we first arrived, we had to be somewhat persistent in finding a spot away from all the construction. We sensed the Lord's message was, "Don't give up!"

The dry dirt surrounding the construction site contrasted with the colorful flower blossoms in barrels nearby. With proper

Interesting Sign

prophetic seeds and water, there will indeed be a harvest of beauty in this county. We declared the Lord would bring beauty to Iowa and the dry, dead places would become alive as in Ezekiel 37. We prayed for the water to bring refreshing to the

land. We asked for captives to be set free and for righteousness to invade the governmental authorities in every county across this state.

This place, known for relaxation and renewal in the natural, is about to bring forth a greater portion in the spiritual. Great, new aspects of the Spirit of God will be revealed in this place.

Old mindsets will give way to the fresh move of God. But persecution may follow. As the picture above indicates, we proclaim this to be a spiritually storm ready county (Rev. 19). When people hear the sound of the Lord's horse, may they stand in readiness!

CLAY COUNTY
Spencer

This was our sixth and last county of our first day's journey to Iowa's 99 county courthouses. It was also our second of only a few that we would visit where construction and renovation was going on. Again, we saw this prophetically as the Lord's way of incorporating 1 Corinthians 15:46 where it says the natural precedes the spiritual. The Lord definitely purposes to bring change and revelation to Clay County!

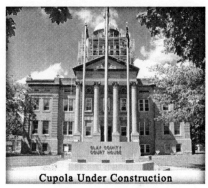

Cupola Under Construction

The busy town square seemed to be unaware of our presence, but the spiritual realm was very active. We sensed oppressive warfare here from small groups, even gang activity. It was rebuked in Jesus Name. We prayed for a cleansing of minds and hearts and for repentance to come. Reshape hearts to match Your heart, Lord!

We declared the Lord to be Most High above and beyond all things. His righteousness and justice were proclaimed over the people.

God's truth is being revealed. *"If you abide in My Word, then you are truly disciples of Mine; and you shall know the truth and the truth shall make you free."* (John 9:31).

Back Shows More Scaffolding

This county is being called to walk in truth. Your proclamation is John 14:6 where Jesus tells you, Oh Clay County, He is the way, the truth and the life! Abide in Him.

As we scanned the grounds and the construction site, we saw a yellow ladder or steps ascending the top of the scaffolding. We saw, as it were, many people's lives that were crumbling. Their idols, whatever those may be, are now being torn down. People living for themselves are about to wake up to the voice of God!

The Lord is extending Revelation 4:1 to this county. They are to *climb* to their higher purposes in God.

The red clay of this courthouse brought us by way of the Holy Spirit to Isaiah 64:8 which was proclaimed over this county. People are like clay but the Lord is the potter, and His desire is to reshape you into His image and into your divine destinies. Clay County, you are being called to be used for noble purposes! (Acts. 17:11; 1 Cor. 1:25-31).

❧ five ❧

WEBSTER, HUMBOLDT, KOSSUTH, PALO ALTO, EMMET, POCAHONTAS, CALHOUN

"Righteousness and justice are the foundation of Thy throne; lovingkindness and truth go before Thee. How blessed are the people who know the joyful sound! O Lord, they walk in the light of Thy countenance." —Psalm 89:14-15

This was a journey we knew would hold great warfare. We would be entering places where there had been great battle grounds and massacres in the civil war era. These events effect generations even up to the present hour. Some of these areas are worn out from all the battles that have lingered in the natural and spiritual realms.

Launching out at 6:27 AM on July 8th, again like the time before, it was 66 degrees. Of course, six is the number of man, but we chose to see it as a chance to turn things around, 99 - if you will; 99 counties where we would proclaim God's healing grace and restoration!

Martie Cornell and Kris Buchanan would meet us later that morning in our first county of the day. Our journeys this time took us 370 miles and it was a glory ride all the way!

Mike said he felt as if we were scouts. We likened it to being a Joshua or Caleb, who upon scouting out the Promised Land, brought back a good report saying they could take the land in spite of the giants living there. They were confident God was with them. (Deut. 1).

Most people have a tendency to see the bad things going on in any given situation. It doesn't take a rocket scientist to see what the enemy is doing and the devastation he leaves in his tracks. But the power of the Holy Spirit within you, allows you to peer into the supernatural spiritual things of God, see what He is doing and then speak it, proclaim it, decree it!

Proverbs 18:21 says, *"Death and life are in the power of the tongue."* Our words form our world. In other words, what you say is what you get. The Lord wants His children to proclaim His Word because it reigns! It's unshakeable, eternal truth. We need to check ourselves every so often to see what words are continually flowing from our mouths. Jesus taught us a good lesson in Matthew 12:37, *"For by your words you shall be justified, and by your words you shall be condemned."*

WEBSTER COUNTY
Fort Dodge

As we drove into Ft. Dodge on our second prophetic prayer journey, we were met by Martie Cornell, who lives here. She was originally going to be my travel companion to all these counties as I indicated in my opening remarks of this book. God had other plans for both of us! However, we are most grateful not only for the time she was able to go

Martie Cornell with Linda

56

with us on this particular journey, but also for her contribution of research of the histories of the counties and their maps.

There had been a massacre in this area when white settlers were beginning to encroach upon Native Americans territories. This brought defilement. We prayed for cleansing from this defilement and that God would heal the land. No shadow of a curse or wickedness shall remain!

> "…And My people who are called by My Name humble themselves and pray, and seek My face and turn from their wicked ways, then I will hear from heaven, and will forgive their sin, and will heal their land. Now My eyes shall be open and My ears attentive to the prayer offered in this place."
>
> —2 Chronicles 7:14-15

Change

We saw a lot of cement around this courthouse. It suggested cold hearts, but those can be changed to hearts of flesh, moldable and shapeable by the Master Potter.

> "And I shall give them one heart, and shall put a new spirit within them. And I shall take the heart of stone out of their flesh and give them a heart of flesh, that they may walk in My statutes and keep My ordinances, and do them. Then they will be My people, and I shall be their God."
>
> —Ezekiel 11:19-20

We decreed truth to be revealed and the veil of deception be removed.

We asked forgiveness of pride. Forgive this region, Lord! We felt there had been an attitude of: "it doesn't matter what we do." We prophesied that they would choose to live Philippians 4:8:

> "Whatever is true, whatever is honorable, whatever is right, whatever is pure, whatever is lovely, whatever is of good repute, if there is any excellence and if anything worthy of praise, let your mind dwell on these things."

We declared "no favoritism" in court decisions.

At 8AM we hear church bells ringing. Thank you Lord!

This Bronze Plaque Reads:
"You triumphed over obstacles which would have overcome men less brave and determined."

We prophesied "enough is enough" (with the bad)! It's time for the good to come forth.

We saw a van whose doors were marked with the name of a local newspaper: MESSENGER. It said 150th Anniversary, so we declared 3 Jubilees over the area (Lev. 25)! Three 50's within the number of 150 represents the Trinity and there is also a hospital in this area called Trinity. We declared the power of the Holy Trinity in this county, declaring Jesus' Name is above every disease. Bring healing here!

We choose life and a new reality in Jesus for this county.

It had been shown to us there had been a spirit of "taking" that had left little.

We declared Ft. Dodge to be a city of refuge and for churches to set aside pride ushering in unity among them.

Linda saw in the spirit "eggs, being broken"… and saw it as new, spiritual births bursting forth!

Warring in families will cease. We declared the mantle of peace upon them.

Mike discovered the IOWA flag was flying upside down at the courthouse! He lowered it, righted it, and raised it again. We saw this as symbolic of the distress in this area. We then prayed against it, declaring clarity of mind and heart, as well as spiritual insight and revelation.

We noted the 13 gargoyles *above* the two lions on the front of the

Mike Righting Upside Down Flag

building. Take note Webster County and be on alert!

HUMBOLDT COUNTY
Dakota City

It was quiet here, almost reverent, hardly a breeze in the trees. It ushered in a greater sense of *hearing.* One of the first things we saw was the MIA/POW flag on the front lawn and began to declare all captives set free. We perceived the Lord is raising up a brave, new generation that's about to come forth.

The landscape showed almost two levels of ground on the front lawn of the courthouse. The Holy Spirit had us declare a higher level of spiritual revelation to come forth.

> "After these things I looked and behold, a door standing open in heaven, and the first voice which I had heard, like the sound of a trumpet speaking with me, said, 'Come up here, and I will show you what things must take place after these things."
>
> —Revelation 4:1

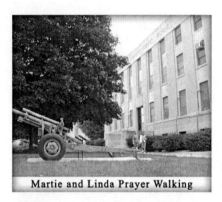

Martie and Linda Prayer Walking

Mike sensed that something was emerging from this county, something significant for the future of Iowa, perhaps leaders.

We rebuked a spirit of sadness and declared it would be replaced with joy. The joy of the Lord is our strength! *"My flesh and my heart may fail, but God is the strength of my heart and my portion forever"* (Ps. 73:26). Psalm 118 is also for this county.

A new SOUND is coming forth. We decreed the sounds of heaven coming to earth in this place.

There were two big oak trees on the front lawn. We declared Isaiah 61, especially verse 3, that "oaks of righteousness will come forth."

Strengthen feeble hands that hang limp. *"Therefore, strengthen the hands that are weak and the knees that are feeble, and make straight paths for your feet, so that the limb which is lame may not be put out of joint, but rather be healed"* (Heb. 12:12-13). Let hands be raised in worship to the Lord all over this county.

We felt some sadness here, perhaps as a result of brow beating. Hopes and visions have been stolen. When hope is deferred it makes the heart sick (Prov. 13:12). But Psalm 42:5 redeems this county: *"Why are you in despair, O my soul? And why have you become disturb*ed

Linda Reads Announcement About Inventor/Entrepreneur Workshop

within me? Hope in God, for I shall again praise Him for the help of His presence. "

Mike and Linda

The eagle statue on the front of the building appeared "still, and not in flight," nor was it attached to a branch or anything else. It looked quite odd. We asked ourselves, "Where have people placed their hope and trust?" We prayed for people to be taken higher in prophetic visions and into the heavenly realms. We prayed for spiritual flight on prophetic eagles' wings to come forth. (Isa. 40).

We declared humility will come forth for divine destinies to be fulfilled. A new day is coming where visions are delivered! Let the land be known for more than corn and soybeans, but more for the people of God that it's raising up.

The bitter cup is being removed, and the Cup of Cana is coming! A cup of celebration! (John 2).

As we left this county, we saw a sign that said, "Creepy Crawlers Immediately Eliminated." Yes! (This apparently was an ad sign for an extermination company for bugs, etc.) We felt this had been done spiritually. Also upon leaving this area, we saw another sign that grabbed our attention. It was a realty sign in a yard speaking of growth. We felt it signaled *spiritual* growth that's going to come forth across this land.

Finally, as we slipped out of town and out of Humboldt County, Mike felt there had either been a tornado here, or there was one coming. This county should stay on alert for things in the natural and in the spiritual!

KOSSUTH COUNTY
Algona

We sensed this county has a big heart but it hasn't yet been fully revealed. It's been known for wrestling but it will become known for "overcoming."

As we approached the county seat, we drove through a town called, Joseph. The map said: <u>Saint Joseph</u>, but the town sign did not have the "saint" part on it, which we saw as a reflection of the attitude of the area. Things of God seem to have been taken away. "Saint" represents holiness, so we declared holiness to come in this region. Joseph represents the fathering spirit and a spirit of adoption. We cry "Abba" for the people! May they call upon their heavenly Daddy. He will protect them.

Driving further, Martie noticed a sign beside the road. It spoke volumes as to what this prophetic prayer journey was all about. Time and time again the Lord would bring confirmation of this journey in delightful and exciting ways. This one read: "Without the past,

A Sign as We Approached This County

there is no future." We all have a past and have made mistakes. But when we repent of those things, asking the Lord to come into our heart, we are redeemed! Then we can move into our future divine destinies! We were called on this tour to find out the past, so we could SPEAK into the future the divine purposes of God.

This is also the area of the West Bend Grotto. While the grotto is impressive, the Holy Spirit is less concerned about monuments and more interested in SEEING LIFE, full, abundant, and sanctification coming into fruition among His people.

Rain

About the time we drove into the parking area of the courthouse to meet Kris Buchanan who lives here, it began raining. We took a few pictures from the car window and began to pray. The rain started to dissipate, so we began our walk around the building and soon were able to shed our umbrellas. The rain

Kris Buchanan, Martie and Linda

signaled the Lord's desire to cleanse the land, bringing a time of

63

spiritual refreshment to this county. However, the rain was sporadic…stopping abruptly…starting again abruptly. We saw this prophetically as an on and off again attitude towards the things of God in this county. Kris has experienced things in her life that attest to this, so she was happy to be a part of this particular portion of that day's journey.

The Holy Spirit is bringing holy balance through righteousness, justice and mercy. *"So speak and so act, as those who are to be judged by the law of liberty. For judgment will be merciless to one who has shown no mercy; mercy triumphs over judgment."* (James 2:12-13).

The information sheet said this was a "grade 5 **tier**" geographic area (whatever that means). But the Holy Spirit revealed that **tears** shed behind closed doors are being wiped away. (Ps. 126; Isa. 25:8; Luke 7:38).

We rebuked the spiritual rituals of the Eastern Star and Masons. We rebuked diluted, deceptive mind sets. Mike declared, "Allow people to wrestle with their destiny in You, Oh Lord, like Jacob did!" (Gen. 32:24-31).

Create in the people a clean heart, especially the judges. (Ps. 51).

Algona is named after a woman. God is releasing a "beautiful spirit," Beulah Land, beauty, holiness and purity for the Bride of Christ. (Isa. 62:4).

We declared hunger for God to grow here.

It's Iowa's largest county. Grant them a spacious place in the Lord, tent pegs being stretched forth for MORE of God to come (Isa. 54:2). They've left the drudgery behind!

Isaiah 28:17, "The waters shall overflow the secret place."

On the grounds was displayed part of the old courthouse which had deteriorated and crumbled. We placed the new "cornerstone" next to it and proclaimed it would now be founded upon this stone and that it would not crumble. (Isa. 28:16-17).

Kris Placed Isaiah 28-Inscribed Stone Beside Original Courthouse Stones

Strange views of the marriage covenant was rebuked as we decreed an honoring of the proper one designed by God. Restore! Grant justice and righteousness here. We also sensed the need to rebuke child abuse. Bring forth holy marital covenants that protect children!

Rain down times of cleansing and refreshing, Oh Lord. Teach us to love ourselves. Teach us to be holy as You are holy. (Lev. 11:44-45).

We saw a lift truck at the back of the building with the sign: JLG Lift. Martie declared: Jehovah Lord God Lifts!

We concluded by proclaiming a holy covering by the spirit of adoption, crying out, "Abba Father!"

PALO ALTO COUNTY
Emmetsburg

Music was heard in the town square as we arrived! Irish tunes that had a distinctive melody. There's a distinction to this county yet to be revealed. We drove into Palo Alto County at 11:41 AM. We were making good time. It was 66 degrees and raining.

Portal Window Atop Courthouse

We noticed a lot of crumbling cracks in the sidewalk leading to the courthouse. We declared repair and restoration coming to people here. This building is located on the corner of 7th and Union Streets. Bring unity Lord.

We saw a grain bin that was blue with a white top and prophesied growth with a harvest of new souls. John 4:35 says the fields white unto harvest. Then we saw a "Harvest Store." New grain - new souls coming forth!

The scales of justice are imbalanced here…because the portal (round window) appeared misaligned at the top of the courthouse. We rebuked blockage of true justice and righteousness. An open heaven and an open gate were declared, as well as a portal of heaven to be opened. God speed! May manifestations of His glory come quickly.

We rebuked the worldly partying spirit and a spirit of stupor. Then we declared unabashed dancing in the streets as King David did, even though he was declared to be undignified in doing so. If the world can party, so can the people of God! We saw dancing in the streets for the joy of the Lord is coming here and it will override the worldly party. A Jesus-party spirit is being released… praise and worship in the spirit of King David. People dancing unashamedly for Jesus!

One noted the name of the county, proclaiming, "Palo Alto - Pals with God!" And may it be known as the friend of God, being pals with Him. Abraham was called the friend of God (James

2:23). "Alto"–means a higher place. The Lord is calling it to a higher place in Him. "Alto" - Altitude…. God is going to take these people high and higher still. They will climb up, up, up. Revelation 4:1 is coming!

The spirit of religion was broken as we rebuked a contentious spirit of personal relationships with the Son of God.

We saw a parking sign that read: "Reserved for the Judge." Yes! This place is reserved for righteous decrees from Judge Jesus!

Definitely!

The Holy Spirit is waiting for an invitation to blow down the walls of Jericho!

A change in thinking is coming. Nobility of godly character will arise…nobility of purpose.

It will bear great fruit.

EMMET COUNTY
Estherville

This stop on our prayer journey was very interesting having discovered an unusual monument on the courthouse grounds to Ft. Defiance which was founded against "marauding Indians" (as seen in the picture below). It was in the form of an

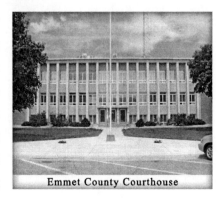

Emmet County Courthouse

obelisk which denotes the Greek word "obelus" meaning "pointed pillar," or "obeisance" which means to "bow, curtsy or pay homage." It also means "fat," where we get the word "obesity." Another meaning involves the spirit of lust. Ancient Greeks built their godless society around false gods in the form of obelisks.

An Obelisk Monument

It's not known the full intent of this unusual monument, but the word "defiance" spoke volumes, as did the term "marauding Indians." The Native Americans of course, were simply defending their *homeland* from being taken away from them. We repented for the "defiance" of many settlers who disregarded the Native American's claims to the land.

We saw this monument in the spiritual realm, as rebellion and rebuked it. It was seen as an Asherah, a false god mentioned in Exodus (34:13-14), *"You are to tear down their altars and smash their sacred pillars and cut down their Asherim—for you shall*

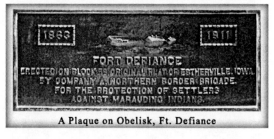
A Plaque on Obelisk, Ft. Defiance

not worship any other god, for the Lord, whose name is Jealous, is a jealous God." We declared: Tear down the idols in people's hearts in this place O Lord!

Judges 3:7, *"And the sons of Israel did what was evil in the sight of the Lord their God, and served the Baals and the*

Asheroth." We repented for the sins of Emmet County and proclaimed people will serve the one true Most High God!

We prayed against a spirit of lawlessness represented in the name of "Ft. Defiance." We declared a spirit of obedience. "To obey is better than sacrifice." (1 Sam. 15:22).

Right the wrongs

The county is named for the Irish orator and patriot, Robert Emmet. The county name was incorrectly spelled "Emmett" for a number of years. Lord, right the wrongs in this county!

History tells us that the county seat of Estherville was named after Robert E. Ridley's wife, Esther, mother of the first white female born in the county. We saw this prophetically as a declaration that in this hour, the Lord desires to raise up Esthers, the women of God in this county. We called forth the courage of Esther to arise in *all* the people here that they might tear down the spirit of Haman. Raise up women in this place Oh God, to carry the strong mantle of an Esther to make intercession to save her people!

In this county and across this region, God is raising up a  nurturing, mothering spirit in the order of Titus 2:3-5. Older godly women are to encourage and strengthen the younger women in the Lord. We declared the Lord is now being "mindful" of the prayers of many mothers and grandmothers in this area for their children and grandchildren. They are passing along their

Picnic on Front Lawn of Courthouse

great faith to the next generation as Lois and Eunice did in 2 Timothy 1:5. Pass the baton! Be a torch-bearer for Christ! These godly women are to provide a holy covering of intercession for the next generation of young people

As we were praying, a caravan of cars went by honking their horns. It was a wedding procession. We decreed: "Raise up the Bride of Christ in this county, O Lord. Get the Gospel message out!"

There was a civil defense tower behind the courthouse. "Send out the message of God! Send it out loud and clear!" says the Lord.

POCAHONTAS COUNTY
Pocahontas

The address was intriguing: 99 Court Square! May the Good Shepherd come, leaving the 99 counties to come after that one lone sheep...this one lone county. We invite the Holy Shepherd Jesus, to come and save that which is lost. (Matt. 18:11-14).

Kris Buchanan, Linda, Martie Cornell

The print out of info said the county was named for the Native Americans Princess Pocahontas. She became famous for her heroic intercession to save the life of Captain John Smith in 1613.

Our information also told us the general design of the courthouse was called: "Classic Revival" whatever that is. But we saw it as prophetic for what God purposes to do here. Thus we declared a "classic revival" by the power of the Holy Spirit in this county!

We rebuked a strong spirit of slumber here.

Ten Native Americans were buried at the SW corner of the foundation of the courthouse. It was our history that told us that because much to our dismay, there was no evidence of it announced on the building. We saw "lifelessness" here, so we

Praying on the Courthouse Steps

declared Ezekiel 37, speaking life and the breath of God to come into dry bones in this area! We prayed against generational bondages and curses. We decreed healing and restoration upon the land in the name of Jesus.

The courthouse structure itself was stark, cold, and looked more like a mausoleum. We continued to pray the Breath of God to come and awaken people to be shaken from their slumbering spirits. I (Linda) felt nausea in my stomach as we were approaching this county. We sensed it was a sign as to the "sanitarium" feeling to this courthouse...the upheaval of certain mind sets. We prayed against it.

Messengers

Interestingly enough, Mike and Martie, upon approaching the property, immediately felt there were sentinels guarding the area....as if they'd been waiting for a "release" to minister as messengers of fire! These were angels! They seemed to be near the grove of trees...waiting...watching, as if they'd been standing

Martie Blowing a Shofar

guard for a long time waiting for someone to come and make decrees in the name of the Most High God! *"Then the Lord said to me, 'You have seen well, for I am watching over My word to perform it'."* (Jer. 1:12; Isa. 55:11). *"Are they not all ministering spirits, sent out to render service, for the sake of those who will inherit salvation?"* (Heb. 1:14; Ps. 91:11).

Martie e-mailed me the following day to say she had awakened to the word "sentry." The previous day while at this county courthouse, she had felt the angels were like "centurions." She decided to look up the word *sentry*. It means: "a soldier placed on guard to see that only authorized persons pass his post and to warn of danger." "Sentinel" means "to protect." Certainly the Lord called us here for a "time such as this!"

Loose negative thinking! The spirit of heaviness was rebuked. We declared blossoms of fruit...the fruits of the Holy Spirit to come forth. Lord, raise up day and night prayer.

Kris and Martie at Indoor Garden

There has been hard ground here, but we asked the Holy Gardener to come and till the ground for holy purposes to be raised up. We discovered a garden-like area that seemed somewhat hidden. (See photo). It's the place where visitors wait to see prisoners in the county jail. It was amazing that we had access inside this place without being approached. There were three beautiful flower pots inside this garden area. We prayed: "Soften the ground, Lord...soften the hearts. Remove stony hearts. Raise up a spirit of boldness and humility. Come forth from the tomb, oh people...the Lord is calling... just as He did with Lazarus - Come forth!" (John 11:43).

The fruit of love is coming. (Gal. 5:22).

We rebuked any spirit of suicide that may have lingered here.

We declared a canopy of glory, a mantle of peace, over each corner of Pocahontas County. We decreed a holy infusion of God's government. A new identity in Jesus will come forth. The sluggard spirit was rebuked and we declared this to be a place of "nourishing" life.

This was the twelfth county on our 99 county prayer tour. We declared it to now be an apostolic county! People here will find their way by reading the Word of God. News media will have to report on signs and wonders here. Snares are now broken!

We rebuked abandonment. "God will never leave you or forsake you." (Deut. 31:6).

CALHOUN COUNTY
Rockwell City

After traveling through six counties, we were beginning to feel somewhat weary by the time we got to Rockwell City, our seventh and last one for the day. It's in those times we knew this assignment had nothing to do with us, but everything to do with God's purposes and plans for Iowa. We needed to rely even more

73

on the Holy Spirit to open our eyes to see prophetically what God's destiny was for this county. He is faithful. But it seems we all have to learn that fact over and over again!

One of the first things we noted was some kind of shield or breast plate high above the entrance of the courthouse. We could

not quite discern what it was supposed to be. (We should have brought binoculars to observe some of these things a bit closer.) However, we were led to declare that the shield of faith be released here! And since it was high atop the

A "Shield" at the Top of the Courthouse

building, we declared that shield of faith to be a banner over Calhoun County. The Lord desires that it be known for its FAITH IN JEHOVAH GOD. This county is called to walk in Ephesians 6.

There were many picnic tables on the property. *"O taste and see that the Lord is good; how blessed is the man who takes refuge in Him. O fear the Lord, you His saints; for those who fear Him, there is no want."* (Ps. 34: 8-9).

There are hidden treasures in secret places here. It's Psalm 42:7 where "deep calls to deep." There are wells of hidden treasures in God in this county. They'll have to dig deep for it...going deeper into the Lord. Job 28 speaks of this kind of search.

The Rock of Ages will make this county healthy and well.

The finger of God

The word, "tight knit" came forth. People want to keep to themselves…but we declared a spirit of unity and bonding in love through the power of the Blood of Jesus. We declared a "coming out"… a supporting of one another. Linda saw the verse in Matthew 23:37-39 where Jesus wept and prayed over Jerusalem and how He wanted so badly to gather the people together *"as a mother hen gathers her chicks under her wings,"* but they refused. So we decreed over this county in Jesus Name, that

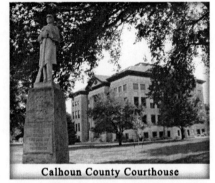

Calhoun County Courthouse

people *WILL* gather together to hear the Word of the Lord, and they WILL gather together for praise and worship! Release that desire, Oh God!

We rebuked the decrees that have been made in this courthouse that have shattered and disturbed many lives.

We prophesied the "Sons of Thunder" to come forth, those whose hearts are like John and James (Mark 3:17). Lord, raise up men of God who will be protectors of wives and children.

Mike saw an "inconsequential" spirit here…a sense in the people that says, "Nothing of consequence takes place here." He then declared lives will not be lost to this "inconsequential spirit" and the "wandering spirit" was rebuked. We proclaimed many will indeed be raised up to MAKE A DIFFERENCE in the Kingdom of God and that difference will come by way of prayers, but also "finances"–<u>giving</u> to the work of God for the advancement of His kingdom. "Let them see their significance." We prophesied JOY for Calhoun County!

The people here have been seen in the spirit as "reaching out, but not able to touch anything." "Touch them, Lord!" Linda saw, as it were, that famous Michelangelo painting of the finger of God touching the finger of man. We knew the Lord was confirming this very declaration.

Concluding this day's journey

As were concluding the day's journey, having gone to **seven** counties, Martie had been aware all day of the numbers "7" and

Martie, Kris, Linda Behind Courthouse;
Note Linda's Prayer Patrol T-shirt

"8." As we were saying our goodbyes, we casually glanced at the bank across the street and the sign read: 5:55 PM - <u>8</u>5 degrees. Five is the number of grace and favor, seven is God's number of perfection and eight means "new beginnings." We had started the day with these significant numbers in various ways and ended with them as well. We knew we had been wonderfully blessed throughout the entire day by God's great grace and His proclamations of divine destinies and new beginnings. We then sealed it by the power of His mighty Name!

I (Linda) awoke two days later with these words in my spirit from Isaiah, "Behold, I am doing a new thing! Do you not now perceive it?!" (Isa. 43:18-19).

Amen Lord, Amen.

✦ six ✦

CARROLL, SAC, BUENA VISTA, CHEROKEE, O'BRIEN, IDA

"And the elders of the Jews were successful in building through the prophesying of Haggai the prophet and Zechariah the son of Iddo." —Ezra 6:14

I had a very interesting vision from the Lord **a few years** before we had set out on this prophetic prayer journey to all of Iowa's 99 county courthouses. In this vision, I saw myself and a number of other people as if we were yellow submarines stealthily gliding through deep waters. Imagine that! People, as submarines! I didn't know what this meant, but when I pondered the vision all I could think of was that old Beatles song, "Yellow Submarine."

It wasn't too far along into this journey when I discovered the Lord had shown me in that vision what we were now doing! Mike and I kept saying we felt like we were scouts going into these counties. Unbeknownst to the people, we'd slip into town quietly like submarines, almost completely unnoticed, and destroy (spiritual) enemies. But God's fragrance, beauty and victory were always left behind.

Imagine my surprise when I received several e-mails regarding this very thing, each coming two days apart and from different people. They had remembered my writing about this in our monthly IWG Journal as we were about to embark on this divine assignment. One read: "A lady on her way back to Minnesota from our meetings said she and her husband saw a real submarine on a flat bed semi truck stopped along the freeway. In Iowa! How strangely wonderful can that be? What a prophetic picture of confirmation. Isn't the Lord fun?!

Another wrote: "Our theme for the meeting was "Underwater!" with a large fishnet, flickering fish lights and swimming gear. The Lord had me to go Hobby Lobby before the last meeting and get yellow construction paper to draw and cut out yellow submarines to add to the decorations. The Lord had told me the reason I was doing this was because the speaker liked to sing the Beatles' song, "Yellow Submarine," and yellow represented the glory of God. She went on to say she felt we were riding on glory waves that summer. Their speaker also felt many secular songs were actually prophetic. I'd have to agree with that. How amazing that our Creator God uses so many things to catch our attention, even secular music! He is not confined in His creativity, nor should we.

The most significant journey

We set out on our third journey on a beautiful August 19th morning. It was 7:15 AM, cloudy, overcast, foggy and rather humid. The temperature was 72 degrees, but it felt warmer. We were accompanied by Donna Bierle who is a beautiful woman of God and who has been a friend of our ministry for a long time. She is one rock solid lady in the Lord and is much loved and appreciated.

This was to be the most significant prayer journey of our entire assignment! Why? Because it was the day our second grandson, Ezra, was born! We even got to hear some of his very first cries via the cell phone. What splendid joy God gave us and a cherished memory forever.

CARROLL COUNTY
Carroll

This is a CRESTED County, standing above others in the region. It's as a shining city/ county in the land. *"You are the light of the world. A city set on a hill cannot be hidden"* (Matt. 5:14). It will have great influence in a righteous way. *"The light of the righteous rejoices, but the lamp of the wicked goes out."* (Prov. 13:9).

Linda and Donna Bierle

As we drove into Carroll, the fog was still somewhat dense, so we proclaimed spiritual fog to lift off people's eyes and hearts.

Heaven and earth are drawing together. Iowa is beginning to experience holy convergence!

The magnificence of God's glory was proclaimed.

This county will be known for the abundance of the Holy Spirit.

We saw and decreed a canopy of love and growth over Carroll County. *"He has brought me to his banquet hall, and his banner over me is love."* (Song of Songs 2:4).

We also noted the color blue on the building's façade as prophetically representing open visions and revelations that are destined for this county. Heaven is to be revealed. (Rev. 4:1).

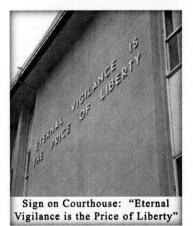

Sign on Courthouse: "Eternal Vigilance is the Price of Liberty"

The snares of the enemy were rebuked.

The old is giving way to the new and people here will begin to experience new insights and fresh revelation of who God really is. Old mindsets are being washed away.

Donna noted the areas of new grass growing on the lawn. We proclaimed "new growth in God" is coming!

Things out of balance in this county have created some injustice. Grant a true plumb line of justice, Oh God.

Depression was also rebuked.

We called forth a "vigil" and for this county to LIGHT UP! Bring forth the "watchman on the wall."

> *"But as for me, I will watch expectantly for the Lord; I will wait for the God of my salvation. My God will hear me. Do not rejoice over me, O my enemy. Though I fall I will rise; though I dwell in darkness, the Lord is a light for me."*
>
> —Micah 7:7-8

We decreed heaviness to lift and for lightheartedness to come, setting souls free in Jesus Name.

Sound the alarm, wake the sleepers! Let them know the price of salvation in them. Let their lamps be ready and full of the anointing. (Matt. 25).

We saw chairs being moved out of the courthouse, as if it were "moving day." The seat of man is being removed as the NEW SEAT of God's government and authority moves in.

There was a sign on the premises that read: "Not all signs posted regarding hazardous material." So Carroll County, beware of hidden hazards!

People here haven't gone far enough into God. They think there isn't any more. We prayed, "Lead them on, Oh God. Let them go deeper."

A new vitality in God will emerge. Praise sounds!

Raise up those who love you, Lord, and may their prayers be dispatched.

Let lives not be patched up, but totally healed by Jesus. Let a desire for the "new" come forth. Let that which inspires come forth.

The Sword of the Lord, the Word of God, is slicing through the atmosphere in this county! Gideon and Samson pulled down that which was unholy. Lord, let the unholy things crumble. (Judg. 6, 7 and 16:28-30).

There will be a new sound coming forth in this area!

SAC COUNTY
Sac City

It was still cloudy and overcast as we drove into Sac County. But we felt the strong presence of the Lord. His prophetic words began to flow through us. While "Sac" is a Native Americans name, we interpreted it spiritually as "womb," or new births, new life. Lord, bring people out of their enclosures, their bondages, things that have held them back. Give them new life, abundant life, pure life, ordained life which was purposed from the foundation of the world!

There has been an unholy umbilical cord (unholy attachments) and but those will now be turned into divine connections to God.

We rebuked shifting sands and prophesied people will come back to the sure foundation of Jesus.

We proclaimed all of Isaiah 28.

Let the mountain of God be seen and the Ark of the Covenant of God be known here.

We saw a "memorial tree" dedicated to those who had died during (and after) World War I. It had been dedicated in 1925. Again, it was strong upon us to proclaim life. We decreed the TREE OF LIFE will be known here. We called forth the knowledge of the Righteous Branch. *"'Behold, the days are coming,' declares the Lord, 'When I shall raise up for David a righteous Branch; and He will reign as king*

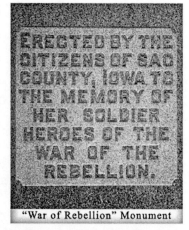

"War of Rebellion" Monument

and act wisely and do justice and righteousness in the land" (Jer. 23:5). Zechariah 6:12 says, *"Then say to him, 'Thus says the Lord of hosts, Behold, a man whose name is Branch, for He will branch out from where He is; and He will build the temple of the Lord.'"*
We had just taken a picture of a sign outside of town about "I spy something green." Lord, we declare "green" to represent growth in the things of God that is about to bud forth in this county.

We ran into a gentleman who was doing some gardening nearby. He came over to give us some in-depth history as he had researched much of it in this county. Since he was gardening, his hands were all covered in mud and dirt, but we still shook his hands heartily thanking him for all the information he'd given us. Moments later, we asked how we could pray for him. He responded, "Well, I don't know if you know of this Fire Man

"*I spy something green.*"

Gathering in the Arizona desert..." (I did know about it and it's not good!), "but it's where different faiths come together in a *rainbow* of unity to pray for world peace, mother earth...etc, etc...." His "dirty hands" reflected his heart, soul, mind and body. But that morning, he got a good dose of our holy God! We even took his picture, which he obviously agreed to. We're still praying for our new found friend.

Only a few would know

One of the interesting things this man told us was of the triangle Native Americans tribal burial grounds we were standing on. It was a crescent shaped burial area with barely any indication of what lie beneath. Most of those remembrances had been removed a number of years ago. Only a few historians would know of this burial ground, unless they combed the county records! How sad. We felt much warfare here and prayed for release.

After our brief prayer with this man, we continued walking around the courthouse grounds, praying against a spirit of deception in this area.

A juvenile detention center is attached to the courthouse. We declared the captives (those held captive to sin and rebellion), will be set free in Jesus Name. We proclaimed the young will arise to  declare NEW LIFE! Lord, turn the curse into a blessing (Neh. 13:2). We actually declared much of the book of Nehemiah in this place because we saw an extensive building of the kingdom of God that will take place in this county. We called

Linda and Donna Bierle

forth the REBUILDING of things that have been devastated. Intimacy with God will be restored.

God will also raise up a Cup Bearer to the King here! (Neh. 1:11; 1 Kings. 10:5).

Nehemiah 4:14 and 20 - fight for your families! God will fight for you! Lord, let many voices rise up as trumpets declaring the Word of God.

We stood against earlier governing powers who placed heavy burdens on the people. (Neh. 5:15).

Then we decreed the joy of the Lord to come forth and a breaking open of the fragrance of Christ.

Interesting

One of the interesting things about this Prophetic Prayer Journey, is that quite often we would begin to see immediate results of our prayers, proclamations and divine decrees. For instance, within months of this particular journey, we clipped a newspaper story about Sac County. The headline read: "Sac County's rural life rates No. **7** in America." There's that number seven again! We saw this report as a "Hallelujah Jesus moment!"

Another story that ran soon afterwards was one of a college student from Sac County, Kevin Peyton, who had begun painting quilt designs on the sides of barns. We didn't know any of this when we started driving past those beautiful designs along the roadways as we traveled. It just fascinated us that someone had done it! This young gentleman was named one of the top 10 youth volunteers in America by the Prudential Spirit of Community Awards.

We praise and thank you Lord for all you are doing as a result of our little submarine efforts!

BUENA VISTA COUNTY
Storm Lake

This day held within its confines the aspect of both death and life. We felt its effects in various ways as we encountered spiritual warfare. Our friend, Donna, who was with us on this particular journey, had gotten word of the death of her sister-in-law's husband. Of course, our prayers were directed to the grieving family.

An Interesting Welcome Sign

Later, as we approached Buena Vista County, Mike and I got a call from our son-in-law in Pennsylvania saying our daughter had just given birth to their second son, Ezra! This little guy squealed with gusto and zeal for life as we intently listened via our cell phone. We heard his first cries! This precious new grandson of ours hadn't even been weighed or cleaned up. He was lying on his mommy's breast, having just come into the world. What a moment to remember! We all began to laugh and rejoice as the sun began to break out overhead. Within a short period of time, we had experienced the circle of life. Lord, have mercy.

Midwives

Prophetically, we saw ourselves as midwives who came to help birth the purposes of God. We decreed new spiritual births. Bring forth life and more of what you desire Lord. And let all the umbilical cords be broken—spiritually, so that holy, living waters can flow over and

Mike and I Moments After Hearing of Our New Grandson!

through this county. *"But the midwives feared God, and did not do as the king of Egypt had commanded them, but let the boys live"* (Exod. 1:17). Lord, raise up godly midwives in this county!

Storm Lake and Buena Vista County—Jesus speaks to you as He did on the stormy Sea of Galilee, "Peace! Be still" (Mark 4:39)!

Let faith be raised up here…no tossing to and fro (James 1:6). Raise up the mature. (Eph. 4:14).

We decreed the Lord is raising up unique giftings upon His people. Speak to them in love, Oh Lord.

Make new the attitudes of minds.

We prophesied a new standard would arise–a King's point.

This next stage of life will be good.

Rocks were all around this courthouse. Let it be founded on the solid Rock of Jesus, the Rock of Ages. Jesus is the Solid Rock on which they will now stand. Different jeweled rocks scattered in the landscaping showed us prophetically that there is an emergence of different people groups that will be working together in peace.

Corner View of Courthouse

We declared a letting go of bitterness and purity of motives to come forth.

This county is called to take care of foreigners and widows (Lev. 19:33-37). This is a place of refuge. God has called this county to place a watch over the most vulnerable - widows and orphans.

"Vista"–a good vista! The dictionary's second meaning is: "mental view of a series of events." Lord, let the view here be a good one! This area will become a new habitation of God.

We were called here as soldiers of Christ and declare, *"Let God arise, let His enemies be scattered."* (Ps. 68:1).

A high standard of living in Christ is coming forth. The old is passing away and the new is coming.

The Lord declares in the opening chapters of Genesis, "It is good!" We knew what we were doing on this tour was *good* and this county is going to benefit from that declaration.

The battles in homes will cease and a godly, holy peace is being released. The Lord God Almighty stands with His arms open wide, bidding them to come home like the prodigal son in scripture. We declared many people in this county will come out of their pit. (Luke 15:11-32).

CHEROKEE COUNTY
Cherokee

Mike and I in Front of Courthouse

This county needs to look beyond that which is in the here and now and together, look to the Creator and King. Look beyond prejudice, beyond skin color, beyond any opportunities missed, beyond religion, in order to have a relationship with the Lord.

This was our fourth county of the day. We had a fun picnic on the courthouse grounds. This area sits on a hill and we munched our lunch with a beautiful, panoramic view of the city of Cherokee and beyond as our backdrop. The sun was now shining brightly and "it was a beautiful day in the neighbor-hood"!

As we began our walk around the courthouse, revelation began to flow.

This was a highly elevated place in the natural, so we declared the people in this county will ascend the hill of the Lord.

Donna, Linda Observe War Memorials

"Who may ascend into the hill of the Lord? And who may stand in His holy place? He who has clean hands and a pure heart, who has not lifted up his soul to falsehood, and has not sworn deceitfully. He shall receive a blessing from the Lord and righteousness from the God of his salvation. This is the generation of those who seek Him, who seek Thy face...."

—Psalm 24:3-6

We sensed generational curses. We prayed those curses would now be broken and that shame would be also break off.

We repented of bloodshed and abuse. Lord, renew! Restore!

We decreed a conquering spirit, an overcoming spirit would emerge. *"But in all these things we overwhelmingly conquer through Him who loved us"* (Rom. 8:37). *"And they overcame him because of the blood of the Lamb and because of the word of their testimony, and they did not love their life even to death."* (Rev. 12:11).

We knew angel watchers were on guard here!

Righteousness and justice will prevail.

We pronounced this to be healing ground by the power of Jesus Name and His redeeming Blood.

Renew minds, Oh Lord. Let fear, doubt and anxiety be let go of.

Release LIGHT, knowledge and revelation of the Savior.

Keys

The Lord is going to release the KEYS of His kingdom here. Cherokee County, you will hear the SOUNDS of KEYS...letting loose...setting bound people free. Let freedom ring! Wherever the Spirit of the Lord is there is liberty! (2 Cor. 3:17; Matt. 16:19; Isa. 33:6).

A man drove by in a van and seeing our Prayer Patrol shirts, he yelled out the window, "No way!" He knew we were praying at the courthouse. He continued to yell something about wanting to know

Donna Bierle Placing Isaiah-Inscribed Stone Next to Boulder Near the Courthouse

more, but another vehicle came up behind him and he had to drive away. As he drove off, he again yelled something about our PRAYER PATROL t-shirts and seemed to be quite interested in them. Since he crossed our path, we prayed for him as well.

We drove to the HOUSE OF PRAYER located here and found no one there at the time. We prayed the Lord's blessing upon it and asked that it would be filled up with praying saints.

We came against prejudices and high mindedness.

We proclaimed that God would bring people in this county into a new season and for the light of God's love to break forth.

Let the people in this county begin to skip with joy and wonder as a child discovering life anew. (Ps. 29:6).

We saw a governmental shift. May the righteous authority of the Lord come forth.

O'BRIEN COUNTY
Primghar

It didn't take long for the Holy Spirit to begin giving us prophecies for this county. Just observing the picture of the SOS on a building across the street spoke volumes to us. The sign is in red and white. Notice the life preserver. Red represents the blood of Jesus; white represents the holiness of God. The Lord purposes to save lives here, physically and spiritually. We

Very Interesting!

knew in the spirit there was urgent prayer needed for O'Brien County. We decreed people are going to know the revelation and power of the saving blood of Jesus and His holiness. Get ready O'Brien County! Begin releasing your faith for great things of God to transpire here. Sing out the old song, "There is power, power, wonder working power in the precious blood of the Lamb!" Believe it!

We began to decree a massive anointing for evangelism. Pre-Christians are about to be saved!

Winds of change are blowing here. The Breath of God is bringing vitality, along with strength of heart and soul.

The streets surrounding the courthouse were of cobblestone. We prophesied people will begin to walk upon the SOLID ROCK of Jesus Christ.

O'Brien County Courthouse

O'Brien County, God has not passed you by! Turn the page (today/now) for a new history to begin.

We declared the light and warmth of a camp fire. People will make their hearts a "camp of the Lord." There will be a pillar of fire by night (Exod. 13:20-22). Verse 22 says, *"He did not take away the pillar of cloud by day, not the pillar of fire by night, from before the people."*

We rebuked the dark night of the soul.

Holy Spirit Gatherings

Lord, let the people arise to drink heavily from the Living Well that will never go dry. Let them be filled with the new wine and drunk with the Holy Spirit (Acts 2). We prophesied there will be HOLY SPIRIT GATHERINGS!

There will be discoveries of hidden things...in the natural... treasures hidden in darkness.

Lord, release a spirit of gentleness.

Nurture the seeds of faith that are here, so they can grow and produce.

Release a firestorm of grace (Rev. 3:16). Raise up hot Christians! Turn up the fire on them!

Release insatiable hunger for You, Oh God.

Release a shepherd for Primghar, Lord, because the sheep have been scattered (Ezek. 34). We perceived by the Spirit that a sword (pain/sorrow/shame…) may have struck a shepherd. God is healing them now. Jesus taught that the GOOD SHEPHERD would leave the 99 (Iowa counties) to go after the one that was lost. (Matt. 18:11-14).

Release a new sound here, Lord, the sound of love, holiness and purity.

Love may have grown cold in this area (Matt. 24:12-28). We rebuked those things (vs. 24) "where the vultures gather" because of death. Therefore, we declare those things cancelled by the Blood of Jesus. God is releasing the four winds of heaven (vs. 30-34)!

IDA COUNTY
Ida Grove

This is the county where a trucker and a former alcoholic became Governor, then senator, and most importantly a Christian believer, Harold Hughes. Certainly God had a great destiny for him and he found it! Therefore, we prophesied people in this county come into their divine destinies! We called forth those divine destinies particularly in little children and for them to begin to walk it out now.

Mike Ready to Anoint Front Door

There was an RV parked in back of the building. Painted on its side were the words: "Ida County Mobile Communications." We proclaimed communication with God will go to a new level.

Many people here are "masked," as if they may have something to hide. Many things are hidden or masked. We rebuked it, proclaiming they find their true identity in the Lord and will begin to move onward and upward in Christ Jesus.

> "Brethren, I do not regard myself as having laid hold of it yet; but one thing I do: forgetting what lies behind and reaching forward to what lies ahead, I press on toward the goal for the prize of the upward call of God in Christ Jesus"
>
> —Philippians 3:13-14

Also Revelation 4 is for this county.

The "cupola" on top of the courthouse gave it the appearance of a Victorian House. We saw the word, "home" stand out. The Lord says, "Come home to Me! Get comfortable and cozy with Me. I will show you great and wonderful things which you do not know." (Jer. 33:3).

Governmental authority in Christ will arise in this place.

People ask just like Nathanael in John 1:46, "Can any good come from Ida Grove?" Yes! The Lord says, "I can use, and will use, the least of these. My servants here look like little Davids, but

I am calling them forth just like a David, rulers for justice and righteousness."

Little talks with Jesus are going to escalate and accelerate.

Let your hand, Oh Lord reshape and renew the land in this county. Reshape the atmosphere.

We declared peace upon the "house," upon peoples' homes, the houses of God, and the courthouse. We decreed peace to come upon every threshold of the houses in this county.

Conclusion

After driving away from Ida County heading toward our home in the Des Moines area, we rejoiced and gave thanks to the Lord for this August 19th prayer journey. It was a day which held many awesome memories after traveling 371.8 miles in His Name!

Linda and Donna in Prayer

❧ seven ❧

SHELBY, CRAWFORD MONONA, WOODBURY, HARRISON

"O give thanks to the Lord, for He is good; for His loving kindness is everlasting. Let the redeemed of the Lord say so, whom He has redeemed from the hand of the adversary, and gathered from the lands, from the east and from the west, from the north and from the south." —Psalm 107:103

As previously stated, we could make our plans, but it was always our holy Commander in Chief, the Lord, who would direct our paths. Every journey was divinely orchestrated by Him and we simply followed. It was rather significant that each time we set out on one of these prophetic prayer journeys the date itself seemed to always hold special meaning. This one held personal significance as it was our youngest daughter's 21st birthday. She lived in Colorado at the time. We called her to send our love and prayers. It was September 23rd, 2006. It was also Rosh Hashanah.

Bob Jones, who is one of our modern day prophets known for the accuracy of his words, recently said that we are moving from intercession into proclamation. This is exactly what this prayer journey was all about! It gave credence that this assignment was strategically designed by the Lord.

Lucy Nieman would also be joining us for a portion of travels on this particular day. At the time, she lived in the tiny Iowa town of Ute in Monona County where we would be heading. What a blessing to have her come alongside of us. We appreciated her gift of blowing the shofar, especially on Rosh Hashanah!

This particular trip would be one of our longest, traveling 472 miles. As we eagerly drove off with anticipation and excitement, the morning air was cool and crisp at **55** degrees. "Good numbers!" Five of course, means grace and favor. Nonetheless, the day held spiritual warfare which God gave us the grace to overcome. Glory!

SHELBY COUNTY
Harlan

Shelby County Courthouse

The Lord revealed to us that this is an OASIS county. Rivers of washing and cleansing are coming. Isaiah 43:19 is for Shelby County. The Lord is bringing forth new beginnings. *"Behold, I will do something new, now it will spring forth, will you not be aware of it? I will even make a roadway in the wilderness, rivers in the desert."*

We were personally excited about going to this county as it holds the name of our only granddaughter, at least at this writing! That's not to say this county was about her, but it was fun to visit a county that had the same name.

We decreed no favoritism in the courts and that there would be proper decisions of lawyers, judges and magistrates in this county.

We proclaimed a fresh openness to God and open heavens to occur. (Rev. 4).

God wants to reveal strength in this area. A new strength in His people will arise. *"The Lord will give strength to His people; the Lord will bless His people with peace."* (Ps. 29:11).

There is a fortress in God here. But it's partly closed, partly opened. An openness to see God is coming forth.

Governmental godly authority is coming with the spoken Word. Let the Word of God become as strong as the stone on the courthouse. A jubilation is coming! The WRITTEN WORD will go forth by the power of revelation, insight and understanding. Open your light of justice!

There is sense of love for the past here, but it's got to come into proper alignment. We called forth Living Stones (1 Pet. 2:5)! The Lord laid His life down for the people of this county and He is the capstone or cornerstone here. He is going to raise up sons and daughters with governmental authority.

War Memorial

Past generations have kept an openness to that which is pure. Defend it Lord!

This county was named after General Isaac Shelby, the first governor of Kentucky. "Shelby" however, is associated with a feminine name in our society. Therefore, we sensed God is about to release the women of this county to come together in a sisterhood of believers to strengthen and support one another.

We saw Isaiah 40 as key for this area. People will be carried on eagles' wings. A "rising" in the things of God will occur. There is a sense of expectancy, and the next generation will proceed in the things of God moving onward and upward. "Lord, take the smallest things and explode them for Your glory!" *Incidentals* of God–really aren't!

An openness to revelation of God is here.

God will raise up writers and poets in this county.

We prayed blessings upon the pulpits… preachers and teachers, those who plant seeds of harvest.

The environment is breaking and changing. Something new is arising! A new atmosphere is coming! Lord, raise up the laborers for the harvest of 30, 60, and 100 fold. Raise up the next generation of godly mothers and fathers. Hebrews 11 was declared as the next lineage of faith that's coming!

CRAWFORD COUNTY
Denison

As we arrived in Crawford County, the skies were partly cloudy and it was about to rain. We quickly went about our Father's business.

Linda and Lucy Nieman By Courthouse

One of the first things we took notice of first was the construction all around the sides of the courthouse and also the street sign "Broadway." The Donna Reed festival occurs here because of the movie, "It's a

Wonderful Life" in which she starred. We then declared a wonderful life in God to come forth right here! We prophesied people will go further in their walk with God than what they could ever imagine. Ephesians 4 was proclaimed. Verse 20 was especially noted: *"Now to Him*

Mike and Lucy Sit Near Courthouse at Corner of Ave C and Broadway

who is able to do exceedingly abundantly beyond all that we ask or think, according to the power that works within us...." "Go farther" is the word for this county!

Let the pastors go farther in the Lord than they ever thought possible! Bring forth fruit that will remain. We also rebuked the spirit of religion that's prevalent in this county.

Lucy Blowing the Shofar

Our history told us the first courthouse was constructed of clay. We prayed, "Lord, have Your way with these people! You are the potter and they/we are the clay. Mold them after Your will." Isaiah 64:8 was declared, *"But now, O Lord, Thou art our Father, we are the clay, and Thou our potter; and all of us are the work of Thy hand."*

The word "wart" was used to describe the unsightly addition to the courthouse many years ago. We read where SEVEN tons of marble rock was used to build the current courthouse. Because the number seven represents God's perfection, we rebuked any

101

spiritual warts the enemy may have tried to leave here and we decreed God's *perfecting* to come forth.   We proclaimed a completion of His divine purposes.

Raise up wise judges for Crawford County, Oh Lord.

Raise up spiritual patriots!

The youthful generation will seek God's face. We prayed they would have the spirit of revelation and the eyes of their understanding opened. Let them be known for the Presence of God.

Raise up the mighty remnant to destroy the "religious" spirits, Oh God. Raise up new leadership. Bring forth divine destinies.

Written on the war memorial was: "Those who answered the call of patriotism…." Let God's people in this area answer the call to God's war of spiritual intercession. Teach them spiritual warfare, Oh Lord. Raise up spiritual patriots!

Bring forth the apostles and prophets and a love for the higher gifts. (1 Cor. 14).

Pour out Your Spirit, Oh Lord on the Latinos in this area. They didn't come here just for a job, but for God.

By the power of the Holy Spirit, we sensed corruption within the law enforcement area. We prayed for redemption and godly justice in that area.

The fragrance of Christ was decreed.

> "But thanks be to God, who always leads us in His triumph in Christ, and manifests through us the sweet aroma of the knowledge of Him in every place. For we

are the fragrance of Christ to God among those who are being saved and among those who are perishing."

—2 Corinthians 2:14-15

Quantum leaps for God will come forth.

This is a welcoming community.

"Lord, allow their prayers to be heard!"

This area was named among the top 100 cities in which to live. Let it be so in the spiritual realm as well. Thank you Lord, for the peace which is settling on the land.

God is ready to bring home the one "farthest away!" Bring back the prodigals. (Luke 15).

Put out the *welcoming mat* of the Holy Spirit! We proclaimed Revelation 4:1 as the sun/Son breaks forth! It only takes a spark to set ablaze a forest. Come Holy Spirit with Your fire!

This is a STRATEGIC COUNTY. We called forth the raising up champions for Jesus. Chariots of fire are coming! Mike saw this as if it were a "flint rock," or "trigger," or a "firing machine." A spiritual explosion is coming to this county as a result.

MONONA COUNTY
Onawa

It seemed rather dismal when we arrived in this county seat. It was dark, cloudy, overcast and had begun to rain. The air was chilly. It was also the place where my worst fears came true. Our camera broke! We went looking to find a quick replacement. We knew part of our assignment for this prophetic prayer journey was to document our travels with photographs. God provided!

Onawa, which is the county seat, is a Native American word meaning "wide awake." It's also known for its <u>wide</u> streets. We prophesied: "Open up the pathways, Lord, that lead to You. Open them wide and wider still!"

Lucy Nieman Blowing the Shofar

Lucy blew the shofar a number of times and kept declaring: "Awake! Awake" (Isa. 52). This county is to *ascend the hill of the Lord.* (Ps. 24).

We prophesied and declared the SOUND of music…sounds of praise and worship to ascend so the people can go up and climb the mountain of the Lord. Monona will kiss the face of God!

A release of Living Waters is coming, fresh waters, fresh brooks of God. *"He who believes in Me, as the Scriptures said, 'From his innermost being shall flow rivers of living water'."* (John 7:38).

"Wake up and kiss the Morning Son!" God is releasing healings here. (Mal. 4:2-3).

We sensed that while there are many believers here, their disbelief is greater than their belief. "Lord, let believers believe! Bring them out of their sleepy, slumbering spirit. Bring forth the action that you require, Lord. Be known here for WHO You are!"

We saw the people here as having been too dependent on their own hands. Give them now the <u>keys</u> to the Kingdom of Heaven (Matt. 16:19). Lucy had a dream the previous week about needing a key to open a door, so we knew this word was right on!

We prophesy breakthroughs of intimacy with You, Lord. Let the true knowledge of God come forth. We call forth the beauty of the Lord. Let grace and mercy fall like rain.

Fertility of the land is coming.

Let them be wide awake, Lord! God will arise with healing in His wings.

Let there be a compelling need for righteousness and justice. Let it flow from this place.

Eskimo pie dessert was invented here. Yum! Bring forth the spiritual desserts of God! (Ps. 34:8).

We rebuked any coldness of heart (Matt. 24:12). We also rebuked the "clamoring of men" and called for the sounds of God to burst forth.

We broke any evil powers of barrenness, declaring fruitfulness. Holy Spirit, we welcome you into Monona County! Crush strongholds.

Let people hear the SOUND in the treetops for strategies in spiritual warfare (2 Sam. 5:24). There is a call for the heritage of the saints to arise. Raise up those who will know how to weather the storms and not be reduced to what is seen, but to what is unseen and to know the power available through the Holy Spirit (2 Cor. 4:18). Let them be pregnant with the Word of God. Bring forth the fathers!

Mike and Linda

WOODBURY COUNTY
Sioux City

It was raining on and off as we approached our fifth county of the day. We experienced much spiritual warfare and found it difficult to "plow through." But the Holy Spirit was always faithful to help us!

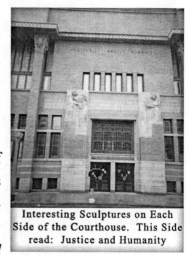

Interesting Sculptures on Each Side of the Courthouse. This Side read: Justice and Humanity

We began by declaring all of Psalm 85 over this county. It speaks of mercy. Verse 10 says, *"Loving-kindness and truth have met together; righteousness and peace have kissed each other."* This county is called to manifest the scripture from James 2:13, *"For judgment will be merciless to one who has shown no mercy; mercy triumphs over judgment."*

The "spirit of Law" is displayed in a huge figure over the courthouse, but it felt somewhat like the spirit of death. No green thing was around this courthouse. There was no lawn, trees, shrubs or flower pots, nothing that displayed life. It appeared void of vibrant growth and life.

Above the sculptures on another side of the building (not the one pictured) are the words: "Justice and Peace have met together. Truth hath sprung out of the Earth." Truth comes from Jehovah God alone. So we

Woodbury County Courthouse

decreed revelation and salvation for those in this county, that they

106

will come into the knowledge that God is TRUTH. *"Jesus said to him, 'I am the way, the truth, and the life; no one comes to the Father, but through Me'"* (John 14:6). We declared the spirit of truth would come and reign/ rain over this county.

Ungodly things that are deeply rooted need to be shaken loose. Shake and awake this county!

> "And this expression, 'Yet once more,' denotes the removing of those things which can be shaken, as of created things, in order that those things which cannot be shaken may remain. Therefore, since we receive a kingdom which cannot be shaken, let us show gratitude, by which we may offer to God an acceptable service with reverence and awe; for our God is a consuming fire."
>
> —Hebrews 12:27-29

We decree this county will become a sweet fragrance in Your nostrils, Lord. We claim holy fire! We claim a holy offering of praise and an offering of love.

"Confining keys" that are imbedded will be exposed. Keys are not to lock up people but to release the kingdom of God. We call forth holy keys to unlock divine destinies. Things that have held people in bondage will be broken in the Name of Jesus!

The Sword of the Lord is being prepared for released here. It will get rid of the Leviathan spirit, the serpent that has held this county. *"In that day the Lord will punish Leviathan the fleeing serpent, with His fierce and great and mighty sword, even Leviathan the twisted serpent; and He will kill the dragon who lives in the sea."* (Isa. 27:1; Ps. 74:14).

Pioneers and forerunners

We decreed Pioneers and forerunners for a new generation. Bring forth the trail blazers!

We declared this will be seen as a shining city on a hill.

Angelic visitations are coming! And instead of oppression–freedom!

We rebuked the mixture of the gods, and unholy fire. People of God, do not eat food (spiritual food) that is cooked over defilement (Ezek. 4:12). We prayed the saints would watch the source from which they are drawing spiritual nourishment. We called forth a sweet fragrance.

The airport's initials are: SUX. Bring forth the heroes again Lord, just as with Flight 232!

The muddy river has defiled the land, but we proclaim a cleansing over it by the purity of the Word of God. Release a flood of your spirit, Oh God!

People here feel like they've been between a rock and a hard place. Mike saw an evil root system…like the roots of a tree that go deep. But we have come to decree the Lord purposes to pull out those roots so that the Righteous Branch will come forth. (Isa. 4:2).

Lord, let them know the Rock of Ages (Isa. 9:7). May the zeal of the Lord accomplish this!

We rebuked generational curses, especially regarding Native Americans. A weeping spirit will arise. However, a "rain" or a "cleansing" will occur by the Spirit of the Lord. A repentant spirit is being released along with humility.

Bring forth the DESIGNS of God. Bring down prideful spirits.

Woodbury county, ascend the hill of the Lord! (Ps. 24). This is a GATEWAY city and county.

We rebuked abortion and decreed life, eternal life! Babies are coming in the natural and spiritual realms. We speak to people's hearts: "Live! Live!" This is similar to Ezekiel 37.

Belligerence was rebuked and we declared obedience to the Lord and obedience to the Most High God will rest here.

HARRISON COUNTY
Logan

We were always able to perceive certain things by the power of the Holy Spirit. We were totally dependent on Him at all times. He showed us this county had a feeling of detachment from the rest of the state. Many have felt alone or abandoned. Re-attach their identity and their prayers to the rest of the state, Oh Lord.

Linda Taking Notes

We began to prophesy this area will be known for its spiritual warriors! They will bring down demonic strongholds by praise and worship.

Let this county be defended by faith in God. May traditional religions become *alive* in the Holy Spirit. Draw the Body of Christ together!

Lord, bring forth the "more"… the "beyond the status quo."

Bring unity and the power of agreement. The differences are really minor.

Break fears and bind people together with love.

Harrison County, you will be known for more than just your farmland!

People here have lost their identity to other states nearby. A distinct flavor of God will mark this place. *"Behold, I've inscribed you on the palms of My hands,"* says the Lord. (Isa. 49:16).

Raise up the arts here, Lord. This is a community of opportunity.

God is dropping fresh dew from heaven here.

We then called forth righteousness. There has also been abandonment...impotence—we prayed for the fathering spirit. Let families be attracted to this county.

There's been lack of bread—spiritual food. Bring forth Living Bread, Oh God! Feed the malnourished souls. May they fall in love with your Word!

Police stopped a car right in front of the courthouse while we were there. We felt eyelids have been closed and they cannot see which way to go. Open spiritual eyes, Lord. *"The lamp of the body is the eye; if therefore your eye is clear, your whole body will be full of light."* (Matt. 6:22).

Let a revival spirit come forth!

Let a warring spirit come forth. We called forth commanders, generals and judges.

There's been a faith without power. Lord, bring holy, reverential fear of God to this place.

We proclaimed Isaiah 55 with restoration and renewal for

Harrison County. Righteousness and justice will be the standards.

We stand in agreement with God's purposes in Logan (town).

There were vultures on top of the courthouse. We rebuked them! We prayed for *watchmen*,

Mike Praying By Courthouse Entrance

those who will pray at night and at all hours. Bring forth vigilance Oh God! We also prayed for the "seer anointing" to arise. Many have been seeing through rose-colored glasses. Their eyes have been nearly closed, not even aware of what's going on. Lord, re-energize the people.

In the spirit, we saw picnics and reunions on the courthouse lawn. Bring forth reunions!

Let the crumbling end and the rebuilding begin. Bring forth those who will help rebuild. *"Let us arise and build"* (Neh. 2:18).

As we were leaving this area, we came across the Museum of Religious Arts. While the displays were insightful and interesting, it caused us to pray for a fresh move of God for Iowa and beyond!

❦ eight ❦

HAMILTON, WRIGHT, HANCOCK, WINNEBAGO, WORTH

"Every place on which the sole of your foot shall tread shall be yours." —Deuteronomy 11:24

B y now, we're well into autumn. It's October 28th, 2006 and the temperature hovered most of the day in the lower 40's with cold, penetrating winds. We put in 358 miles and were blessed every inch of the way!

We were privileged to have Craig and Diane Leaming join us on this cool October day. Craig has a story of his own to tell! This godly gentleman was directed by the Lord to <u>walk</u> the length and breadth of the entire United States repenting for the sins of this nation. You can find out more about his incredible journey at www.acrosswalk.com. It's ironic, or maybe not, that Craig began his walk the same month we began our Prophetic Prayer Journey to Iowa's 99 County courthouses in June 2006. We also finished the same month! God is calling **Iowans** to arise, go forth, and **walk** into their divine destinies for the glory of God!

HAMILTON COUNTY
Webster City

Arriving in Hamilton County, the weather was a good reflection of what we were sensing in the spirit. There's a coolness here. It made you feel as if you were a prisoner in jail. We began by proclaiming Palm 146, especially verse 7 *"[God]...Who executes justice for the oppressed; who gives food to the hungry. The Lord sets the prisoners free."*

The county sign was burrowed in the side of a hill. There was no other one like it on our entire journey throughout Iowa. It

Linda Standing With Craig and Diane

looked somewhat like a tombstone...a grave. We began to proclaimed freedom and a breaking of shackles. Set the captives free! As we walked around the courthouse, we ran into a man smoking a cigarette. We asked who he was and if we could pray for him? He refused saying, "I'm *just* a jailer." Immediately we thought of the jailer in Acts 16:22-34. As we walked on, we prayed for him, declaring his household would be saved.

People have been weighed down, bowed down to a lesser destiny. Let them look up to you Oh Lord! Do not let them bow down to the weight of the world.

We decreed open gates of possibilities.

This is a place where aliens, people who have moved here from other countries, must begin to know their identity and self esteem.

People here seem older than they should be, seemingly having been bowed over by their burdens. Release them from their burdens Oh God!

Release pastors and teachers to minister freedom. Bring forth a spirit of freedom, not just doctrine.

Release the people from the "law that condemns" and let them know the Holy Spirit brings freedom. (2 Cor. 3:17).

We noted a "smelly" kind of thing…as might have been when Lazarus came forth out of the tomb. Linda felt an earthquake (almost literally), as when Jesus raised Lazarus! Resurrection power is being released here (John 11)! Again, looking at the subterranean sign, it seemed like a hollow grave representing a shallowness or emptiness in the lives of people. Loose them like Lazarus! Feed them with the

Mike and Craig

food Jesus spoke of when He said to the mother and father after raising their daughter from the dead: *"Give her something to eat"* (Mark 5:35-43). Jesus is the LIVING BREAD, take Him and eat!

There's been a lack of pride, as the courthouse sign denotes, having been placed in the ground. This county has been beaten down. There's been a ground level mentality, having felt no significance in rising above. But Revelation 4:1 is beckoning. "Come up here!" We declared Revelation 3:16 that passion for God would arise. Revelation 1:5-6 was read as we decreed the blood of Jesus sets this county free. Bring forth the message of Calvary, Lord, and let it be proclaimed from the roof tops. Let fullness of God's glory come forth.

Black stones

We perceived the black stones on the front of the courthouse (see Photo), may have been extracted by forced labor or prisoners. Again, the mound that held the courthouse sign, to Diane, gave her the impression of a mass grave. There have been too many issues of captivity in this area. There are hog confinements here. "Confinement" reminded us of jails. We sensed some people feel unredeemable. But we've all fallen short of the glory of God. We're all redeemable by the Blood of Jesus (Rom. 3)! We proclaimed hope to those who don't know it's available. We also declared a replacement of the rock on the courthouse with the spiritual cornerstone from Isaiah 28:16-17, proclaiming solid foundations. Let the Rock of Ages be known here.

We sensed there's been improper use of justice. Bring forth godly justice, Oh Lord. We came against the spirit of lawlessness and prayed the armor of light, the armor of God, to come upon the people. May righteous civil leaders come forth. (Eph. 6).

We decreed the cloud of depression to lift. Bring forth godly destiny. Give the people of Hamilton County the keys to the Kingdom of God (Isa. 22). Those locked will be released!

Let there be no coldness, grieving, or being "held back" any longer. Bring new revelation, Lord. Generations have been held back. No more detention! Cut the curtain/veil so they can see, Oh God! Touch them with truth. Raise up visionaries with new hope. Let them cling to God and to one another.

We rebuked any incest that's occurred in this county. Heal broken lives, Lord.

Craig had a vision and he saw as it were, a beast over a man and child. The beast held them both down. The child tried to get up, but the beast would not let them and kept pushing them down. The dad was teaching the child not to move because it was just easier that way. No movement. No progression. No growth. Lord, let them now arise! (Rev. 4:1).

WRIGHT COUNTY
Clarion

We felt a sense of urgency in this county. The clock is ticking! We declared a "clarion call" and that the trumpet of God would sound. There's a need for watchman to be on high alert–open up spiritual ears, Lord. Release the watchman. Awaken the people! (Isa. 52:1-2).

There have been murky, contaminated spiritual waters. Bring forth clear, fresh waters Lord! Living waters! (John 4:10).

There is a window of opportunity that's arising. We decreed openness to the Gospel as there's been too much closure. Make the wrongs right and right the wrongs in Wright County.

Diane and Craig Leaming

We proclaimed repentance, humbling and bowing of knees in homes.

The theatre across the street was showing the movie: The Grudge. We rebuked vengefulness.

There's been a chip on people's shoulders. They've been looking for their own vengeance. We declared: *"Vengeance is mine,"* says the Lord.

(Deut. 32:35; Isa. 63:4).

At 10 AM the bells in the clock tower of the courthouse sounded. God's timing is never late! Craig noted that it had been prophesied to him that as he began his walk across America, he was to take note whenever he heard "bells" ringing because it meant: CAUTION! This took us back to the first things we felt and proclaimed as we entered this county regarding the clock. 10 AM – **Ten** also represents the 10 Commandments. Judgment may be near for this county, but we asked for mercy. We asked for at least **ten** righteous people to arise! (Gen. 18:32).

May people turn their battles over to God (1 Tim. 3). Vindication is available by the Holy Spirit.

Craig saw a line around this county. It was a red line indicating the Blood of Jesus. We repented for the sins in this county. Show them Your timing, Lord! Let them not make decisions based on the past, but on the TRUTH. Revelations 7 speaks of the ones who had been "sealed" so we declare this county SEALED with the Blood Line of the Lamb of God. Let His atoning Blood bring healing here for all the people.

Many have not walked in righteousness, so we proclaimed they'll discover a need to pursue the Lord in great faith. Christ is the end of the law. May they come to *gentle* salvation. (Rom. 9, 10).

We rebuked the abused authority of some pastors, church board members, or deacons, who have used their position for religious superiority or power. They are the ones who have taught wrong doctrines using "religion" for manipulation (Rom. 10:17). Raise up the authorities you want Lord.

God wants to raise up sons and daughters into their divine destinies.

We rebuked the ungodly emotion of envy, decreeing in its place the graciousness of God. We proclaimed the Good News! We declared Jesus Name, and that a gentle humility will come forth. There's a remnant here chosen by grace. Let them not fall short of it. (Rom. 11:5-6).

Golden harvest

God wants to bring a golden harvest here. Bring forth Your special "move" and the fruit of harvest, Lord!

Seeing a florist shop on the corner, we began to proclaim the *fragrance* of Christ be known here, the Lily of the Valley, the sweet Rose of Sharon (Song of Songs 2:1). Reveal the Chief Cornerstone, the Lord Jesus! (Isa. 28:16).

Mike saw this as a lightning rod county! Lord, let Your glory shine here. Open the heavens. Withdraw the darkness.

Linda and Diane

We decreed a complete shift from upside down to right side up! The corner windows on the courthouse appeared to be new and had "cross-like" beams in them. Thus, we proclaimed the Cross of Jesus to rule and reign here.

Shake one small county for the universe, Lord!

Capture those who consistently do evil. Demonic darkness was rebuked.

We felt a sense of urgency for Wright County. There is a window of opportunity in the Spirit. Lord, give that person/or persons a clarion call.

We came across a closed down, abandoned Masonic Temple. There was a chain-like draw bridge in the overhang portion covering the front door. The place was rotting away, which is what happens when people are corrupted by the power of the enemy. We prayed fervently against this and for people to be set free.

Proclamation was made that churches and "children" come into alignment.

Driving out of town, we noted a STAIRCASE or STEPS that led up to a sawed off, empty, hollow tree stump. It made absolutely no sense! We perceived many people have been doing things their own way which only leads to emptiness and a hollow life. We decreed they will discover the ascending/descending of angels in this county and that the Lord Jesus Christ DOES INDEED LEAD US UPWARD AND ONWARD into heavenly places! (Gen. 28:12; Rev. 4).

HANCOCK COUNTY
Garner

Upon entering this county, Linda quickly wrote that she felt a dishevelment and disorder. No sooner had we arrived in front of the courthouse, when a man with a somber looking face came running up to our car looking for help. He said he'd seen a man slumped over the steering wheel in a parked car beside the road outside of town. He asked if we knew where the police department was. He said he'd already found two people dead this year and didn't want to find a third! We directed him to where we thought it was and then took off to check it out, all the while making declarations of life! Talk about being strategically placed! We, nor the police, ever found this person. Praise the Lord! We feel God answered our prayers and that this person was revived!

After our search, we went back to the courthouse.

We saw the "Good Nature" store and declared people to be of a good and godly nature. May they have their identity in Christ, aligning with God's wisdom, not their own. They must put off the old and put on the new according to Ephesians 4.

Craig & Diane Leaming with Mike

The Lord wants to garner, gather, embellish and bring much growth to Hancock County. We declared an invitation to those in this county to feast at the table of the Lord. (Gal. 5:22; James 3:13-18).

We have come to this county according to 1 Peter 1:10, *"As to this salvation, the prophets who prophesied of the grace that would come to you made careful search & inquiry."* (See 1 Peter 1:1-10).

A decree was made this county not carry forward any malice contained in it (Phil. 4:8). Proverbs 9 is an invitation for you. Proverbs 8:14 is wisdom's call to you. By virtue of Proverbs 8:34 we proclaim, "Raise up the watchman!"

We rebuked confusion.

Raise the banner of victory! We decreed Jehovah Nissi over Hancock County. *"We will sing for joy over your victory, and in the name of our God we will set up our banners. May the Lord fulfill all your petitions."* (Ps. 20:5).

At noon the bells rang on the clock tower. It's time for faith in God to arise. We proclaimed Hebrews 11 praying for faith to overcome this area…faith that is sent by God….pure, unadulterated faith!

God had earlier stimulated us to *action* as we went looking for the man in the car beside the road. Let the people be *stimulated* to active faith! Let them not be deceived or presumptuous any longer. We rebuked the fears of the people declaring Revelation 3:21 that they would become OVERCOMERS. Revelation 12:11 was also declared over Hancock County that people

Respect For Our Flag Engraved in Stone

would rise up with testimonies in their mouths as to the goodness of God….even unto death. Garner the overcoming spirit, Lord.

The roadway that went past the courthouse seemed more like a busy highway then just a regular street in town. Therefore, we felt led to declare a highway of holiness is being released here. (Isa. 35:8).

WINNEBAGO COUNTY
Forest City

One thing for sure, this particular journey was filled with many gongs, bells and whistles! We felt that was the result of the "word" that had been given to Craig Leaming when he had started his walk across America and we claimed it for this day's travels.

So it wasn't ironic that, again, as we are driving into a town, we hear bells sounding off in the courthouse clock tower. However, this time it was unusual since it was 1:24 PM. This was a God thing. What a welcome!

We began to decree Daniel 11:14 that God would invade the "Beautiful Land" (Winnebago County). We then prayed from Daniel 12:2-3 for the multitudes who sleep to be awakened.

Linda and the Leamings Under the Gazebo

The bell rang again at 2 PM, at the top of the hour, which might be expected. Nonetheless, we were quite aware of the Lord's blessing upon this holy invasion into Winnebago County.

Chief Winnebago Carved in Stone

We felt those here celebrate the past, but they need to look more to the future. It was wonderful to see the honoring statue (see Photo) of Chief Winnebago. But we sensed our God will bring forth a likeness of the Lord Jesus by reason of some miracle that takes place here! Pray for it, people!

Lawmakers, leaders, have been wishy-washy trying to please everyone, being all things to all people. We saw by the Holy Spirit there has been a "yes" person who doesn't like confrontation. There's been no continuity. God's perfect intentions have been compromised. People's position has been their god. But "without a vision the people perish." We declare clear, godly vision! (Prov. 29; Hab. 2).

Linda beside a war monument: "Freedom is never Free"

We felt conflict, indecisions and warring here as the grounds had a lot of things *scattered* around it: a war memorial, an army tank, a soldier statue, a sitting area protruding into the street and a gazebo. We saw the people as feeling "lost in the woods."

This county has come to their defining point. Tip the scales of justice in your favor through God!

His perfect intentions have been compromised with the result that too many people have become "accommodating" to the point of not knowing perfect obedience in the Lord. Obedience is better than sacrifice (1 Sam. 15:22). Follow God, not man.

A blanket of love and new depth of God was decreed. Lord, blanket this county with love...a new depth of love! The Lord is giving a trumpet call to the people because He desires to take them down a different road.

Raise up new, young warriors in the Spirit at Waldorf College. They will be *tender* warriors. There is a release of gentleness and kindness. People's strength in God will become the talk of the town.

This county is in transition. Some have not been able to go forward because they haven't dealt with the past. The Lord is building a new thing!

We were elated when the sun broke through the clouds at 1:50 PM warming our bodies and hearts after a very cool day of temps mostly in the 30's. When the sun broke through, we could not help but declare BREAKTHROUGH for this county!

A store across the street had the address of: 111. Therefore, we proclaimed the Lord is bringing a revelation of the power of the Godhead, the Holy Trinity - Father, Son, and Holy Spirit.

We asked for forgiveness of the unrighteousness in this area, and prayed for the widows and orphans who have come into unjust judgment here.

We called forth a "transitioning" spirit to begin flowing. People will now begin moving into the newness and freshness of God! They'll be revived, as they put on the full armor of God. (Eph. 6).

WORTH COUNTY
Northwood

The area just around the courthouse had a number of instruments of war not the least of which was the huge army tank pictured on the next page. Therefore, we discerned much unrest and spiritual warfare here.

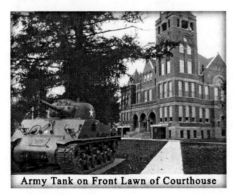
Army Tank on Front Lawn of Courthouse

We decreed <u>divine worth</u> to come into people's lives.

Because this county has a significantly higher national and statewide average for recorded tornadoes, Hosea 8:7 came to mind, "those who sow to the wind will reap the whirlwind." We rebuked destructive winds in the natural and spiritual realms, where the enemy has wanted to destroy people's lives. We decreed the Lord God Almighty desires to bring holy winds of change! (Nahum 1:3).

> "Behold, I have made you a new, sharp threshing sledge with double edges; you will thresh the mountains and pulverize them, and will make the hills like chaff. You will winnow them, and the wind will carry them away, and the storm will scatter them; but you will rejoice in the Lord, you will glory in the Holy One of Israel"
>
> —Isaiah 41:15-16

James 1 speaks of the tossing wind, so we declared clarity of mind for the things of God and for the people here not be double-minded.

Linda felt there is going to be a pertinent newspaper story that will come forth about the "tornadic activity of God"!

We saw a softening of the land and a harvest of holiness.

What the enemy meant for evil, God will turn it to good. (Gen. 50:20-21).

This county will become a bread-basket. It has great worth and significance in the spiritual realm.

Its main street is very wide. Lord, make the way of the people go

The Lemings Sit Nearby as Linda Proclaims Scripture

126

wider, higher and deeper in You (2 Sam. 22:20)! A broad street of godly wisdom was prophesied to come here. Craig prayed there would be an uncontrollable desire for godly wisdom in Worth County!

Lord, release the gifts of the Holy Spirit in maturity.

We perceived a spirit of illegitimacy, but God says, "You are mine!" This county is invited to come into "the church of the first-born" (Heb. 12: 8-24)! It will regain its *birthright* or *name value: Worth County.* The Lamb of God brings *worth* into people's lives.

A softening

All the store fronts lined up quite beautifully, which we found amazing since there was a mixture of old and new buildings. The main street is six lanes wide! Lord, align the people perfectly according to Your will and to Your ways.

God will bring a softening of the land.

The famous tornado activity of the enemy will change into the famous movement of a mighty rushing wind of the Holy Spirit! We bound the spirits that intend to do a destructive work here. We proclaimed a replacement with God's love and power.

Lord, take away things that are not of You. Destructive spirits that would come through here, we bind them in the Name of Jesus! Replace them with revelations of God.

An unforgiving spirit was rebuked. God says, "Give up your spirit of judgment and unforgiveness."

1 Corinthians 2:6-12 was proclaimed. The spirit searches the deep things of God. Let the people begin to search deeply.

There have been winds of immaturity. Reverse the destructive winds! We decreed maturity in God. (Heb. 6:1).

We asked the Lord to make this a Gateway County as it borders the state of Minnesota. Open up the gates! People here must ascend the hill of the Lord. (Ps. 24).

We prayed the blessing of God to saturate the land and people.

Stopping on our way out of town at a convenience store, Diane asked the woman clerk behind the counter how could we pray for this town/county? Looking a bit puzzled, she was a bit startled by the question. She must have thought, "Who would ask such a thing?!" But it didn't take her long to say: "Pray about *communication.*" We did! We prayed about the gossip and backbiting she spoke of, declaring communications and conversations would be according to Philippians 4:7-8. Finally, we pronounced Matthew 12:36 over this county: *"And I say to you, that every careless word men shall speak, they shall render account for in the Day of Judgment."*

❦ nine ❦

CERRO GORDO, FRANKLIN, HARDIN, STORY

"Arise, proceed on your journey ahead of the people, that they may go in and possess the land which I swore to their fathers to give them." —Deuteronomy 10:11

O ur 272 mile trip this day would wrap up one third of our divine assignment. It was a strategic day in that it was Veteran's Day, November 11th, 2006. Mike and I felt like soldiers of the Most High God. Indeed we are. We prayed the heavenly host would protect us. It was just Mike and I on this trip and we prayed a number of scriptures as we took off from our driveway. Leviticus 26:7 was one of them, *"But you will chase your enemies, and they will fall before you...."* Like David, we ran to Goliath–fearless! (1 Sam. 17:48).

Mary Ellen Earles who is from Independence Iowa and is the Aglow State Prayer Coordinator, had called the day before saying some ladies from Aglow, after a time of prayer at the state capital, had seen "golden snow" falling as they drove home. We'd had rain, but no snow. However, our Most High God loves to give us little surprises from His Throne Room. They had felt this was somehow a prophetic act of God. We agree! The Lord is indeed blanketing Iowa with His glorious Presence in new and fresh ways as saints from all over the state pray. We give Him praise!

I-80 Revelations

Progressing down Interstate 80 toward our first county of the day, we pulled into a Rest Stop. This was Veteran's Day and by the design of the Lord, it was no coincidence that we stopped at this particular one. Walking in, we discovered its theme was all about commemoration of different wars. Our prophetic prayer journey was all about spiritual warfare, and we knew our holy Commander in Chief would lead us into victory! *"But in all these things we overwhelmingly conquer through Him who loved us."* (Rom. 8:37).

Getting back into our car that cool morning, we also noticed three smoke stacks going up into the sky. We prayed, "Lord let the smoke of false altars go up in destruction! Let agents of terror be taken out!" (Gen. 19:27-28).

CERRO GORDO COUNTY
Mason City

On our way to Mason City, we discovered the town was first named: "Shibboleth." Very interesting to say the least. We immediately went to Judges 12:6 where we find this very word. In this passage, Israel is in civil war. We prayed the people would be able to proclaim accurate spiritual truth and life. Let them not say, "Sibboleth"! Our intercession took us deeper as we sensed a clashing of the swords in the heavens for the people that they might not die and that they'd get "right" with God.

Open gates were declared for this county through praise and worship.

We knew we were headed into great warfare in this county knowing full well the city had many pioneers of the Masonic Order that settled here. We prayed that secret rites be torn down. Split the altar, Lord (1 Kings. 13:1-6)! Let every enemy be discerned and rebuked.

We came against polluted waters. Lord, bring forth clear waters.

There was a war in this area on July 4, 1854 (in Clear Lake) a Native American uprising called the *Grind Stone War.* Begin a new work today, Lord. Take hearts of stone and turn them into flesh. (Ezek. 11:19-20).

In the photo you can see Mike standing in front of a statue of a soldier with his fist raised to the sky. A wreath lay beside it because it's Veteran's Day. We raised our fists into the air proclaiming holy victory over this county in Jesus Name! Judges 12:12 says, "...they've been engaged in a great struggle."

Mike By a Monument

Kathryn Kuhlman, the great healing evangelist, had preached here years ago. But this is also where her ministry came under assault because of her relationship with a man whom she would later marry. However, a few years later she was completely restored with an even greater anointing having repented for past mistakes. She gave up *everything* in order to preach the gospel in holiness and purity once again. While here, we declared holy relationships for Cerro Gordo County.

The sign on the bank read 33 degrees. We declared Jeremiah 33. Reveal Your plans, Lord, to the pastors and civil leaders.

This is the home of Trinity Hospital. We declared truth, holiness and righteousness, and the POWER of the Holy Trinity to bring forth healing.

We called forth law enforcement officials, county supervisors, city council, etc. to walk in righteousness. We prayed for divinely placed law enforcement to thwart any evil.

Cerro Gordo County Courthouse

There have been pot holes of evil in some areas of this county representing gaping wounds and we decreed a filling up of those cracks by the righteous Blood of the Lamb of God. Healing and deliverance was proclaimed! We prayed against patchwork repairs, declaring the Lord is the repairer of broken lives (Isa. 61). May there now be open passageways into His heart! We prophesied "renewal" for this county.

At 11:35 AM we prayed with a young couple and their infant, who had come to the courthouse for whatever reason, but found it to be locked. We knew we had been strategically placed there for "such a time as this." Before we'd prayed with them, they looked rather contentious with one another, not walking together. After our prayer, they walked side by side with a more peaceful countenance on their faces. We may never know till we get to heaven, how much effect these prayers have had.

We pronounced "permission" for people to come into alignment with God. We proclaimed the full circle of God's plans to come forth! No breakages, Lord, just like the old song, "May the circle...be unbroken...."

FRANKLIN COUNTY
Hampton

Partridge Avenue leads into this county seat, so we prayed, "Lord, release the *dove* that Noah released so that the people of this county will find a resting place in you" (Gen. 8:8-12). "Release the power of the Holy Spirit. Come Sweet Dove as on the day of Jesus' baptism and bring forth the shifting in the natural and spiritual realms. Shift the people here towards the ways of God. Let eyes, ears and hearts be lifted up to You!"

Restoration

It was 12:34 PM as we drove into town. We prayed those numbers in sequence: 1,2,3,4. Set all things in order! May people here prioritize their lives according to the will of God. Get your own "house" in order as well as your "tabernacles" (Houses of God). Destroy such sins as smoking, drinking, spousal abuse... pornography. If you do not praise the Lord, "even the trees and rocks will cry out...!" (Luke 19:40-41).

Keyhole-Like Opening

Of course the date was 11/11/06 and it seemed significant to us their War Memorial had been dedicated at 11 AM with their Clock Tower dedicated at 12:00 Noon. Twelve of course, is the number of authority. Mike saw a "key-like" hole or an opening on the façade of the entrance to the building (see Photo). We declared Isaiah 22. Lord, release Your kingdom keys over Franklin County. Let the people arise with a new spiritual authority. Authenticate their walk with you, Oh God.

We prayed Daniel 9:23. The command has been issued! These people are highly esteemed in God's eyes. We declared that they would give heed to the message of the Cross and gain understanding. Lord, raise up brave and mighty spiritual warriors that will be fearless. (Dan. 10:13, 19).

Mike saw TREES of WHITE in the spirit; felt it represented "fertility" (like Jacob and the spotted/speckled poplar trees of Genesis 30). Bring forth fertility of sons and daughters of the Spirit.

Mike heard a guy who was walking around one of the war memorials on the grounds saying to himself, "I guess I'm lost..." Mike wasn't exactly sure what he meant but perhaps it was because he couldn't find a name or place of someone on the monument. We then declared, "Those once lost, are now found.

War Monuments

Let eyes and ears be opened to salvation." Jesus came to seek and save that which was lost. (Luke 19:10).

We prayed for the spirit of Issachar that the people here would know the time they are in and have spiritual discernment and revelation (1 Chron. 12:32). Raise up leaders for Your kingdom, Lord.

With "no hands on the clock tower," which was under construction and yet was still being dedicated that day, we sensed

TIME has stood still here. But now God wants people to be shaken and awakened to His love, mercy and forgiveness.

We felt good about this county.

HARDIN COUNTY
Eldora

Coming into town we saw a sign leading to the Eagle City Winery. We prayed, "Lord, let this county rise up as eagles," and then declared Isaiah 40:29-31. Let the new wine of the Holy Spirit be poured out here. (Acts 2).

Hardin County Courthouse

We rebuked abuse in this county. Mike saw as it were, "a dead child," one in which *hope* was stolen by the enemy. In the Name of Jesus, we broke the spirit of lawlessness, pain and hurt of the young.

Raise up great leaders for Your kingdom, Lord. Put a minister in place to help set captives free in the state's juvenile facility located here.

Mike saw something that had to do with a "trigger." Let it be said, "God has "triggered" something for the state that's shot or propelled the people of God into new heights of glory!"

We declared justice and righteousness. We prayed against stiff necks and generational curses...hard hearts...abandonment.

Release JOY! This is the opposite of what they've seen. We proclaimed, "Hosanna! Hosanna in the highest!" (Matt. 21:9).

Declared husbands and wives will "cleave together." Let families embrace each other. We praised God for the changes taking place here. (Matt. 19:5).

We rebuked a spirit of abortion and robbed destinies. Decreed divine destinies to come forth! Isaiah 11:6, "*A little boy will lead them.*" Youth will arise in the power of David.

We saw tiredness. We prayed for a release of fresh energy for the things of God and fresh love for Him. A FIRST LOVE anointing was proclaimed to fall on the young and the old. (Rev. 2:4).

Sign in a Resident's Front Yard

Upon driving out of town, we saw a yard sign: "Say No To Torture." Another one read: "Who Would Jesus Torture?" (Probably had to do with Iraq prisoners being held in a US island prison; however, we weren't sure what they meant by those signs.) Nevertheless, we prayed regarding "tortured minds" in this county. We prayed against strongholds of abuse and torture (whether mental, emotional or physical) be broken. Samson was also tortured. The Philistines gouged out his eyes, but he still won against his enemy. (Judg. 15, 16).

We decreed the youth would not be driven to a "base level" or act out of their lower nature.

Full, abundant life with freedom and honor was proclaimed with true honor as "place markers" or SIGNS which are the opposite of these yard signs! May there be true honors for those who are righteous decision makers. Set hearts free, Lord! Thank you Lord!

STORY COUNTY
Nevada

The old song came to mind, "This is my story, this is my song, praising my Savior all the day long," which we prophesied to this county...that they would begin to fall so deeply in love with Jesus, they would sing His praises all day long! Lord burn

Entrance to Story County Courthouse

this desire into this county with Holy Spirit fire so that day and night worship will begin to ascend here. Raise up a 24/7 House of Prayer!

A "musty smell," like something that had been stored for a long time in a basement, was discerned. We noticed an old AND a new/current water tower. The old one had rusty panels on it. We prayed rusty hinges be blown off doors and gates in the spiritual realm. The Lord wants to OIL the doors of people's hearts, so they will open up to Him. His Word tells us He is the "The Door" (Rev. 3:18-22; Rev. 4; John 14:6). He is the way, the Truth and the Life. May this county now have an in-depth revelation of that.

The Lord says, "I've seen your tears, Story County, I've heard your cries. Those who have cried to Me, I've inclined My Face to you. Continue to pursue Me and I will grant you the governmental power you long for."

There is a highway in this area called "Lincoln Highway." As President Abraham Lincoln stood for freedom for all people, we declared freedom from all spiritual bondages upon those in this county.

We decreed the spiritually dead to arise into new life in Jesus.

The Lord says, "You are important to Me. I grant you victory in your prayers. Come together and be united."

"Story County, you must care for the oppressed, widows and orphans!" says the Lord. (James 1:27).

We prayed Ephesians 6 and for the full armor of *light* to come here, as we noted the front panels on the courthouse resembled

A Rusty Water Tower

armor. We saw a sign about a "security" company and prayed, "May the people in this county know true security in Christ!" We prayed for protection.

The Lord is bringing "cleanness" to Story County. "Character counts" was on a mural across a whole building opposite the courthouse. The Lord says, "Clean your closets...the secret places of your hearts" (Ps. 51). Release the fresh fragrance of the Lord! Release Living, Fresh waters! Bring forth the oil of gladness in knowing the King of glory!

As we observed the new water tower upon leaving town, we sensed this spoke of those fresh waters being released here. It represents change coming to this county. Landscaping was yet to be put in place around this water tower. We declared "new and improved" Christians in this county would fall under the anointing of the Holy Spirit! Bring forth many abundant blessings, Lord.

As we left town, our prayer was: "Thank you Lord for the privilege of being scouts and prophets on this Veteran's Day. We hear freedom bells ringing! Let freedom ring! On this Lincoln Highway, we speak freedom, unity and victory. May those who are slaves to sin now be set free. Be free in Jesus Name! Release the pools of Bethesda, Oh Lord. Stir fresh waters! God's releasing pools of healing waters! (John 5: 1-9).

While we were in this county, the Lord gave a personal word to Mike and I: "Because you are doing this assignment, I am going to bring IOWA into pre-eminence!" Praise His Name!

❧ ten ❧

FLOYD, MITCHELL, HOWARD, WINNESHIEK, ALLAMAKEE, CHICKASAW

"And you shall teach them to your sons, talking of them when you sit in your house and when you walk along the road and when you lie down and when you rise up. And you shall write them on the doorposts of your house and on your gates." —Deut. 11:19-20

Setting our sights on this trip within days after Thanksgiving, our hearts were filled to overflowing with remembrances of many blessings. God had given us an incredible year with family, friends, and now this prophetic prayer journey. We knew the holidays would fill up the calendar till after the first of the new year, so leaving at 6:44 AM on November 25th, 2006 we were amazed at the availability in our schedule for another day of travels to the county courthouses. We looked forward to meeting a small group from Winneshiek County who were also offering lunch at their Coffee House. This day, there would be no cold picnic lunch inside our car! How delightful!

We rounded out the day with 461 miles on our odometer and experienced one of the most amazing things yet! Without having realized it, we were actually fulfilling a prophecy that Chuck Pierce had given over Iowa in 2003. He had said that Iowa was to glean from the four corners of the state so that the oppression in the middle could lift. He said, "And this is literal." Toward the end of the day as we were driving home, we saw something we'd never seen before in all the years we've lived in Iowa. We saw a man and woman "gleaning" a harvested field! *See the footnote to Allamakee County.

FLOYD COUNTY
Charles City

Upon arrival in our first county of the day in Charles City, we began to pray a cleansing from any and all defilement. Unseal the skies over Floyd County, Lord!

Linda at the Courthouse

Known for its marble-like stone in this area, we proclaimed a "polishing" of the "living stones" to come forth with foundational beauty (1 Pet. 2:5). Also Zechariah 9:16, *"And the Lord their God will save them in that day as the flock of His people; for they are as the stones of a crown, sparkling in His land."*

We prophesy melodies to come forth and new inventions and applications. Release the beauty of children and their destinies. May discoveries of the Lord and knowing Him more deeply become prevalent.

Expressiveness has been suppressed. We proclaim open heavens for holy expressiveness–open, unabashed feelings for God! May children in this county be known for their arts, poetry and songs.

Let the jewels of the land - the people, come forth. People will begin to act according to Matthew 13:44–52. *"The kingdom of heaven is like a treasure hidden in the field, which a man found and hid; and from the joy over it he goes and sells all that he has, and buys that field."* They will treasure the kingdom of God more than anything else! May they discover their value and be as one who would "go out to buy a field to find that precious jewel." They've been bought for a price by the Blood of Jesus. Let them know they are precious, living jewels of the Lord! Let them come alive with that knowledge (1 Pet. 2:4-8). Raise up godly men with an honorable spirit.

This county is turning a corner. Old things have passed away. Be born again! Restore children's destinies. Bring forth justice for the children.

American's *hometown!* Let the *home* be treasured.

The Shulamite's land restored (2 Kings 8:6). *"Give back everything that belonged to her."* We proclaim a break-through for families and children.

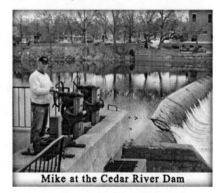
Mike at the Cedar River Dam

There were five eagle statues on the front of the building. We declare this county will rise up as with eagles' wings. (Isa. 40:20-31).

Floodgates here! (See Photo). Open them up! Open the floodgates of heaven!

The voice of the Lord is like mighty rushing waters (Rev. 1:15). Open up people's ears in this county to hear the mighty voice of God beckoning them to come into great revelations and

143

understandings. We declare they will now see Him in a *depth* they could not otherwise have known. (Ps. 34:8).

MITCHELL COUNTY
Osage

The Walk Up to the Courthouse

Show Your Face Lord in this county. Show them Your mercy and favor. Lord, gather together all the hot spots or connecting links to make a huge bonfire in the spirit for Your glory.

The sun began to break through the cloudy day. It was 9:**58** AM. We declared Isaiah **58**, especially verse 12. Raise the people up to repair, rebuild, and restore what the enemy has stolen.

We felt a cleanness and an order to this county.

Let the tornadic whirlwinds be only holy winds of God! We called forth the four winds of the four corners of the state, and the foundational things of God (Ezek. 37:9-10; Rev. 7:1-2). Release them to their destiny. Let the light shine in darkness.

There were four huge white pillars on the front of the court house and an enclosed glass cupola on the top, but no clock in it. According to Isaiah 58:4, we rebuked contention, strife and fighting.

Lord raise up people to wield Your authority, which dwells within them, that they may know victories over long standing sins in their lives. Give a revelation of Your holy, divine authority.

144

Trees placed in order along the street caused us to declare, "Bring all things into divine order!" Let new growth emerge in their walk with God. Let the "ordered things" of God come to fruition. *"Truly is not my house so with God? For He has made an everlasting covenant with me, ordered in all things, and secured; for all my salvation and all my desire, will He not indeed make it grow?"* (2 Sam. 23:5).

Linda saw long awaited dreams and visions coming to fulfillment, but only as God's people begin to humble themselves anew to Him. Let a humbling of heart come forth. We saw a gentleness of spirit arising.

War Monument Honoring Women

Harshness is being eradicated. This shall be known as a county of *gentle people*, kind hearted, giving, and generous.

Great works of God will flow from here because people will fund those things through their excitement and growth for the heart of God. This will come because of a fresh move and excitement for all the Lord is doing because of humility in the saints.

A gentle people of God are rising up! Old arguments are being stilled by the power of God's love and forgiveness.

HOWARD COUNTY
Cresco

We discovered from history that the Royal Arch Masons have been grounded here. The architectural designs on the front of the courthouse showed "arches" over each window. We rebuked the gates of the enemy. Let Masonry fall from its prideful ways. Let people bow their hearts and knees in their prayer closets and "come out" for Jesus! Let them declare the righteousness of God. No "arch" or gateway of manipulation or corruption will take place here, in Jesus Name!

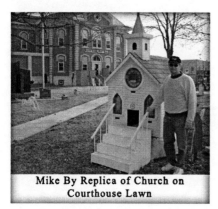

Mike By Replica of Church on Courthouse Lawn

We proclaimed Isaiah 22. Bring forth godly authority into this county, Lord. The gates of hell shall not prevail against it (Matt. 16:17-18). Psalm 24– Pass through the gates, Oh people!

We declared: "Greater is He who is in them, then he that is in the world." May there be a revelation of that to people in Howard County (1 John 4:4). Jeremiah 29:11 was decreed, *I know the plans I have for You,* says the Lord.

As the sun shown *full face*, a haze came over the land as we drove into this county. Lord, lift clouded minds and bring people into clarity of mind to the purposes of God to His will and His ways. Bring clear vision to people's eyes that they may see Your glory and grow.

Bring forth the "splendor of God!"

Let people here passionately pursue the prophecies of God spoken over this county.

Bring forth purity of mind, heart and body.

Lord, open doors for the light of revelation to occur (Rev. 4.1). Open the highways, roadways and streets leading to this courthouse and release openness to the Holy Spirit that hearts may expand and grow in this area.

Bring the latter day rain/reign of Your Spirit, Oh Lord.

> "So rejoice, O sons of Zion, and be glad in the Lord, your God; for He has given you the early rain (for your vindication). He has poured down for you the rain, the early and the latter rain as before…."
>
> —Joel 2:23

Repair the broken streets and broken pathways of God that have been wrecked by religious spirits. Release afresh the power and the joy of your Holy Spirit, Oh God. Raise up a banner of victory! Trample down your enemies, Oh Lord.

We saw "joyful" things in all the Christmas decorations….an angel, a church, a manger, an advent wreath… amazing! Where in America does this happen anymore but in middle America?! The American Civil Liberties Union has not destroyed these holy expressions in this county!

Manger Scene By Courthouse!

We declared residents of this county: "chosen people." You've been called from death into light, from being ordinary, to being a *chosen people*! You are the people of God! (1 Pet. 2:4-11).

WINNESHIEK COUNTY
Decorah

Soldiers. Linda's the Real One!

Anton Dvorak was from the city of Spillville in this county. He is known world-wide for his New World Symphony. We declared a "new world" here where God's Presence would be known in a greater degree. Let the rocks and hills cry out! Soften hearts. Bring forth a gigantic move of God! Cause the people here to prophesy! Bring forth the fragrance of the land, the fruit of the harvest, the "fat of the land" with praise!

This area is also known for clocks. Lord, we declare a download of Your perfect timing!

We were joined at this courthouse by a few members of the group Souled Out Decorah, which included Melanie Kleiner, Nick Gross, Russ Abbot. (Melanie and her husband operated a Coffee House at the time and provided lunch that day!) The scripture for their ministry is from Mark 12:30 which says to love the Lord our God with everything within us. We indeed proclaimed this over Winneshiek County.

This county is named after the Native American chief of the Winnebago Tribe, whose name was Chief Winneshiek. He was

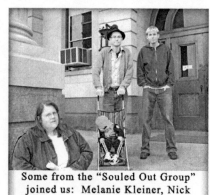

Some from the "Souled Out Group" joined us: Melanie Kleiner, Nick Gross, Russ Abbot and his little son

148

the adviser to the War Chief Black Hawk. Winneshiek has several meanings: "Has them tied up" and "coming thunder." We prayed against all "bindings" in this county. We then proclaimed a "coming thunder" of God. May it release the holy, reverential fear of the Lord! *The voice of the Lord is upon the waters; the God of glory thunders, the Lord is over many waters."* (Ps. 29:3).

An increase of haze came as we approached Decorah. The sun became more and more obscured.

We declared decisions made here would be just and right. Teach ministers the way they should go that they may run and not faint. (Isa. 40 and also 28).

Bring forth the prophetic gifting in this county, so they can see the revelatory things of God. Let not the spirit of religion take over. Let the blood, sweat, tears of those who have gone before (see Photo) inspire those who are here now. May the Blood of Jesus cleanse this county, cover it in the protection of the great I AM GOD (1 Pet. 1:1-2). We decreed strength for the people of God.

Mike By War Monument: "Blood, Sweat, Tears"

We saw Jacob's Ladder here...angels ascending and descending to open up the heavens (Gen. 28:12). Take away the restraints, Oh God. Cut soulish ties. Swing open the gates through praise.

"Decorah! Decorah! We declare the *decoration* of God over you, His favor and fruits!"

Luther College

Impact and inspire the students at Luther College. The government of God is upon your shoulders…not man's government. Let there be divine supervision and conduct upon county officials, supervisors, sheriff, school boards and policemen.

There is a bridge from the past to the future. Break through! Break through with the anointing. What is not possible with man is possible with God. (Mark 10:27).

We prayed people would seek the Lord's face with fasting and prayer, that they be fused with God's spirit and power to pray. May the Body of Christ step out in demonstrations of signs, miracles and wonders.

Let righteousness and the wisdom of Solomon prevail. Wounded families will be healed. Healing will become a reality here!

We bound any spirits of witchcraft and deception. Declared the people of God to stand together in love. Declared great fruit and abundance of God like that which Joshua and Caleb saw. (Num. 13).

There is a greater dimensional thing….it's been a "ridge line" of protection around this county and yet, it has not fully allowed them to experience the fullness of God. A new dimension of God's love and abundance is forthcoming!

Let people accurately divide the Truth…preaching the Word in and out of season. It is to the glory of God to seek out a matter. Stone cold hearts are turning into hot hearts for Jesus! (Rev. 3:16).

Rebuked the battle that has been going on between the old and the new. Let the new wine come forth now!

ALLAMAKEE COUNTY
Waukon

There was much to pray about here with ungodly influences such as the secret societies of the Masons and the Templars. We rebuked the corruption of contaminated religious establishments.

The county is named after the Chief of a Native American tribe called the Winnebago, whose name signifies: "spirit, whirling thunder, great doctor" or "something of great and powerful of the supernatural." But false gods cannot be mixed in with

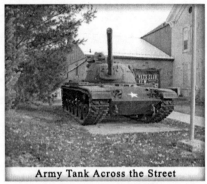
Army Tank Across the Street

the one true God! We declared some-thing powerful and wonderful is coming here. Give the people of this county the keys that will reveal the mysteries of God: holiness, purity, righteousness and truth.

Prayed for healing, cleansing and an awakening. "Step up" is what Mike heard for this county. Revelation 4 is for them so they can go higher into the things of the Lord God Almighty. Step into the waters of the Lord. Be washed and made clean. Lightings and the thunder of God will be released here. It will begin to roll over the land! (Ps. 29).

The emblem of corn over the courthouse door caused us to proclaim fruitfulness. The fruits of the Holy Spirit were called forth.

Declared an awakening for the people. (Isa. 52).

Allamakee County Courthouse

Declared the people to *step up to the next level of God's destiny for them. Step into holy ground.*

Captives set free here.

*There is going to be a "**gleaning of the edges**" of the field for those wanting to be fed or provided for. The book of Ruth is for this county! Bring forth the manna of heaven upon the people, O Lord. Bring forth the threshing floor for those who don't feel they belong. Bring the kinsman Redeemer and a **gleaning** that will bring forth the next generation of godly men and women.*

Dutch Sheets and Chuck Pierce's prophecy fulfilled!

Amazingly, the above prophetic phraseology about "gleaning" the fields played out before our very eyes later that afternoon! The Lord has a magnificent way of orchestrating His prophetic words. At 4:40 PM, as we were traveling down the interstate on our way home at the end of the day, we saw something we had never seen before in all our years of being raised in Iowa. There was a farmer and his wife picking up corn from a harvested field. They were actually "**gleaning**" ears of corn. Immediately we knew this was a *significant sign from the Lord.* It was an exact fulfillment of Dutch Sheets and Chuck Pierce's prophecy over Iowa in 2003! Briefly, *one of the things* prophesied at that time was that Iowa must first **literally glean spiritually** from the four corners of the state in order for it to come into its full destiny, thereby affecting the core or center of the state. The center of course is the location of the

State Capital where *statewide* governmental decrees and decisions flow. The manifestation of that prophecy was now literally being fulfilled by this Prophetic Prayer Journey! Glory to God!

This day we had gone to one of the farthest northeast corners of the state. We'd already been to the farthest northwest corner. We were shocked to say the least. We knew God had been ordaining every step of this Prophetic Prayer Journey, but it was quite another to have it manifested and confirmed in this dramatic way. Quite frankly, we wondered if these two people gleaning in the field were actually angels!

We were again reminded of the book of **Ruth and the kinsmen Redeemer**. The Lord continues to unfurl His blessings and destinies over Iowa. We saw it with each unfolding journey. The anointing, power and authority of God that was declared and established in places of man's government (county courthouses), is fast changing the spiritual landscape of Iowa!

CHICKASAW COUNTY
New Hampton

Approaching the city there was a sign that read: "A city of expanding horizons." We declared it to be so in the spiritual realm. Give them eyes to see, Oh Lord, and a heart of under-standing toward the things of God.

We declared light and that the darkness upon minds and hearts be dispelled.

We sensed God's purpose for this county is *purity..* Pure hearts must be raised up to walk out the purposes of God. *"Blessed are the pure in heart, for they shall see God."* (Matt. 5:8).

153

There was a round window-type, portal-like opening at the top of the courthouse. It represents what the Lord wants to do here in

bringing about spiritual revelation and insight. It spoke to us as the "Eye of God." *"...A land for which the Lord your God cares; the eyes of the Lord your God are always on it, from the beginning even to the end of the year"* (Deut. 11:12). This opening or portal had a spot light on it so it could be seen at night. Lord, shine your spot light on Chickasaw County! Let them see what You see. Give them an epiphany experi-

Seal of Iowa and Engraving of Chief Chickasaw

ence so that the awe of God will come upon the people (2 Chron. 16:9). Let the eyes of the Lord be fixed here.

We rebuked foolishness and family wars.

All four corners of this court-house garner a "shield" with a cross-like emblem on it, which we declared to be one of *faith*. We decree the Cross of Christ to be known here!

Portal-Like Window at the Very Top

The journey back home began at 4:05 PM. How fun that we saw a "sun dog"/rainbow in the sky! We felt it was a signature mark by the Lord of His confirmation for this day's travels. Additionally, there was a more powerful one yet to be discovered down the road! (See notes from Allamakee County, page 152)

❧ eleven ❧

BOONE, GREENE

"Then we journeyed from the river Ahava on the twelfth of the first of the month to go to Jerusalem; and the hand of our God was over us, and He delivered us from the hand of the enemy and the ambushes by the way." —Ezra 8:31

W e were always fascinated how the Lord would time after time open up opportunities for us to travel. With it now being winter, we knew our days were numbered on the amount of miles we could put into this prophetic prayer journey.

On December 30th, 2006 after a hearty breakfast, Mike said something to the effect, "I think we could get in two more counties today." I was game! Nonetheless, I was quite surprised at his suggestion considering it was also the day of the Iowa/Texas Alamo Bowl Game! My husband is a diehard Hawkeye fan so this was a miracle to hit the road with this impending game at hand. However, we made it home in time to watch the whole thing!

By 11 AM we were out the door, much later than we would normally set out. It was a balmy, wintry 46 degrees with a little rain. This day would be one of our shortest journeys, just 90 miles, but filled with intense spiritual warfare. Maybe that's why the Lord kept it short! Nonetheless, we were always excited and filled with anticipation for what the Lord would show us. Everyone ought to do this! It's so much fun! Travel around your state, your city, your neighborhood and prophesy. Paul prods us in 1 Corinthians 14:1 that we all ought to prophesy!

I do want to note something rather significant about this particular journey. Mike felt that we are coming into a time of <u>CIVIL UNREST</u> for the entire country of the United States of America. There may be some kind of civil war that will touch institutions and families. Rest will come in God. The battle will be in the civil realm verses the spiritual realm.

BOONE COUNTY
Boone

On our way to Boone we took a different route than we had planned, but the Lord always ordered our paths in the ways He wanted us to go. He had something for us to take note of. Driving along Highway 17 in Dallas County, we came upon a Hindu

A Spiritual Caution Sign

"Peace Palace," seemingly in the middle of nowhere. This was new to us, not realizing the impact these "palaces" are making in Iowa. The fight was now on! Spiritual warfare was engaged and we began to pray that Iowa will not be known for these places of idolatry that contaminate our countryside. We rebuked these places filled with Hindu prayers. (We took pictures of the *full parking lot* which I'm not going to include in this book, but we must realize this was a Saturday morning!) Oh God, let Iowa be known for true, holy prayers unto the Most High, Jehovah

God, and the Lamb who sits upon the Throne! Let there be a cleansing in the mid-heavens over this state.

As we traveled on, we took note of all the flags flying at half mast for the death of former President Gerald Ford. Saddam Hussein had also just been executed! One man honored, one man disgraced before the world. Ford represented freedom, Hussein represented oppression. We had clear signs of the true "clashing of the swords" in the spiritual realm in

Linda Deposits Isaiah Stone

the mid-heavens! We prayed the Lord would give supernatural intelligence to our fighting troops in Iraq and Afghanistan. "Give them insight to see where the terrorists, our enemies, are hiding, Oh Lord!"

Open up eyes, Lord. Lift the "eye lids" of those who are asleep. Let them begin to see truth and light in Jesus. Let there be a change in the atmosphere.

Let the bread basket of this nation–IOWA–feed the Bread of Life to the nation.

The town of Boone was shrouded in fog and rain. The Iowa High School Athletic Association is here. Lord, raise up spiritual athletes. Youths are being contended for.

Mamie Eisenhower

This is also the home of Mamie Eisenhower. Let righteous leaders come forth and go to the nations. Raise up mothers and wives of leaders who will have ties to world events.

Street Honors Mamie Eisenhower

We saw a sign in a window across the street that read: "Genesis Development." Lord, we proclaim a new beginning for this county…a new spiritual beginning so that people here will begin to flow in the true streams of Living Waters.

The bulging stones on the court-house brought to Linda's heart the fact that the Lord wants to burst forth in this county…even into cold, stony hearts! The "protruding stones" represent the Lord's *showing* Himself in odd places, unexpected places! A bursting forth will occur as a few "called" saints begin to pray. The rain today represents a cleansing and that purifying waters will begin to emerge.

Daniel 9 was proclaimed over this county. *"As soon as you began to pray, I heard your prayer…"* (verse 23). But they've not listened to you, Oh God (vs. 16). Lord, turn your anger away from the people of this county (vs. 19). Hear our prayers! Don't delay! PRAY! PRAY! Understand the vision Boone County! People here will begin to understand the visions God has given them. We decree as soon as they begin to PRAY they'll gain understanding. We decree everlasting righteousness upon this county.

Beat your plows into swords for spiritual warfare! (Isa. 2:4).

People, take captive your thought life (2 Cor. 10: 3-5). Don't tear people down, but rather build each other up. Don't make comparisons. Let the people here boast in God, and God alone!

We stand in godly authority against misused authority in county government.

Let the people here sense the true and divine way.

GREENE COUNTY
Jefferson

We crossed the county line at 1:06 PM and our thoughts turned towards the New Year that would soon be ushered in. We prayed Greene County would leave behind all the hurts, the anger, the resentment and bitterness of 2006 and get on with new and improved life in Jesus!

We decree in Jesus' Name a new establishment in mercy, love and forgiveness that will begin to unfold in 2007 and grow and grow according to the growth represented in the color green.

Carillon Tower Next to Courthouse

O Lord, let our prayers be like arrows and strike the enemy. As we fire our prayers, we pray it hits our target.

Take scales off people's eyes. Remove layer upon layer of generational curses.

This is a day filled with tears, but it will turn to tears of joy! Psalm 12:6 is for this county, *"The words of the Lord are pure words; as silver tried in a furnace on the earth, refined **seven** times."* We also decreed Isaiah 30:18-23.

It was 46 degrees. 4 + 6 = 10! Lord, we decree in Your Name that good, sound, foundational, godly government will come to this county. Let the 10 Commandments be lived here in a fashion of humility and love.

Bring a soaking of Your Presence, Lord. As the ground is drinking up the rain, so too let the people begin to drink deeper of You. (Ps. 42).

We saw a bell tower monument on the courthouse grounds with a "reflecting pool" inside. (See Earlier Photo). It was closed on Saturdays so we weren't able to get inside. But interestingly enough, the plaque on the tower said it had been *dedicated* to God. We prayed it was to the true, most High Jehovah God! Lord, bring forth a *spiritual dedication* for the *birth* of many *spiritual babies* in Your kingdom!

Bell Tower Dedication to God's Glory

We bless the governmental officials that they would look to You, Oh God. Bring forth the divine destinies you've had in your heart for the people of this county.

The Lord says to Greene County: "Come! Come and soak in My Presence that I may take you to new depths in Me that you could not imagine, for I am well able," says the Lord, "to do above and beyond all you think or ask." (Eph. 3).

❧ twelve ❧

MARSHALL, GRUNDY, BUTLER

"Blessed shall you be in the city, and blessed shall you be in the country." —Deuteronomy 28:3

P aul says in 2 Corinthians 12:10, *"When I am weak, then I am strong,"* and this is exactly how I felt as we left for another prayer journey across Iowa. Neither Mike nor I was feeling particularly well, having fought the "bug" that had been going around. Nonetheless, after a hearty breakfast on Saturday morning January 27th, 2007 we felt we had enough energy to hit the road. This prophetic prayer journey is a divine call! We always felt the unction of the Holy Spirit drawing us into this holy assignment. And as the saying goes, "Whom He calls, He enables." It's true!

Leaving home about 10:45 AM, little did we realize the bitter cold of single digit temperatures, strong winds, swirling clouds and snow squalls that awaited us. I didn't pack a picnic lunch this time as we knew it was too cold to eat in the car. This would be one of those days we would have to find a good hot meal in a restaurant along our route.

We went first to Marshall County, then Grundy and on to Butler. The 220 miles we traveled that day went rather quickly in spite of it all.

MARSHALL COUNTY
Marshalltown

There were cloudy skies as we approached. We asked the Lord to bring forth the sentinels, both angelic ones and those of men to "watch" and keep an eye on this county.

A friend, Rev. Marc Jackson, had walked the perimeter of this

Marshall County Courthouse

county praying a year earlier. Later he was afflicted with a disease and died. So we knew we were walking into a lot of spiritual warfare! Whatever Rev. Jackson saw and proclaimed, let it continue Lord! Deuteronomy 11:24 was proclaimed for Marc's walk, *"Every place on which the sole of your foot shall tread shall be yours."*

A Sad Cornerstone

We knew this county needed much prayer. Nevertheless, we were shocked to see one of the cornerstones on the courthouse had been laid by the Masons. There was a Masonic Temple across the street. We rebuked lies and falsehoods that have clouded Marshall County. We also rebuked this ungodly influence and happily deposited our stone nearby with Isaiah 28:16-17 written on it.

There had just been a well publicized raid at the Swift Meat Packing Plant with many illegal immigrants being arrested. Many families were torn apart. We prayed for the aliens. Let the justice of God come swiftly. *"Show your love for the alien, for you were aliens in the land of Egypt"* (Deut. 10:19-21). Let the administration of justice be applied without partiality and straight forth.

We decreed holy justice be seen in this county, not men's version of justice, which can be twisted and distorted. Break bondages of prejudice, Oh Lord. Let this be a city of refuge. Let this be a safe place.

The courthouse is situated at Church St. & 1st with the other corner, 1st & Center. Let this county be *centered* on You, Oh Lord. Fill up the *churches* for Your glory! We declared Psalm 89:14-19 over this county.

Clear the spiritual pathways for righteousness.

Raise up those who believe in you, Oh Lord. We called for the power of the Sword of the Spirit (Heb. 4:12). Marshall County– live up to your destiny in Christ as per your name sake and *marshal* the resources of heaven in the fight for righteousness and justice. Bring forth righteous laws and order.

Open eyes!

> "Lord, when did we see You hungry, and feed You, or thirsty, and give You drink? And when did we see You a stranger, and invite You in, or naked, and clothe You? And when did we see you sick, or in prison, and come to You?"
>
> —Matthew 25:31-46

The people of God must open their eyes! This county is known for an Eye Clinic. Open up spiritual eyes, Lord. Let this county be seen as a *portal county*!

False testimony was bound and rebuked. Prayed for awesome wonders to occur here.

We prayed for a "completing anointing" in Marshall County. "Be complete and whole," says the Lord. (As this was being written, Chuck Pierce had a word for that exact kind of anointing.)

May the people here elect righteous leaders.

We prayed against any evil forces coming against the HOP (House of Prayer in this area and for all of Iowa).

Lord, do your unusual and extraordinary "alien" work here (Isa. 28:21)! We declared breakthrough for this county. Let the threshing floor make ready a harvest of souls. Divine destinies will now break forth! Look with compassion on this county and not judgment.

We rebuked a spirit of deception, destruction and death.

Access to the power of the Sword of Solomon was proclaimed. Declared the forces of evil diminished. Break off unholy fires and unholy alliances! A breakthrough of the Holy Spirit is forthcoming!

Snow Squall With "Sun Dog" at Right

The skies grew darker and darker while we were here. The winds picked up and we ran into a blinding snow squall as we were leaving town. We knew the mid heavens had been stirred! We definitely felt the "clashing of the swords." After driving through the snow squall, it immediately disappeared on the outskirts of town.

GRUNDY COUNTY
Grundy Center

This county was named in honor of Felix Grundy who was born on Sept. 11, 1777. Look again at those numbers! First of all, in regard to "9/11," we declared protection from any enemy attacks here. We also declared a "completion" of the things of God to take place according to the three "7's" of this man's birthday. Bring favor, Lord!

Grundy County Courthouse

Our history told us that the first courthouse built here was in the shape of an octagon. Octagon of course means eight sides. Eight means new beginnings which is what we declared for this county. The old has passed away! We decreed the people in Grundy County can, and will "start fresh and new." Isaiah 42:9 and a portion of verse 10 says, *"Behold, the former things have come to pass, now I declare new things; before they spring forth I proclaim them to you. Sing to the Lord a new song..."*

1:11 PM was the time we actually drove into this county, so we declared the power of the Holy Trinity to come forth and "Thy kingdom come, Thy will be done on earth as it is in heaven."

We rebuked contentious spirits here.

Let this county not look to another place for its identity. But let its identity be rich and full in Christ Jesus. Let them exchange current views for God's views. Let them ask, "What does God say?!" (Jer. 29:11).

Reveal holy, spiritual mysteries in this county, Oh God.

Masonic influences were rebuked.

There was a balcony-like structure over the front door. We saw this as an invitation of the Lord for the people here to go higher and higher in Him and to *see* what things look like from His perspective!

Ornate Stone Work

We then proclaimed county government officials to be administrators of righteousness and justice.

Let the sweet oil of the Holy Spirit drench and baptize this county. Let the fragrance of the sweet oil come forth and bring peace!

We prayed for divine "connectedness" as people may have felt "short-circuited." They've felt short-circuited in the spiritual realm of God's purposes and plans. We decreed that it will now come into fruition.

We left the courthouse and stopped to get a sandwich at a gas station. We knew the word the Lord had given us regarding "divine connectedness" was a true word of prophecy for this county and God is going to bring it forth. The precious girl behind the counter seemed totally "disconnected," not being able to carry on a conversation, answer simple questions or able to make change. We knew this county has been short-circuited in the spiritual realm, but it's about to change!

BUTLER COUNTY
Allison

It was a whopping **12 degrees** when we got here, which felt warmer if you can believe that because most of the day the temp had hovered around 9 degrees. We came into the county at 2:21 PM. With the temp being what it was, we felt we were to declare the power of the significance of the number "12" which represents governmental authority. We then released godly, governmental authority over Butler County.

Butler County Courthouse

We prayed against negative generational spirits and proclaimed God's spirit of "adoption" to bring favor breaking bondages of illegitimacy and children without destiny. *"For you have not received a spirit of slavery leading to fear again, but you have*

Cross-Like Window Connections

received a spirit of adoption as sons by which we cry out, 'Abba! Father!'" (Rom. 8:15).

Raise up more leaders like Senator Charles Grassley and those who will rule righteously from the nation's capitol.

We declared a warmth and *fire glow* of the Holy Spirit to come here.

167

The cross-like connections in between the windows caused us to declare that the Cross and the Name of Jesus are the final authority in this place–not man's government, but God's!

Bring forth dramatic transformations in people's lives, Oh Lord. Bring forth the supremacy of Christ!

The wire "butterfly emblem" on the temperature gauge behind the courthouse (see Photo), spoke of transformations. We decreed

the people of this county are now "emerging" into new and holy identities in Christ. They have been cocooned for long enough! It's time to break forth and be all you can be in the Lord. New beginnings are soon coming!

Wire Butterfly Ornament on Rain Gauge

We proclaimed there will be an epiphany in many hearts…insights, revelations, knowledge and the fear of the Lord. This is an EMERGING COUNTY. The people here are emerging into the insights of God that will direct their divine destinies. Isaiah 11 is for Butler County.

At 3:17 PM, we headed home, running into heavy snow squalls once again–those quick rising, blizzard like conditions. I photographed much of it, as they were saturated with sun dogs/rainbows! They were intriguing and beautiful to say the least. They seemed to us as jewels in the heavens crowning our prophetic prayer journey for that day. It had been a day filled with feisty things going on in the atmosphere and the mid-heavens. Most certainly we had stirred things up! But our God reigns!

♣ thirteen ♣

JASPER, TAMA, BENTON, IOWA, POWESHIEK

*"By the blessing of the upright, a city is
exalted."* —Proverbs 11:11

Sunshine and a clear sky opened up our March 3rd, 2007 journey of 274.4 miles of Iowa territory. Just the day before, Iowa was hit with its second blizzard in a week. Venturing out on the roads after two back to back blizzards took a lot of faith! We counted 71 cars, trucks and other vehicles in ditches by the end of the day. God protected us

The 3/3 date caused us to declare Jeremiah 33:3 over the counties we were about to visit. I-35 and I-80 had been closed because of the blizzard and just reopened, so we declared Isaiah 35 over the state as well as Psalm 80. We prayed that people on the interstates would experience *open heavens*, which **we** did at the close of the day! Oh my!

The Lord allowed us to experience an amazing phenomenon. What a wonder! What joy to see God's glory revealed in the heavens! See the end of this chapter for details. Precious friends, we've come into a time where we need to approach Almighty God with holy, reverential fear!

As we took off that day, I (Linda) heard the Holy Spirit say, "They're getting it!" I wasn't totally sure what that meant other than we knew beyond a shadow of a doubt this prayer journey was making an impact in people's lives. Things are beginning to shift and change in lives across this state. Iowa <u>is</u> beginning to "get it!" Many are opening up to spiritual things. They're on alert for more of God. When I told Michael what I'd heard, he said a similar statement was boldly proclaimed that very week in the Business Record newspaper: "Iowa is on the *verge* of great things!" We say, "Yes and Amen!" We do not have room in this book to share all the newspaper clippings of great things that have been unfolding since we began this assignment. All praise and thanksgiving to God and God alone!

Prophetic signs

Another significant factor of this trip was a word Mike got from the Lord at 11:09 AM. Reversing those numbers reads: 911. By the Spirit of the Lord he declared: "God is going to reverse the curse of 911 and all the enemy has done!" (Re: our whole nation).

Bald Eagles in Our Backyard

With our home situated along the Des Moines River, we have the privilege of observing wild life. We enjoy watching bald eagles on a rather frequent basis. However, on this strategic day, we saw four of them just outside our windows as **close as** they'd ever been. Eagles, of course, represent the prophetic. We knew it was going to be a great day. And it was!

JASPER COUNTY
Newton

Just as the statue of a soldier in the photo is crying out for his fallen comrade, we also cried out for fallen comrades in the family of God. We felt God sent us here to proclaim His divine assistance to those who are willing to come to Him. *"For consider Him who has endured such hostility by sinners against Himself, so that you may not grow weary and lose heart."* (Heb. 12:3).

Summoning Help for a Fallen Comrade

In the natural realm, it was a bright, sunny day. We declared wide open, bright, eyes of revelation are coming. Let nothing block your revelation! As with the Golden Rule inscribed above the front of the courthouse, we proclaim its fruit over this county.

"Raise up a new way! Having invented the modern washing machine in Newton, it's now time to raise up a new way!" The Lord says, "You shall not be known for old manufacturing, but you will discover new ways and new turns!" New turns in the road are coming.

Jasper winery is in this area. Bring forth the new wine of the Holy Spirit!

The Newton Correctional Facility is located here. We proclaimed release from spiritual bondages. The best is yet to come (Isa. 58:6)! Loose the bonds of wickedness, Oh Lord. Paul and Silas went from prison to praise, and doors opened! *"A light shone in the cell"* (Acts 12: 7). We decree revelation and insight

Golden Rule Inscribed
Atop Courthouse

(Acts. 16:22-26). We declared people in this county will now see the newness of God. "It's a new day, a new season of bounty," says the Lord. "Look up, your redemption draws near." (Luke 21:28).

We rebuked generational curses. We heard in the spirit: "Course correction! Course correction!" as when a ship needs to adjust its rudder to avoid a collision. There will be rudder correction/course. There will be a "correction" to put people on the right way.

Jasper County, you will not just be bountiful in the soil, but bountiful in the heavens. You are destined to go from bounty to bounty; from the loss of Maytag to God's holy provisions. (We didn't feel the oppression we expected from the closing of Maytag.)

We decreed people here will become FRIENDS OF GOD. *"He was called the friend of God"* (James 2:23). Exodus 33:11 says *"face to face,"* as one speaks to a friend. Jasper County, seek intimacy with God! Also, people here must stick together in holy unity and friendship. Proverbs 18:24, *"A friend who sticks closer than a brother."*

We declared Ezra 9:9:

> "For we are slaves; yet in our bondage, our God has not forsaken us, but has extended loving kindness to us in the sight of the kings of Persia, to give us reviving to

raise up the house of our God, to restore its ruins and to give us a wall in Judah and Jerusalem."

In regard to the Speedway now located here, we declared, "Speed the cause of righteousness" (Isa. 16:5)! "Lord, accelerate Your work here. RENEW! REBUILD! RESTORE!" (Isa. 61).

TAMA COUNTY
Toledo

We entered this county at ll:28 AM, it was 21 degrees but we still had sunshine!

We declared the freshness of God, just as spring is around the corner, so too is the fresh dew of the Presence of the Lord!

This county is named for a Native American Chief from the Fox Tribe. It is also the location of a Native

Tama County Courthouse

American settlement/reservation. They have "Sovereign Nation Status." But we declared they recognize the Lord God's Sovereign power. Let people here not be left behind or taken advantage of.

Do not gamble with eternal life. Choose this day who you will serve. God chooses you! Now choose Him above all others.

New vision was decreed for this county and prosperity like they've never seen before. The Lord owns the cattle on a 1,000 hills (Ps. 50:10). But because they belong to your heavenly Father, they also belong to you, if you will recognize *His* sovereignty!

This county is no longer cornered or bound.

Regarding the Native Americans, they will be part of the first fruit bounty. The bounty of the Lord will be upon them with great revival. We prophesied reconciliation between the tribes as well as the white people.

We decreed a spirit of reconciliation over Tama County. Heal old wounds, Lord!

Bring heavenly health in mind, body and soul.

We called forth the capstone (1 Pet. 2). People shall become as "living stones, living tabernacles." May a spirit of worship arise here.

Poinsettias Mark Snowy War Memorial

Felt an unsettling. We declared the Prince of Peace to come. "Peace, peace. Be still and know God!" says the Lord (Ps. 46:10). "Peace! My peace I give to you" (John 14:27). "Worship the Prince of Peace that your souls may stop striving and be at peace." We rebuked the warring spirit.

Romans 8:37 is a declaration for you, that in all things you are more than conquerors.

We heard a spirit of groaning for the Native Americans. May they know the height and breadth of God (Eph. 3:18)! We rebuked the bad names Native Americans had been called and pronounced the spirit of adoption and reconciliation where we "call them brothers" (Rom. 8:23)! They never were or have been, savages, but they only fought for their homeland. May the truth of Christ come and break generational bondages.

Tama County, do not put your trust in men, but in God. With the Lord there is no gamble, no chances taken. He is all that He says He is! Come and see! Come and see! Rest assured in Him and Him alone. He who comes to Him <u>wins</u>! He is victory!

Let the Son rise upon you with healing His wings. Submit, surrender to the One, True, Sovereign God! *But for you who fear My Name the sun of righteousness will rise with healing in its wings; and you will go forth and skip about like calves from the stall.* (Mal. 4:2).

Malachi 4:6, *And he will restore the hearts of the fathers to their children, and the hearts of the children to their fathers, lest I come and smite the land with a curse.* We prayed for the children here that they be given a place of destiny in Iowa.

Bring forth the unexpected, Lord!

BENTON COUNTY
Vinton

We declared the people in this county will chase hard after God like King David. *The Lord has sought out for Himself a man after His own heart* (1 Sam. 13:14). May they build on the faith of the righteous fore-fathers.

Linda by Benton County Courthouse

We declared "cleanness." The Lord is going to make a "clean sweep of things!"

Olympic Torch Passed Through in 1996

The Olympic Torch passed through here in May of 1996 (see photo). We declare Psalm 119:105, *"Thy Word is a lamp to my feet and a light to my path."* May the people of Benton County fall in love with the Word of God. It will set fire to their souls!

The children here will keep the Name of the Lord holy! There will be a reverential fear of God arising from this county. *"Praise the Lord! How blessed is the man who fears the Lord, who greatly delights in His commandments."* (Ps. 112:1).

Sons and daughters have left for other places, but "keep them in You, Oh God!"

Make a broad way for your work here, Lord.

Establish something here that cannot be done anywhere else. It's a solid and foundational work of God.

The scroll-like carvings on the courthouse building were artistic and interesting. The Lord is going to *rewrite* some things in this county. He is going to make things *right*. He is going to *right* the wrongs. He is writing a new destiny! Linda saw these carvings in the spiritual realm as resembling some kind of musical notes and sensed new songs of joy emerging. Intimacy with God will produce new songs of the heart, giving Him great glory! These songs will become well known and sung far and wide. People will be reading the scriptures more than ever before resulting in fresh, vibrant music coming forth. Revelations of deliverance, healing, joy and restoration, along with intimacy with God are about to emerge.

Scroll-Like Carvings

We proclaimed Psalm 146:1-3 and all of Psalm149.

This was the 45th county on our Prophetic Prayer Journey, therefore we declared Psalm 45 over Benton County. Verse 6 was especially strong because God is extending the scepter of uprightness. *"Thy throne, O God, is forever and ever; a scepter of uprightness is the scepter of Thy kingdom."*

We prophesied a new beginning!

IOWA COUNTY
Marengo

I (Linda) was astounded to learn some of the names of Iowa or "Ioway" is: *Sleepy Ones, Drowsy Ones, Dusty Faces, Beautiful Land* and, *This Is the Place*. I recalled an amazing dream I had a number of years ago. The dream was so dramatic and vivid that I recorded it. In the dream, there was a clown standing beside the highway that led into a town. (Quite often as you approach city limits, there will be a billboard with the town's name, as well

Castle-Like Courthouse

as what they're known for.) In my dream, this clown didn't have a

Seal of Iowa County – A Flame!

particularly fun or happy expression on his face. In fact, he looked rather scary, almost evil. He held up a sign as people were passing by that read: "Stop! Stop here! We are a *sleepy* town! We like to take naps!" That was in the fall of 1998. Nine years later I am living that very dream! Unbelievable!

Iowa County and the entire **state of Iowa** need to embrace Isaiah 52, especially verse one and two where it says, *"Awake! Awake! Shake yourself from the dust…rise up…loose yourself from the chains around your neck."* (Bold emphasis is mine) Revelation 3:2-3 is also relevant which in part says, *"Wake up, and strengthen the things that remain…"* Wake up Iowa! Remember Psalm 121 that says our God does **not sleep or slumber**! *"And this do, knowing the time, that it is already the hour for you to awaken from sleep; for now salvation is nearer to us than when we believed."* (Rom. 13:11).

Another dream

Also within days of taking this Prayer Journey, I had another dream where I saw the United States from high above in an aerial view–or God's view. His eyes went to and fro and then I heard Him proclaim as in a **big announcement** from some stage: "And now…(pause/drum roll)…I choose…IOWA!" So Hallelujah for the divine destiny of this state!

In light of this, we declared an arousal and an awakening to the Spirit of the Lord! We saw people beginning to rise from their sleep in the night to pray. Oh God, awaken the watchmen to pray. We speak to the churches of this county to awaken!

We proclaimed a cleansing from shame in order to make the people pure and worthy so that they may prepare to become the Bride of Christ. The "turrets" on the courthouse speak of darkness. We speak light! We decree in the Name of Jesus, there is a gate of heaven here. Healing is that gate! Silver and gold we may not have, but we have Jesus. In the name of Jesus, we command you to walk, jump and praise, in Iowa County! We proclaimed the gates of heaven to open up and people will walk, jump, and leap before the Lord with healings and deliverances. Declared the Gate Beautiful! (Acts 3:1-10).

"Dust" in one of the meanings of *Iowa*, represents death. We rebuked the spirit of death and decreed new life in Jesus.

We declared great faith in this county and repentance according to Acts 3:19. Repent! Repent, so that times of refreshing can enter in.

This county caused us to realize God still wants to create divine connections. We met Rev. Morris C. Hurd of the First United Methodist Church shoveling ice and snow from the front of his church. We hadn't realized it before, but we had all met about a year earlier at a meeting in Des Moines. Given a moment or two earlier, we would have missed him

Mike With Rev. Morris C. Hurd

this particular afternoon. But it was a divine set-up by the Lord in order that we might pray with him giving renewed hope and encouragement to his soul.

We decreed the breaking off of coldness on so many hearts and lives in this county and prayed Revelation 3:16 will come to fruition.

Lord, minister to any dysfunctional lives in this area that they may be healed.

We sensed a mighty breakthrough as we drove out of town at 3:03 PM on 3/3/07. What a match of numbers! There had been divine connections made in the natural and in the spiritual realms. Holy. Holy. Holy. The temperature had actually gone up. It was now 21 degrees. Not warm by any means, but at least it was climbing!

POWESHIEK COUNTY
Montezuma

We arrived at our last county of the day at 3:30 PM and the temperature was beginning to drop again. The roads, packed with ice and snow were becoming more treacherous.

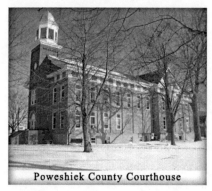
Poweshiek County Courthouse

I (Linda) had an unusual experience as we drove into town. In the spirit, I explicitly heard the sound of weeping. Suddenly a spirit of weeping was very strong on me. I broke into sobs not understanding what was happening. I heard "crying and weeping" as if someone were crying out, "Save me!

Save me!" Release the pain, Lord! And may the name of Jesus permeate the homes in this county.

Release the spiritual warriors here, Lord. Release the watchmen.

When we got to the courthouse we saw an unusual brick–just one lone brick, lying between two stones that mentioned a Mother's Club from long ago. Linda heard the scripture from Matthew, chapter 2 and verse 18, "Rachael weeping for her child-ren." My heart ached for some undisclosed reason. We began to prophesy from Psalm 30, that *"weeping may last for a night, but joy comes in the morn-ing...Thou hast turned for me my*

Unusual Marker

mourning into dancing; Thou hast loosed my sackcloth and girded me with gladness...."

Those who sow in tears shall reap joy (Ps. 126:3-5). Losses have occurred. But no more! For those who have been in the valley, they will now be taken to mountain top experiences with You, Oh God!

The name of this city has its roots in the Aztec Empire, which was known for violence and worshipping false gods. We rebuked that inheritance over this county. Let there be a bending of knees to the one true God. We decreed the presence and power of the Lord Jesus to be revealed. The Lord is releasing redemption here. Things lost, such as virginity, innocence, family relationships, etc. are being restored by the revelation of the saving Blood of Jesus.

We also found something we had seen in one other place–the doors of the court house were open! (They're always closed on Saturdays.) We declared open doors for justice, mercy, righteousness and forgiveness to come forth. Lord, raise up living stones according to 1 Peter 2.

We heard bells ringing and declared "freedom." This is God's perfect timing for His special work to begin here!

A Phenomenon

Setting out for the drive home, we were overwhelmed by what the Lord had revealed to us. We just praised and thanked Him for His loving kindness that never fails. But He had more in store for us!

We were given yet another spiritual marker that this holy journey has been ordained by Him for a "time such as this." He is truly opening the heavens over Iowa!

Mike was at the wheel driving down I-80 when I saw him leaning forward to see something on the horizon. I didn't want to say anything about what *I* was also seeing, because it was simply indescribable! It was so profound; I was thinking it was something in my imagination. But Mike saw it too!

We saw the heavens opening up creating a cloud-like cylinder to the earth, then rising back up again. It was approximately 4:30 PM and the sun was still bright and beautiful in the clear, wintry skies. But suddenly, we saw as it were, a vertical cylinder, funnel-like (but not swirling) cloud formation that descended, touched the earth, and then pulled back into the heavens.

It lasted less than a minute. The clouds within it were fluffy, translucent, with a gold overtone and multiple colors inside of it. It appeared to have invisible borders around it that kept it in cylinder form.

Our majestic and holy, Lord *is* indeed sending signs and wonders to confirm His desire for Iowa and beyond! All I could think of is how the Lord gave the Hebrew children a cloud by day and a pillar of fire by night.

> "And the angel of God, who had been going before the camp of Israel, moved and went behind them; and the pillar of cloud moved from before them and stood behind them. So it came between the camp of Egypt and the camp of Israel; and there was a cloud along with the darkness, yet it gave light at night. Thus the one did not come near the other all night."
> —Exodus 14:19-20

This describes this prophetic journey. The Lord God is decreeing a holy demarcation between those who are His and those who are not. Let us cry out for mercy, and praise Him with a shout of victory!

❦ fourteen ❦

DALLAS, GUTHRIE, AUDUBON

"Blessed is the nation whose God is the Lord, the people whom He has chosen for His own inheritance." —Psalm 33:12

B y now we were getting this down to a routine and our preparation list was hardly needed any more. One of the main things was to make sure the camera was not only charged, but not left behind. We didn't want to have to backtrack, especially in winter! One day we did forget it. However, we had driven only a few blocks from home when we realized what happened. God always protected us. Additionally, with each journey we would take plenty of worship CD's, so our entire day was spent in praise, worship and prayer. We would come home tired, but rejoicing all the way.

This particular prayer journey held a "first" for us, taking off in the afternoon at 2:28 PM instead of early morning. I had spoke at the Des Moines Women Aglow Meeting in the morning and Mike decided since it was a beautiful sunny day, we would try to get in a few more counties. The balmy 55 degrees was unusual for March 10th, 2007 in Iowa, but fantastic for our ordained pathway. What fun! We used the "55" degree temperature as a prophetic gauge to prophesy double favor to the three counties we were about to visit. Two hundred miles later we were *aglow* with all the good reports God gave us.

Note: The Lord gave us a personal word of prophecy while on this journey, but we felt it also applied to the entire state as well. Remember the *dedication* of this book is for those who have gone before us, come along side and coming behind us. Mike said we've turned the corner into the realm of passing the natural, into the supernatural! Then he heard the Lord say: "There is an angel ahead of you for this Prayer Journey. Little by little, county by county, you are taking possession of the land. Prayer by prayer, proclamation by proclamation, decree by decree you are driving out the enemy in Jesus Name. Governmental authority is on these prayers. The enemy is fleeing in SEVEN different directions!"

Iowa, let's give a shout of Hallelujah!

We always sensed that a certain aspect of each county had significance to Iowa as a whole. For example, a certain characteristic or attribute of a particular county was also part of the prophetic DNA of the entire state. The Lord is weaving a beautiful destiny over Iowa by connecting all the prophetic dots!

DALLAS COUNTY
Adel

With all the restoration going on in the natural realm at this courthouse, we were led to declare this entire county to be a place of restoration. 1 Corinthians 15:46 says that the natural proceeds the spiritual.

Mike heard in his spirit the words: "far away," sensing perhaps the influence of the prayers of this county will impact regions far away, even to the Mideast. He also sensed an unexplainable love for Israel coming forth from this area. We declared Ephesians

186

2:17, *"And He came and preached peace to you who were far away and peace to those who were near."* Verses 18-22 were also applied, especially since the court-house is going through reconstruction, remodeling and trans-formation:

Renovation Construction Sign

"Christ Jesus Himself being the corner stone, in whom the whole building being fitted together is growing into a holy temple in the Lord; in whom you also are being built together into a dwelling of God in the Spirit."

The scales of justice and a sword were on the statue of Lady Justice atop the courthouse. We then proclaimed justice and freedom in this place that righteous judgments would come forth. We decreed an *expansion* in this area of justice and righteousness.

This is a gateway county! We had discovered on an earlier prayer journey that on one of the corners or perimeters of this county, there is a Hindu Temple. We declared those attending that place would soon know the one, true, holy Jehovah God, and that their knees would bend to Him alone.

This is a county that is turning a corner. What seems far away is not far away, and the move of God is near!

Things shrouded in secrecy will be exposed so that the true Light of Christ can be known and grasped here. We proclaimed a holy shroud of God's Presence to descend on Dallas County.

Engraving of 1858 Courthouse

As we've discovered in many cities in Iowa, there was a building with a Masonic emblem on it across the street. We rebuked any unholy influence in this area as well.

We prayed for the *balance* between the old and new wine-skins.

Prayed for the *right now* word of God to be given, let fresh revelation come.

Let them know **who** they are! Let this county have eyes to see, ears to hear.

From their French heritage, bring forth freedom in the spirit. We came against the spirit of religion. Let old spiritual wells be dug and fresh waters begin to gush forth in this county.

Declared the hearts of the children be restored to their parents and parents to their children. (Hag. 4:6).

Stagnant waters and pools were rebuked as Isaiah 35:6-7 was proclaimed. Bring forth springs of Living water, Lord. Let joy be upon their heads! (Isa. 35:10).

We declared Isaiah 66:9-12 that "peace like a river" would flow over this county; also verses 18 and 19, "gather nations and tongues," and "declare God's glory to the nations." Bring forth unity, Oh God.

The Lord extends peace to the people.

This county is a *gathering place*. Gather here to put down new roots of praise and worship unto God!

GUTHRIE COUNTY
Guthrie Center

This was an enjoyable county to visit! We had some delightful finds. In the photo, Mike is anointing a stone that we found on the grounds. There was an Anti-Profanity Association in the 1800's. This righteous act began to produce good fruit in

Anointing the "Pioneer Rock"

this county. In fact, this unusual stone gave honor to those pioneers, men and women, who had gone before and planted. It acknowledged the Lord with the inscription: "Seed time. God giveth the increase. We enjoy the harvest." Praise the Lord!

Mike by Guthrie County Courthouse

So it was quite natural to decree a harvest of souls to come forth for this county and this state. We proclaimed seed time *and* harvest. God is giving the 30, 60, and 100 fold increase of His Spirit here (Matt. 13:1-9). Let the Word of God spring up! Oh Lord, it is You who provides the warmth for fertile ground.

The word for this county is *harvest* and *fertility* - Beautiful Land, Beulah Land, God's land (Isa. 62:4). This is a place that is not ashamed of You Oh Lord!

There was yet another stone on the grounds honoring only women. We don't recall seeing anything else like it in Iowa. It read: "Names of women pioneers in the settlement and development of Guthrie Center, co-workers at planting time, for their practical service and inspiring ideals are here acknowledged and memorialized." So women of Guthrie County—you have a divine destiny in the Lord! Find it. Live it. The book of Esther is for you. (See also 2 Timothy 1:5 and Titus 2:3-5).

We prayed for pioneers and forerunners to come forth once again. Draw them to You, Oh Lord.

Let this county not be defiled. Show them the difference between the holy and common, Lord.

Bless the history and heritage of this county in being a House of Refuge and being a part of the Underground Railroad helping to hide, feed, clothe and transport runaway slaves on their journey to freedom in the 1800's. This is still a refuge county. Let freedom ring!

Lord, set Your eyes upon Guthrie County!

This county is fertile ground for God's Word to grow. Grant it much favor, Lord.

This is a quiet and humble place for sons, daughters and grandchildren to be raised here. There is much peace in this county.

Simplicity and humility abounds in this area. There's nothing showy here, just the salt of the earth people. We proclaimed kindness that's accompanied by great humility.

There were two jets in the sky whose trails made a cross directly overhead as we were making our proclamations. "The

Cross" marks the spot! This place is marked for much favor from the Lord.

Let the fragrance of Christ rise up!

We decreed no lawlessness! May there be complete reverence for God.

This county is pressing in, moving out, and strengthening their stakes. (Isa. 54:2-3).

AUDUBON COUNTY
Audubon

This was the **50**th county we have visited. It was the tipping county! We excitedly declared Jubilee here, freedom for captives! We also proclaimed restoration.

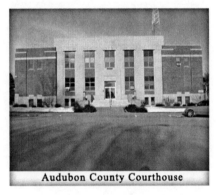

Audubon County Courthouse

Leviticus 25 speaks of the Year of Jubilee. We declared the people of this county would follow God's decrees. Be holy unto the Lord. God declares a walk of holiness here. (Lev. 26: 1-13).

God promises to send rain. Your "threshing floor" will continue. Five will chase 100 and ten will chase 10,000. (Deut. 32:29-30).

No striving for position.

Renew. Rebuild. Restore, Lord!

Located on Highway 71, we declared Psalm 71 over this county. We proclaimed righteousness and justice will rule. Laws and decrees will be righteous.

There was a parked truck in the back of the courthouse with a sign on it that read: Audubon County/Secondary Road Dept. Many people here may feel secondary or downtrodden, but God is going to lift them up to new heights.

There is fresh revelation and knowledge of God that is coming.

Stop judging by the appearance– instead, judge rightfully (John 7:24). Declared no inadequacy! There will be righteous judgments.

This is a critical time and a critical place. We raise up the name of Jesus! We lift it above those who

Statue in Park Across the Street

walk through the county doors.

May words of fresh revelation and insight come to the pastors. Churches will begin to be known for fresh revelation.

Send forth Your mighty Prince, Michael, the archangel, Oh God, to fight the battles in the heavenly realm. Let the Book of Truth, the Word of God, be given.

Let the Masonic influence become tarnished and fall to the ground.

Prophesied people take flight into the fresh move of God. Take them higher! Let them see things they've never seen before.

One of the photos shows a statue of John James Audubon, who was a famous artist and naturalist and whom the county is named after. We proclaimed godly creativity will begin to abound in this county.

Leaving this area at 5:54 PM, there was a sundog/rainbow in the sky just as the sun was setting. How beautiful! We thanked the Lord for this sign and that what we had proclaimed in His Name, is being fulfilled.

✦ fifteen ✦

BLACK HAWK, BREMER, FAYETTE, CLAYTON, BUCHANAN, DELAWARE

"'Everywhere I send you, you shall go, and all that I command you, you shall speak. Do not be afraid of them, for I am with you to deliver you,' declares the Lord. 'See, I have appointed you this day over the nations and over the kingdoms, to pluck up and to break down, to destroy and to overthrow, to build and to plant.'"
—Jeremiah 1:7,8,10

The anticipation of spring was beginning to take control of my thoughts as we journeyed on another cold March day. It was 28 degrees on St. Patrick's Day and we were ready for *green* to be sure! The winter months of 2007 had been fun traveling to different Iowa counties, but spring fever was upon me!

Mike and I dashed out of the house, climbed in the car and drove off at 7:30 AM. There were fat, fluffy snowflakes falling heavily. It made for beautiful scenery, but we wondered if this was wise! It is amazing how the Lord wooed us, even when it didn't seem practical in the natural realm. He protected us through 405 miles on this day's journey.

195

BLACK HAWK COUNTY
Waterloo

By the time we arrived, it was 34 degrees and the snow had stopped with sunshine peeking through. This filled me with delight because this is the county where I was born, raised, and lived for a few years after our marriage. Thank you Lord for opening up the skies! What a wonderful welcome! Since we knew so much of this place, it was somewhat difficult to keep a perspective that was from the Lord and not from the flesh. But God was faithful to reveal the following things to us.

Black Hawk County Courthouse

This county is named after the Native American leader of the Sauk Tribe, Chief Black Hawk, who apparently at one time had unfortunately pronounced a curse over this area because of a broken treaty. We proclaimed a reverse of the curse! Mike and I saw this is a covenant county. We declared a spirit of reconciliation and for healing to come forth. We came against contention and declared a spirit of unity to arise. Ezekiel 37:17-27 was proclaimed over this county.

Pride and greed were also rebuked. Humble yourselves before God! This county is #7 alphabetically. And God's favor and perfection was decreed to fall in this area.

Declared an end to unholy covenants. Daniel 9:20-27 was also prayed for Black Hawk County.

Build and restore.

We prophesied the sweet Presence of the Holy Spirit to come and fall like rain. May they not be known for "hawkish" ways, but the ways of the Holy Dove, the Holy Spirit.

Isaiah 11:13-16 was proclaimed. Oh God, break down the barriers of dividing rivers, so people can cross over in their sandals. We thus declared a new and holy standard to be lifted up.

We prayed the power and control of drugs, and drug lords will be broken.

Heard: "steel heavens," so we decreed those be torn down and an open heaven to occur. We then declared Deuteronomy 11:16-28 pronouncing no more steel heavens! The heavens have been shut up, but we prophesied that the heavens will now be opened! (Rev. 4).

Lord, bring forth a teaching anointing to arise from godly teachers.

Heal divisions

We prayed that Waterloo and Cedar Falls will no longer contend with each other. We call forth a spirit of agreement to draw them together. When that happens, they will achieve their covenant destinies.

Desolation in many hearts will end. Healing will occur. People sick at heart will now be healed! Heal hearts, Oh God, heal divisions! Gather them from the four corners of this county in spiritual unity.

People here will raise up a "plowing in prayer." Plowing! Plowing through in prayer! A harvest is coming as a result of *plowing prayer.* 1 Corinthians 9:10 says, *"Or is He speaking altogether for our sake? Yes, for our sake it was written, because the plowman ought to plow in hope and the thresher to thresh in hope of sharing the crops.* " (See also Isaiah 2:4).

We confessed sins of disbelief, pride, greed and competition.

There have been governmental issues here.

Declared freedom for captives and prayed for the oppressed to be set free. Prayed there will be no prejudicial division between African Americans and Caucasians.

Two Interesting Signs in this County

Close to the courthouse was a billboard that read: "All I know is everything. God." Driving away from this area we saw yet another billboard. This one said: "That 'Love Thy Neighbor' Thing...I meant that. God." What an added blessing for this county!

It was now 10:20 AM and the sun had broken through quite nicely. Thank you Lord for the warmth of Your Presence!

BREMER COUNTY
Waverly

This is the only Iowa county named after a prominent woman in literature, Fredricka Bremer. Lord, raise up youth who will be anointed to write good and godly literature (Dan. 1:4 & 17). Give the people of this county godly dreams and visions.

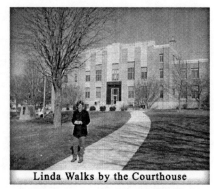
Linda Walks by the Courthouse

Waverly was first settled in 1850 and soon grew to importance due to water power that was used by the flour and saw mills. No more grinding in the spirit! There's the fresh grinding of the corn...abundance of the fruit of the land is coming forth. *"The angel of the Lord was at the threshing floor."* (2 Sam. 24:16-25; Ruth 3; Luke 3:17). We declared fresh, Living Waters of God will begin to flow in great abundance here. (John 4:10).

Holiness, righteousness, justice and mercy will flow in this area.

John 12:23-24 was declared. There will be much more fruit for the kingdom of God.

Bremer County Courthouse

It's time for Jesus to be glorified here in a miraculous way! God says to humble yourselves, die to self so Jesus can be exalted. God ordains much fruit for you. But you must die to your own desires. Bring people out of their self-centeredness and let them center on You, Oh Lord!

The Lord had us proclaim 2 Tim. 2:1-13. God has a *victor's crown* for this county (vs. 5). Let people compete and contend to win God's favor so His will might be done. There's a "running" to complete the race that's being

199

established here. There is a holy planting God is doing. Let purity of purpose come forth.

Hosea 14:1-2 and 4-8 was declared over Bremer County. Take holy words with you wherever you go. We declared restoration and righteousness because Native Americans were taken off this land and sent to Minnesota (Amos 9:13-15). Rebuilding of broken relationships in families and in government will come forth.

The Lord desires prayer to go up from here so a harvest of souls can come. God says He will "do His marvelous harvest work." This is holy ground.

Things stolen by the enemy are going to be restored (Isa. 28:23-29). Your time of difficulty and hard work is about to end as the Lord breaks through Bremer County!

FAYETTE COUNTY
West Union

Fayette County Courthouse

It was now warming up to a balmy 34 degrees as we journeyed into Fayette County. We arrived at a significant time: 12:12 PM. Twelve is an apostolic number, and this is an apostolic journey! We read and proclaimed 1 Thessalonians 2:4-13, declaring apostolic gifts and other blessings to flow. Likewise, according to this scripture, we have been gentle among you as a "nursing mother."

God's authority is going to reign here!

This county was named for Marquis de La Fayette, a French explorer. Bring forth holy expectations in the Most High God!

Mike by Wounded Soldier Sign

Mike is standing beside a sign on the county courthouse lawn (see Photo) regarding one of their wounded soldiers. It grabbed our hearts. We prayed for him and also for the wounded *spiritual* soldiers of this county. We also prayed for encouragement and comfort in order to build lives worthy unto God.

Unfortunately, we saw that one of the cornerstones was set by the Masons. Oh God, bring forth godly authority. Break all covenants with death! No more false gods! We rebuked ungodly influences in this county and declared truth and righteousness.

We prophesied new visions of God. People here have been standing still. They must now move on and upward. There's not enough progression in God. We proclaimed an awakening in order to press in (1 Pet. 5). God will lift you up in due time. Cast your anxieties on the Lord because He cares for you. (vs.7).

We prayed for the children of this county. Show Thyself compassion-ate here, Lord (1 Thes. 2:4-7). There's been a fear of moving on because of past hurts. The Lord says, "Be healed by the power of My Name. Lift Me up and you shall be lifted up."

We read and loudly proclaimed Ephesians 3 over Fayette County.

Ornate Indian Sconces

In the spirit we heard: "Heavy rains!" We proclaimed 1 Kings 18:41-45. Let this place soak in revelation. This county may have been stuck in miry clay, but Living Waters of insight and revelation are coming! We called forth a *rain of revelation* (Also verse 1). There is the sound of heavy rain! <u>This is a "triggering" county for revelation.</u> Unfreeze and thaw those who have been bordered and bundled.

We decreed an awakening to press in to know God more and to know Him intimately.

Saw a bench that said: "Caring County." It was evident in the picture of the wounded soldier on the court house lawn. Bring forth a *godly*, compassionate caring.

Lord, thaw the things frozen in time. We rebuke the fear of moving on. Perfect love casts out fear. (1 John 4:18).

We stand at the point where revelation will be released to this county. Mysteries not seen by previous generations will now be seen (comprehended). Release insight! It's now the fullness of time. Revelations of God will come forth. (Eph. 3:2-6).

CLAYTON COUNTY
Elkader

111 High Street! The address alone caused us to prophesy that the Holy Trinity would be lifted up on high! (See photo). The county is named after a former Secretary of State.

The courthouse is located directly beside the river and a little dam. A sign said it was the largest *stone arched bridge* west of the Mississippi River. (See photo). It's built prominently of *red brick*. We prayed people come out of their "hard labors"

Address: 111 High Street

as the Hebrew children did (Exod. 3). Take people from the "arch" enemy and bring them into Living Waters. Do not let them be deceived (Gen. 3). Let not hearts be as stone, but as flesh. (Ezek. 11:19).

Oldest Stone Bridge in Iowa!

Mike saw the arch of a foot. God is causing people of this county to *step up* into the Beautiful Land or Promised Land of their prayers. Isaiah 52:7 was declared: "*How beautiful are the feet of those who bring good news....*" And according to verse 10, we proclaimed all portions of the county will see the salvation of God.

This county is primed for a mighty move of God! Release the fulfillment of "Beautiful Land" (Beulah Land) for this county! Joshua 1:2-9 was decreed. God is causing the people here to step into His beautiful, heavenly land, the Promised Land. "Step into it! Step into the Living, refreshing waters of God!"

We sensed a fulfillment of many prayers coming forth. Ezekiel 3:17 and Isaiah 52:7 and 10 were proclaimed. Bring forth missionaries from Clayton County.

Linda Beside Dam Behind Courthouse

There are *natural ridges in the landscape* of this county. "Lookouts" and "watchman" have a great anointing here. God loves your devotion. The forces of righteousness will find victory. Let people's prayers know they are touching and changing the world! Your prayers have international power and influence with the Throne of God. As people seek intimacy with God, these things shall unfold. The Lord says, "I will make your face shine with My glory. You shall look different from all the rest, for this day, I have chosen you for My own and for this special assignment. Pray! Pray as never before and see what My Presence upon you shall do."

Let the prayers of Iowa change Iraq just as has been prophesied by Dutch Sheets and Chuck Pierce. Let the prayers here affect the world!

The glory of all the lands was declared to be upon this county. (Ezek. 20:6).

There was a monument with the Gettysburg Address on it, showing this county's respect, honor. It was highly esteemed. Let the esteemed things of the Most High God be released here.

Let those who pray know that their prayers indeed make a difference. Prayed a flooding and a rushing comes forth for the things of God. People in this county will begin to seek intimacy with God day and night.

We declared to this county: "As you know God, you'll know His ways and what to do, where to go. Seek Him. Draw close to Him. He'll draw close to you."

Mike at War Memorial

Prophesied greater and deeper relationship with God will come forth from here.

We declared Isaiah 49:8-9. Declared the people here are a "covenant people" with God. This now is the favorable time of the Lord upon Clayton County. "Go forth!"

DELAWARE COUNTY
Manchester

Delaware County Courthouse

This was now our 55th county and we proclaimed Isaiah 55 over it, especially verses 4 and 11. Raise up leaders and commanders here, Lord. The words of God that are preached and proclaimed here will not return to Him void, but will accomplish the purpose for which it was sent.

As we crossed the county line, a signed read: 11 miles to Manchester. Eleven is a transitional number. This is a county in transition! Change is coming–and soon!

We rebuked a desolate spirit and proclaimed Isaiah 61, especially verse 4. We decreed people will fall in love with God's Word. "God is about to give you good gifts as a Father loves to give gifts to His children. You shall not go hungry. You shall have an abundance of Bread. An abundance of God's Word is coming. Share the Bread! Pass the Bread! Bring a spirit of revelation and insight, understanding and fear of the Lord." (Isa. 43:18-20).

There are discouraged spiritual leaders here. Encourage and strengthen them with dreams that will give fresh and renewed hope for the future.

A Mirrored War Memorial

"A crossing over" is happening here. Some lives have been ravaged by the enemy but God says, "I am your Savior, your deliverer. No longer shall you feel ravaged and desolate. I am giving you a fresh start, fresh air, fresh view, fresh per-spective, fresh manna from heaven. My Son has set you free. Whom the Lord has set free is free indeed" (John 8:36). We prophesied a bridge from desolation to delight! (Ps. 37:23).

The favor of God was decreed for Delaware County.

A hawkish spirit was rebuked and we prayed the Holy Dove (Holy Spirit) descend here.

On a building we saw these words, "Operation New View." Proclaimed it to be spiritually true!

Mike saw in the spirit "iron foreheads." We rebuked stubbornness, obstinacy, and iron foreheads. (Isa. 48:4-6).

Rebuild and restore the godly foundations that have crumbled.

George Washington crossed the Delaware River. "A crossing over" is ready for this county. People are moving from previous spiritual boundaries to new victories and breakthroughs. This is a Bridge County! It's passing over into deeper, Living Waters.

Delaware County, you have something to say about presidential elections! A strategic importance will emerge here. We prayed wisdom, counsel and power in order for people to cross over into their divine destinies "for a time such as this." We saw the Seer anointing rising up.

BUCHANAN COUNTY
Independence

This county was named for the 15th President of the United States.

Buchanan County Courthouse

Blow the bugle! Blow the trumpet in Zion! Sound the alarm! It's not so much the sound of war, as it's the *sound* of something good coming to this county! Don't miss it! Pay attention to receive it (Joel 2:15-32). It's a good sounding alarm. The Lord says, "If you don't look for the blessing, you will miss it. If you don't look for Me, you surely will miss Me!" Watch. Wait and see. (1 Sam. 12:16,18-20, 24).

Linda saw "wide open eyes" almost like a child who has wonder and faith as in seeing something awesome for the very first time. The Lord is releasing child-like faith, a new level of trusting in God.

The Lord is calling His people here to climb higher. Do not kick against the goads (Eccles. 12:9-11; Judg. 3:21). We prayed against the self-will of those who live independent of God. Prayed for dependence on Him! Complete surrender, as well as holy allegiance to the One and only God Jehovah was proclaimed.

This area is known for a mental health facility. We decreed in the Name of Jesus, emotional healing and clarity upon minds, hearts and emotions (Rom. 12:2; 1 Tim. 1:7). Set captives free!

We heard piano music in the spirit, floating through the air as we walked around the courthouse. Lord, bring a new song of deliverance and freedom to this area! The new sound for this county is the *roar of worship, praise and adoration to God*! We declared Galatians 5:13-16. Serve one another in love.

Raise up the trumpet of God with voices to declare, prophesy, decree and sing God's Word. We saw in the spirit an arrow being shot from the earth going through the heavens. The new "sound" (prayer, praise and worship) will break open the heavens! Lord, give eyes to see it and ears to hear it.

Do not use your freedom to indulge. (Gal. 5:13).

In the new freedom of worship, let there be no condemnation, but only the beauty of holiness. The Lord is releasing a new atmosphere here. The music will be an aural picture of God's beauty. ("Aura" means distinctive atmosphere; "Aural" - means "of the ear; or hearing"). Let the new sounds of the Lord come forth from Buchanan County!

A horse is released here! The end days are filled with righteousness, mercy and justice. Ride on these things! (Jer. 22:1-4; Rev. 19).

This 12th journey ended beautifully as we made a quick stop by IHOPE (Iowa House of Prayer) in Waterloo. We were warmed by the grace and love so evident there. It had been a long day so we were not able to stay for long. However, upon their recognizing our presence, they called us forward to share a few brief moments about our Prophetic Prayer Journey. Afterwards, they formed a circle around us and prayed. How comforting to have that power of prayer surrounding us. We felt renewed and refreshed in our divine purposes of traveling to Iowa's county courthouses. So thank you IHOPE! We love you and bless you!

♣ sixteen ♣

MAHASKA, KEOKUK, WASHINGTON, JOHNSON

"But let justice roll down like waters and righteousness like an everflowing stream." —Amos 5:24

During these divine journeys, I often felt as though we were God's postmen delivering holy mail throughout Iowa! My husband, Michael, and I traveled every weekend in March going through blizzards, snow squalls, snow showers, heavy rain, mist, fog and sometimes, even sunshine–hallelujah! As this was our 13th Journey, we were now two-thirds of the way through this divine assignment. Going to the county seats of man's government and prophesying righteousness, justice and mercy according to God's government has greatly boosted our faith.

Often we felt more like we were taking a one day vacation as we set out to declare the words of the Lord on each county tour. On a basic level, just seeing the seasonal landscape changes of Iowa in all its beauty, its heritage, its precious people, was sheer delight!

This day, we woke up to thunder, lightening, mist and fog, but at least it wasn't snowing. We packed up and were out the door by 8:10 AM. In spite of heavy fog and rain, it was an unusually warm March 23rd (2006) at 59 degrees. Our holy adventure took us through 283 miles of Iowa terrain. Arriving back home hours later at 5:31 PM, we were bathed in 73 degrees worth of sunshine. Incredible!

This date was also significant for us in that it was our granddaughter's 11th birthday. We called her long distance to tell her we were thinking of her and praying for her. We felt led to declare Proverbs 11:11 for all of Iowa: *"By the blessing of the upright a city is exalted."* I'd noticed in my Bible I had claimed that verse on 11-11-00 when we were on Prayer Patrol in the inner city of Des Moines. Amazingly, I'd also written the date of 2-**11**-02. These things are not coincidental. God had now broadened that prayer assignment to the entire state and He will be faithful to bring it to fruition! I personally love the number eleven. Its symbolic meaning is "transition." We knew the Lord was transitioning Iowa into its divine destiny "for a time such as this." The Presidential Caucuses were now nine months away and Iowa is strategic!

Something significant was brought to our attention by a gentleman who recently moved here from the west coast and had already made an observation about Iowa. He said, "There is an inferiority complex on the people of this state." We perceived it to be aligned with false humility as well. We rebuked these negative prevailing spirits and began to prophesy godly, divine destinies to come forth. *"'Not by might nor by power, but by My Spirit,' says the Lord."* (Zech. 4:6).

MAHASKA COUNTY
Oskaloosa

This county is named for one of the most noted Ioway Chiefs, Mahaska. The county seat, Oskaloosa, is named in honor of a

Creek Tribe Native American **Princess**. This was wonderful to see, because much to our dismay, there has not been much honoring of the native peoples who first cared for this land. Because of these two significant recognitions we were led to declare daughters in this county

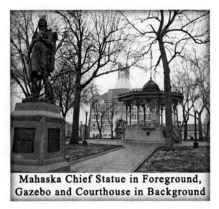

Mahaska Chief Statue in Foreground, Gazebo and Courthouse in Background

will be like pillars in the house of God and sons will be as grown up plants according to Ps. 144:**12**! Twelve being a governmental number, we prayed for divine authority to rule in this place.

We arrived at 9:22 AM and were quickened to the number "9." We decreed the 9 fruits and 9 gifts of the Holy Spirit from Galatians 5:22 and 1 Corinthians 12. The "22" in the 9:22 caused us to declare Isaiah 22:22.

Declared a new spiritual destiny begins here today.

The Lord says, "Why did you strike the arrow only 3 times" (2

Mike Stands by a Torpedo

Kings 13:18-19)? We have come to strike the arrows over and over...five or six times, or more! We proclaimed a double blessing. Elisha had twice the anointing of Elijah. (2 Kings 2:9).

You will no longer be under-achieving. You will bless others now. When the arrow strikes, the valve will release a flow of the Holy Spirit...divine waters will flow.

213

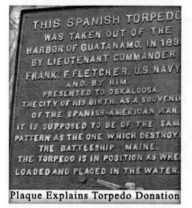

We saw a <u>torpedo</u> monument across the street. (See photo). The Spanish torpedo was taken out of the harbor of Guantanamo in 1899 by Lt. Commander Frank Fletcher, of the United States Navy. It was presented to Oskaloosa, the city of his birth, as a souvenir of the Spanish American War. The torpedo (says the monument) is placed in the *position* as when loaded and placed in the *water* (ready for an attack!).

*As this Prophetic Prayer Journey began in June, 2006, this was the "word" that had been previously given to us before we set out - that we would be like "a yellow **submarine**"...coming into each Iowa county silently, somewhat unseen, blowing up things of spiritual darkness! How wonderful that the Lord confirmed this word in such a unique way! The torpedo of course, is a hidden weapon. It's under the surface. It's not noticed until it explodes. We declared the arrow of victory and that the enemy will be completely destroyed in this county.*

Mike declared: "As arrows are struck, You, Oh Lord, will be the secret weapon. The torpedo of Your Spirit will flow unseen and yet You will perfect its mark. Arrows of victory will then be seen! The spiritual torpedo of God is ready to strike!"

It felt good here. Part of that overall good feeling was that we observed something we haven't seen in too many places and it warmed out hearts greatly. It was good to see the Native American Chief, Mahaska, honored so magnificently in a monument. This "honoring" spirit is going to yield fruit! (i.e., 9:22 AM as stated above)

There was a beautiful gazebo bandstand across the street. Part of the base underneath had a portal-like window in it which looked similar to one in a submarine! Ironic? I think not. The Lord continued to confirm what we were declaring by His Spirit. There will be a gushing forth of His purposes as the "torpedo of God" strikes. This county is about to expand and explode in the things of God with divine revelation, insight, understanding.

The gazebo bandstand caused us to see bandstand notes or music. A *celebration* is coming to this county! We declared 2 Corinthians 5:17: *"Therefore if any man is in Christ, he is a new creature; the old things have passed away; behold, new things have come."* The old is gone. The new has come!

There is also a pioneering spirit here and you shall share it with the rest of the state.

The sun was hiding most of our time here, but shone through again as we got back into the car. We sensed it was God's smile on Mahaska County! Amen!

KEOKUK COUNTY
Sigourney

Michael was raised in this county.

The Holy Spirit caused us to declared Isaiah 66:1, *"Thus says the Lord, 'Heaven is My throne, and earth is My footstool. Where then is a house you could build for Me? And where is a place that I may rest?' says the Lord."* Declared people here will discover the mighty Throne of God. Asked God to rend the heavens and

215

Keokuk County Courthouse

come down (Isa. 64:1). Lord, remove the spiritual ceiling in Keokuk County.

We proclaimed Psalm 29 for open heavens to occur and the voice of God to be heard.

The Lord's voice is breaking through to people's hearts. Let them hear clearly the holy sounds of heaven and God's voice. Verse 8, shake people from wilderness experiences so that they will see new spiritual births. Verse 9, the knowledge of Calvary's redemption causes the "calving" or birthing to come forth. Verses 10-11, give new and renewed spiritual strength to this county.

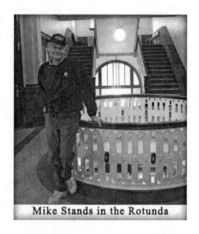

Mike Stands in the Rotunda

We asked for a Joseph anointing to come here. This county will now discover a new anointing of spiritual provision as well as material provision. We called forth dreams and interpretation of dreams. This county has an importance in dreams. As soon as we declared this, a portal of sun broke forth...at 11:09 AM. Eleven denotes transition and change. This is a county of dreams and dreamers. God is raising up people like Joseph to reveal their divine destinies, dreamers who are able to act.

"Be alive in the night season, Oh God!"

Put the <u>signet ring</u> on this county like Joseph. (Gen. 41:42-43).

Psalm 126 is also for this county. "We were like those who dream."

The "K" over the courthouse door looked like a throne or a chair. It caused us to declare a kingly anointing and Throne Room of heaven experiences for the people of this county. We decreed Revelation 4:1.

An Old Flag on Display in Courthouse

This was one of very few courthouses we were able to enter on a Saturday. When we saw the door open, we quietly stepped inside to look around. There was a meeting going on, so we were able to take a mini tour. We discovered an old flag that had been framed and put on an easel. It was wonderful to see the preservation of this unique artifact. We took a picture of a poster (see photo) showing every courthouse in all 99 Iowa counties. This was our first find for something like this, so it really blessed us. We found a window display of Native American artifacts as well. As we left the building, Mike and I noted the beautiful dome inside the rotunda. We were having so much fun discovering these things since we both love history. It was amazing that God had called us to declare HIS STORY over all the counties in Iowa!

First Find of all 99 Counties on a Poster

WASHINGTON COUNTY
Washington

Washington County Courthouse

Before going to the courthouse in this county, we visited Mike's mother in Keota near Washington. We left Keota at 1:11 PM. Three ones! We proclaimed the Presence and power of the Father, Son and Holy Spirit–the Holy Trinity–over Washington County. It was 66 degrees. Six represents the number of man. So we prayed, "Lord, by the power of Your Name, we cancel men's stubborn ways and decree discovery of Your ways!"

This county is named after the father of our country so we believe it holds special significance. Upon seeing statues of both George Washington and also one of a woman, we declared this to be a "mothering county." It takes fathers *and mothers* to birth in the natural, and in the spiritual. We prophesied new spiritual births to come forth.

We proclaimed deliverance from evil. There was a Woman of Justice statue on the front of the courthouse. On the side of the courthouse was another statue of a woman. It resembled that of Joan of Arc as she was holding a shield and a sword. (See photos). We declared people will put on the full

Lady With Sword and Shield

armor of God (Eph. 6:10-18). The shield seemed like a mirror which reflected or directed our attention to the opposite or "opposing corner" to the courthouse. Like opposing corners of fighters in a boxing ring, we knew there is a battle going on here for souls. Across the street was the Planned Parenthood office. We prayed a shield of protection for the unborn. We declared: No abortions! Bring forth innocence, Oh God! Bring forth that which is from heaven and God's will, not man's will. We called forth new births, physically and spiritually! Isaiah 66 was pronounced over Washington County.

President Washington Monument

This will be a county born in a day (Isa. 66:8)! Labor and birth is here. This "mothering" county will nurse people in this area. The Lord will bring it forth! *That which is born of the flesh is flesh, and that which is born of the Spirit is spirit"* (John 3:6). The Lord will give new life here, new life in the Lord Jesus! Let joy arise in this county because of new spiritual births, born out of the labor of love, God's love.

We proclaimed justice, mercy and righteousness. Establish these things in this county, Oh Lord.

Innocence has been lost. We prayed it is regained.

This county has been vulnerable spiritually. We prophesied prayers in the Spirit to come forth. Be alert!

Linda by Statue of a Woman

We called forth *overcomers* and those who don't look to the world, but to the things of God. (Rev. 3:21).

Many have had patchwork lives. God says, "I want to lay a firm foundation in your hearts with My Word. No more crumbling hearts, minds or lives. Restoration! Restoration!" There's been a shattering and brokenness in many lives. But God says, "I am your healer, deliverer and restorer. Come to Me you who are weary and I will refresh you." Matthew 11:28-30 and Isaiah 28 was declared.

Reveal truth, purity and clarity. Heaven rules! (Dan. 4:25-27).

We rebuked any corruption in city government. Lies and deceit by any county or city officials were also rebuked.

We decreed the generational blessings of Abraham, Isaac and Jacob.

JOHNSON COUNTY
Iowa City

We arrived at 3:16 PM and immediately declared Revelation 3:16! There were only a few moments of sunshine during our time here. The address of 417 S. Clinton St. stood out: $4 + 1 + 7 = 12$. Twelve is the governmental number representing authority. We proclaimed a new found spiritual, godly authority for this county and that a holy governmental power will descend from on high.

We proclaimed the youth to come forth in righteousness and with justice.

The Lord wants the people here to make a "toast" to raise their "glasses," raise their "eyes" and allow their hearts to drink of Him more deeply than ever

Johnson County Courthouse

before. 2 Samuel 6:21, *"I will celebrate before the Lord."*

Hebron, the first capital city under King David is likened to Iowa City which was originally the first designated seat of state government (2 Sam. 5:1-3). Restore the rights of the first born. There are "rights" granted to all God's first born into His family, His kingdom. We rebuked the Esau spirit; people have despised their birthrights here. Deception and loss of divine destiny was rebuked as we prayed, "Lord, establish a divine and holy birthright." We declared the people of this county will honor their birthright.

There is a transitional position being established here, people will move into godly unity and authority. Drink in the fullness of God.

Multicultural

This is a multicultural area. We rebuked any divisions. 1 Corinthians 12:13-14 was proclaimed, which says in part: *"Whether Jews or Greeks, whether slaves or free, we were all made to drink of one Spirit...."*

Ornate Archway Over Entrance

Declared John 7:37-38, *"If any man is thirsty, let him come to Me and drink. He who believes in Me, as the Scripture said, 'From his innermost being shall flow rivers of living water.'"*

People here have sought intellectual gifts. But God proclaims to them: "Seek Me! Seek My spiritual gifts and grow and mature in Me." The Lord is ready to show you a more excellent way! 1 Corinthians 12, especially verse 31; Zechariah 4:6, and 1 Corinthians 2:10-13 was pronounced over this county. We prophesied the fear of the Lord to come. It's the beginning of knowledge and understanding. Proverbs 1:7 and Psalm 122:1 were also declared.

We rebuked a suicidal spirit. Declared all of Psalm 42.

Some have mocked the one true God. "Where is your God?!" they ask. They are about to find out! Psalm 2 was prayed over Johnson County along with Acts 4:24-31. The place where they prayed was shaken and we believe this is what God is releasing as we prayed in this county.

The wisdom of men leaves them thirsty. Bring revelation of the secrets of God and the well of deep artesian waters, the Living Waters of God.

We sensed we had stirred up a hornets' nest in the "other realm." We began to plead the Blood of Jesus over Iowa City and Johnson County. Holy protection was decreed by the Blood of the Lamb of God for all Christians in this region. Let them emerge in this hour with a divine warring spirit of worship and praise to God, for "God inhabits the praises of His people." (Ps. 122:3).

We heard: "War and win!" We declared a holy habitation of God's Presence to emerge and be made known here.

Awake this county from their slouchy spiritual lives. Let hearts arise to newness of life in Christ Jesus. Let passionate praise and worship begin to ascend from the four corners of this county. Let them be as David and unabashedly adore the King of Kings.

Day and night

Let Jesus parties arise here, as in day and night prayer, day and night songs that will fill the heavens. Then, God is going to tip the heavens over upon Johnson County. Praise, sing, dance, shout and let godly, holy love and purity come forth!

A gate of heaven was prophesied to be opened here and we called forth an apostolic anointing.

Spiritual wells initially dug here will now be uncovered. Open the wells!

Lord, mark this county as a place of warring angels standing guard.

Wheat has been blown away with the chaff. This is also a Threshing Floor County. Its destiny is being challenged. Bring forth the divine destiny of the threshing floor. Establish a harvest of souls here (2 Sam. 24:18; Ruth 3; Luke 3:17)! Let holy altars be built. Lord, receive the prayers of this county.

We broke off inferiority and nailed it on the altar.

Let the land no longer be viewed as defiled.

Raise up anointed leaders, pastors, teachers. Lord, put Your Sword in their hands (the Word of God). (Heb. 4:12)

Multitudes are now in the valley of decision! (Joel 3:14)

❧ seventeen ❧

LINN, JONES, DUBUQUE, JACKSON, CLINTON, CEDAR

"From Aroer which is on the edge of the valley of Arnon and from the city which is in the valley, even to Gilead, there was no city that was too high for us; the Lord our God delivered all over to us." —Deuteronomy 2:36

On March 31st 2007, we set out on our 14th Prophetic Prayer Journey. We were as surprised as anyone that we toured each of the five Saturdays in March. This is quite a feat considering the temperament of Iowa weather. We certainly didn't plan it that way, but it seemed the dawning of the weekend would beckon us to this holy adventure. Every trip was always filled with so much anticipation and excitement for what the Lord would reveal to us. We wondered what we would do when it was all over! However, it didn't take long to realize there was so much God was releasing over Iowa that it would require a book to inform the people! Thus the messages you hold in your hands. But it goes far beyond the borders of this state. The world is about to see that Iowa is strategic for the next great, epic move of God!

This particular journey was one of our longest, traveling 15 hours and clocking nearly 550 miles that included two side trips. One of those was to the Abbey where I take ladies for Solitude Retreats. Michael had not yet been there and I wanted him to see it since we were within a few miles of it. Likewise, we visited the motion picture site of the Field of Dreams.

Miracle

One of the most significant things about this particular journey was the miracle of my strength that day! I had been very sick in the days leading up to it. It was diagnosed by our family doctor for contracting some form of a virus. It was debilitating. I was as weak physically as I've ever been and could barely walk across a room.   It had completely taken the wind out of my sails. I had a contingent of precious people praying for me and prayer always changes things! We've all heard the phrase, "God equips those whom He sends." Nonetheless, in light of my health **and** the weather, we were on "stand-by" the night before, wondering if we were really going to attempt this journey.

Upon waking up that Saturday morning, Michael asked how I felt. I told him feebly I thought I might be just a tad bit better. He took that and ran with it! He asked me if I thought I could travel? My body said no, but my heart said yes (Matt. 26:41). Now, you've got know the miracle of this. With each mile, I got stronger and stronger. I felt like I had emerged like Samson! It was unbelievable! At times, I even asked Michael to catch up with me as we'd walk around the county courthouses. Upon our arrival at home late that evening, as exhausted as we both were, I felt I could go out and whip the world! Hallelujah!

God is so gracious.

Passion

However, the night before, the weather forecast was cautionary as severe storms were predicted throughout much of the state. (In fact, some tornadoes did touch down in some of the counties south of us that day!) We left the driveway in pounding rain, dark clouds and dense fog. What in the world we were doing anyway? That's a good question!

What you and I need to know is that passionate desire to fulfill God's divine directives can propel you to do things you wouldn't *ordinarily* do. We happily took off and thought of the **highway of holiness** in Isaiah 35:8. However, we had no sooner hit the interstate when the weather seemed to be worsening. It was difficult to see through the deluge of rain. Many cars were pulling off to the side of the road. Michael said at one point, "If this keeps up another few miles, we will have to turn back." My heart sank and I began to pray out loud rebuking the weather patterns and asking God to make a way where there seemed to be no way!

I had already journaled the following prayer upon leaving our driveway. "Lord, instead of the rain being a distraction today, I pray it's a double blessing of a soaking rain of your Spirit upon this land. No adversity today, only blessing!" Remember the temp was 55 when we left. Favor! Favor! As Michael continued to drive, I raised my hands over the road and declared God's Word, quoting Deuteronomy 3:5-6; Isaiah 40:3 and 35:8. We were embarking upon the **highway of holiness** so all would be well, I just knew it! I also prayed, "Let truck drivers across this state begin to sense something different here."

Amazing grace, how sweet the sound and its wondrous effects!

On this day, we were just beginning to see the emergence of tiny, green buds on all the trees. After trekking through all kinds of wintry weather the last number of months, this turned out to be an immensely beautiful spring day. The month of March came in like lamb. But it went out like a *lamb* <u>and</u> *a lion*!

LINN COUNTY
Cedar Rapids

After driving through a lot of hard rain, it stopped as we arrived at the courthouse. Amazingly, this occurred on every prayer journey where bad weather had been forecast. God makes a way where there seems to be no way.

We began by linking our prayers with the prayers of this county. There is a powerful House of Prayer here and because of that, righteousness, justice, mercy, truth and holiness are being birthed. Lord, we know You are hearing those prayers!

This county is named after Lewis <u>Fields</u> Linn (1795-1843), a senator from Missouri. He was a champion of the Western territories who enthusiastically supported every initiative for their advancement.

We experienced the smell of oats (from a plant nearby) and declared the fruit of the harvest <u>fields</u> to come forth. We declared the aroma of the harvest and for the memorial offering to be given to the Lord. This place is an altar unto God (Mal. 1:10-12, Luke 8:8). There is a royal priesthood, a chosen generation being raised up here. (1 Pet. 2:9).

New ideas were decreed. Streams of entrepreneurial strategies will come forth.

Proclaimed a love for God's Word is coming…the skies are opened up and there will be national recognition of people who like Francis Frangipane, will be furthered. Bring forth the prophets!

Cornucopia Carved in Stone Near Entrance

A cornucopia is engraved on the front of the courthouse (see photo) and confirmed what we proclaimed as we were driving into Linn County. This is a Cornucopia County! It's a **bridge** to the harvest!

No man is an island

Courthouse on an Island

The courthouse is built in the middle of the Cedar River on an island. No man is an island. Do not think you can accomplish things on your own! You need each other. You need unity. (While editing this book, there was a headline in the newspaper regarding the floods of 2008 in Iowa which read: "We will have done all we can.") Man can only do so much. We all need the Lord God! Deuteronomy 9, verse 6 says, *"Know then, it is not because of your righteousness that the Lord your God is giving you this good land to possess, for you are a stubborn people."*

Gargoyles are on the façade of the courthouse. We rebuked any evil influence in governmental affairs here. There were also 10 huge pillars, so we declared obedience of The Ten Commandments to come forth.

This county is strategic for the generation that will bring forth the harvest of souls! "They have honored Me in the past," says the Lord, "I will honor them in the day of harvest. The harvest will be for FOOD and FUEL for the nation."

There is a huge Veteran's building across the street. United we stand! People here will accomplish great things through the power of unity. We rebuked competition. If the people "agree" even more, they'll see the remarkable things God will do. The Lord says, "Unite even more! Build on the foundation I've built and stretch higher and farther than any previous generation. My grace is upon you. Raise up your prophets and kings!"

This County is strategically placed for the nations.

This was the 61st county on our Prophetic Prayer Journey. Isaiah 61 was declared for Linn County.

We proclaimed 1 Corinthians 3:4-9, especially the verses about how one person waters, another plants…etc., but God gives the growth.

"Lord, let this be an encouraging county. Let it disperse hope. Reveal to the people here the importance of their county!"

JONES COUNTY
Anamosa

Anamosa was previously called "Lexington," but was later renamed after the daughter of Winnebago Chief Nasinus whose

name was Anamosa. In this county, the town of Stone City is
where Grant Wood's famous
picture of the farmer and his
wife with the pitchfork was
painted. Lord, we proclaim the
joy of the Lord to come here.
Remove sadness and weeping.
Psalm 126, especially verse 5,
"Those who sow in tears shall
reap with joyful shouting."

Courthouse and Distant Correctional Facility

State records indicate this county has a high percentage of
crime, especially incest. We called forth a spirit of repentance.
Wash and cleanse this county by the power of the Blood of the
Lamb of God!

We come against the spirit of lawlessness. Let justice flow here
like a river, purifying the land, lives and homes in Jones County.

Let the SON shine here! Break through and break in to
people's lives in a greater degree. Break in! Break in!

JONES COUNTY REMEMBERS
ALL VETERANS WHO HONORABLY
SERVED OUR COUNTRY

Mike at Jones County Courthouse

There's been a dormancy
here…something lying still and
forgotten…something has been
lost. Hope deferred makes the
heart sick, says Proverbs 13:12.
This entire chapter in Proverbs
deals with wickedness and righteousness. Note this contrast in
the picture above with the courthouse in the foreground and the
correctional facility in the background. Remember the story of
David in the Bible when he was hiding from Saul in the cave?

231

That cold cave must have seemed "prison-like." Nevertheless, it was the discontented that gathered together with him in that difficult place because they wanted to be with the true king–David. God says to gather the discontented in this county to the true King Jesus! (1 Sam. 22:2).

Let a holy fear of the commandments of God come forth. May this county heed correction and find honor in their lives.

Proverbs 13: 14 says, *"Bring forth the fountain of life,"* and verse 17 speaks of the "faithful envoy that brings healing." Mike and I have come in the Name of the Lord as a faithful envoy. Bring healing, Lord! We proclaim healing…healing in broken minds (depression, bi-polar, etc), anxiety, fear, broken bodies, broken relationships. God speaks healing and restoration over this county!

Guard what has been entrusted to your care. Let opposing ideas to God be struck down. (1 Tim. 6:20-21).

Raise eyes to see You, Lord!

We prayed the entire chapter of 2 Corinthians 4 over Jones County. Take away spiritual blindness, Oh God. Do not let them loose heart here; verse 13–we speak life! Also, Ezekiel 37 is for this county. We speak manifestations of truth, which is God Himself.

Lift the dark clouds, Lord. Bring forth Your holy cloud by day and Your holy pillar of fire by night. (Exod. 14).

Side trip of the day

"IS THIS HEAVEN?! …NO, IT'S IOWA!"

A Field of Dreams, just as the Lord told me in October 2005 (see page 9)! That is what this prayer journey was all about! Psalm 126:1 says, "...We were like those who dream."

In Dyersville "Field of Dreams" Movie Site. Like Our Prayer Journey. Psalm 126:1..."We were like those who dream"

Linda By Encouraging Sign on Premises

DUBUQUE COUNTY
Dubuque

Sac and Fox Native American Tribes were in the land. A young lad, Julien Dubuque, 24 years of age, had a kind and wonderful relationship with the Native Americans here. James 3:18, *"And the seed whose fruit is righteousness is sown in peace by those who make peace."* Lord, again, sow peace in this county through relationships that were once established between the white man and the Native Americans.

Dubuque County Courthouse

Our oldest daughter was adopted from this county, therefore we felt led to declare a spirit of adoption. *"He predestined us to adoption as sons*

233

through Jesus Christ to Himself, according to the kind intention of His will" (Eph. 1:5). *"For you have not received a spirit of slavery leading to fear again, but you have received a spirit of adoption as sons by which we cry out, 'Abba! Father'!"* (Rom. 8:15).

Thank you Lord for the mothers who choose life! Protect the innocent ones. Let sons and daughters of the Most High God arise and walk in newness of life and prosperity of spirit. We also decreed Deuteronomy 30:15 and verses 19-20 which, in part, says, *"I have set before you life and death, the blessing and the curse. So choose life in order that you may live, you and your descendants."*

Linda Stands By Unusual Shop Beside Courthouse. The Open Sign Reads: "Do Some Time With Us."

Let people know they are loved by God the Father. This is a county that will continue to uphold life! Declared this to be a GATEWAY county of peace and life! Declared the power of the Holy Spirit to bring these things forth.

Bring to light things in secret places, Lord.

Raise up the intercessors! (Isa. 59:16).

We rebuked the religious spirit. Let the reverence in churches be transformed into holy, reverential fear of the Lord.

Isaiah 43:18-19 was proclaimed which in part says, *"Do not call to mind the former things of the past...behold, I will do something new...."*

You will be renewed like an eagle says Psalm 103:5. We also pronounced verses 13 and 14 over Dubuque County.

This is a GATEWAY FOR RENEWAL!

The Clock Tower Square in the middle of the street (see photo) caused us to decree in the Name of the Lord, "Raise up the *watchman* and the prophets to declare fresh insights and revelation of God."

Town Clock Tower

Keep in step with the Lord. Do not go to the right or the left. Isaiah 30:21 was proclaimed. There is a VOICE behind you that says, "Go this way!" Do not deviate from God's path. Deuteronomy 5:33 and all of Deuteronomy 6 was declared over this county. Wide is the road to destruction and narrow the road that leads to righteousness and few who take it (Matt. 7:13). We declared righteousness of the Lord's Spirit to be established.

We heard the word, "mouth" (Deut. 30:14!). May a love for God's Word go to new heights...insatiable hunger for God's Word is coming! Also regarding "mouth," we heard Isaiah 44:5 where one says, "I am the Lords"...another says, "Belonging to the Lord."

Heaviness of heart was rebuked and we pronounced a joy of the Lord to arise. Lord, comfort many hearts here!

Linda saw in the spirit people crying into pillows behind closed doors. God says, "I see your tears and your screams. Turn to Me and I'll turn to you. Draw near to Me and I'll draw near to you." (James 4:8).

Grant them their divine inheritance, Oh God! (Ps. 78:54-55).

JACKSON COUNTY
Maquoketa

Jackson County Courthouse

When we first arrived, we declared truth to come forth and a holy circumcision of heart to take place. This is a county in conflict, but if they'll turn to God, conflict will cease. A movement into righteousness according to Isaiah 56:1 was proclaimed for Jackson County. Oh God, raise up righteous policemen, lawyers, judges in this county!

The Native American tribes Winnebago, Sac and Fox resided here first. In 1840, desperadoes known as the Brown Gang, roamed the area stealing horses, counterfeiting and committing murder. Outraged citizens began to fight back and the "Bellevue War" was fought between them. Some were killed, some were whipped on their bare backs, some exiled down the Mississippi River.

The prevalent old "spirit of Maquoketa" has been one of lawlessness going back to the Battle of Bellevue. But God says, "Don't judge according to appearance, but judge rightly" (John 7:24). Make good judgments. Stop trying to find short cuts. Too often you have looked to others to make decisions. We declared, "Heaven rules!" (Dan. 4:26).

We felt turmoil in this county. The above photo does not adequately show the turbulent sky conditions. Clouds were really beginning to swirl around with dark ones, lighter ones, sunshine and shafts of light here and there. The atmospheric conditions told the story spiritually. We sensed conflicts here to a great degree. We prayed, "Open up the heavens, Lord, just as we've seen in the natural a few moments ago!"

We declared light and life in the Lord Jesus to prevail. Jesus is the Light of the world. "Jesus, let Your Light shine on the darkness here, exposing hidden sins and let repentance fill the cities of this county!"

The courthouse seemed in disrepair. We saw a very strange, crooked, "gnarling" kind of tree next to the courthouse. The dictionary defines gnarled as: "twisted; rugged." Things have been twisted here. Contempt of truth has taken place. God says, "No more! I will make crooked paths straight." Beware of Isaiah 59:8. It's time to walk in Matthew 3:2, 8-12 which in part says, *"Bring forth fruit in keep-ing with repentance...the axe is already laid at the root of the trees; every tree therefore that does not bear good fruit is cut down and thrown into the fire."*

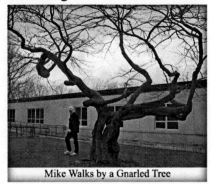
Mike Walks by a Gnarled Tree

It began to rain while we were here. We called forth a refreshing to come to the people. Let them begin to drink deep from the well of Living Waters. May they become *drunk* in the Holy Spirit wine that's being poured out on this county. The Lord says, "You need a Pentecost here! I send forth My Fire upon you. Will you receive it? Baptism of fire is available to you! Reach for it now!"

At 4:30 PM, it began to rain more heavily.

At 4:35 PM sunshine broke in!

This is a county in <u>transition</u>! Break through, Lord! Bring a respect and honoring of one another.

Joshua and Caleb (i.e., Mike and Linda) have scouted out this county and we decree a good report is forthcoming and this will be a land flowing with milk and honey!

The Lord is looking for those who are servants, who value truth and righteousness. No favoritism here! But equal justice for all, God's justice, holy justice!

This county has never lived up to its potential because of conflict, but an open heavens is about to change that!

We left at 4:44 PM. Three fours! Four is a strategic foundational number, as in four strong corners or cornerstones on which to build. Jackson County - build on the four Gospels of Matthew, Mark, Luke and John. Build on God's Word!

CLINTON COUNTY
Clinton

We were often given the warmth of the Lord's hugs and assurances in many ways. Arriving at 5:16 PM, the 70 degree temperature for this last day of March was a blessing!

This county is on the eastern edge of Iowa. It's one of the first places to receive the rays of the morning sun and dawn's early light. Thus we proclaimed, 2 Peter 1:19, *"And so we have the prophetic word made more sure, to which you do well to pay attention as to a lamp shining in a dark place, until the day dawns and the morning star arises in your hearts."* We decreed the Bright Morning Star over Clinton County (Rev. 2:28; 22:16)! We proclaimed this to be a place of *awakening*, as when a rooster crows and the alarms go off–that this county will awaken to God! There is even a clock on the tower portion of the courthouse. "Shake off sleepiness and slumber!" says the Lord. (Isa. 52:1-3).

We call this the AWAKENING PLACE! And as the red sky sets over Iowa, there will be delight in the hearts of people here.

"Show Yourself, Oh God, in night dreams. Give them rest."

The color of the bricks in the courthouse building was very red. We declared the Blood of Jesus here to cover this county with redemption. Lord, bring an epiphany of the Cross of Calvary. The red bricks speak prophetically of red clay or

Clinton County Courthouse

earthen-like vessels. Lord, let the people of this county be as clay in the Master Potter's hand. Form them into Your likeness! *"But now, O Lord, Thou art our Father, we are the clay, and Thou our potter; and all of us are the work of Thy hand."* (Isa. 64:8).

There was mold and mildew on the front of the building. We declared fresh manna, fresh bread–the Living Bread to be known here. (John 6:35).

At the furthest and highest point on the courthouse, there was a green, cone-like top to the building. It spoke to us of reaching further and further, upward and onward into new heights in the Lord. We proclaimed rapid and astounding growth in the knowledge and revelation of God.

We also prayed for protection.

There is also a "welcoming" spirit here, one that welcomes the alien and foreigners. Justice and righteousness were proclaimed.

The winds of change are blowing and shaking the land!

We decreed for the people of Clinton County that the Word of God will become a *lamp* unto their feet. (Ps. 119:105).

Wisdom will strengthen the cities in this county. (Eccles. 7:19).

Clinton County is in the refiner's fire! But you will come forth as silver and gold (Mal. 3:2; Job 23:10)! The Lord says, "Where there may have been unholy sacrifices in the past, I have called you to be a place, an altar with My lamp stands in place. By the power of the Holy Spirit you will offer holy sacrifices of praise to the Throne Room of the Most High God." (Lev. 10 and Num. 16 & 17).

CEDAR COUNTY
Tipton

Gorgeous Fiery Clouds!

Cedar County was not on our radar for the day, but as the sun was setting fast in the western sky, we were within miles of the courthouse and simply had to go there! This was a delightful find and a pleasant county to visit.

The skies were absolutely spectacular while we were here with billowy, fiery clouds, which the black and white photo cannot justify! While driving into town, we even photographed a beautiful rainbow! We saw this as God's signature for His covenant promises to be fulfilled in this county.

240

There was a good, clean feeling here. We had a sense that we were among friends. God has friends in this county!

Observing Turbulent Skies During Drive

This county is named for the cedar tree, but also the Cedar River is nearby. It caused us to declare aloud, "The 'cedars of Lebanon' are here and this county is a delight to God."

> "The righteous man will flourish like the palm tree, he will grow like the cedar in Lebanon. Planted in the house of the Lord, they will flourish in the courts of our God. They will still yield fruit in old age; they shall be full of sap and very green, to declare that the Lord is upright; He is my rock, and there is no unrighteousness in Him."
>
> —Psalm 92:12-15

Lush Lawn for March 31st!

We declared the *fragrances* of the Cedars of Lebanon to come forth– holiness. Linda saw "cedar chests" as when a bride stores things waiting for her big day. The Lord is building a divine trousseau here. As people learn intimacy with God, they will become "clothed" in purity and holiness. Song of Songs 1:16-17. Trousseaus are about to be opened up. Promises locked up are now released, just as the rainbow indicated!

The Arrow Points to Heaven;
Hands Give Time Here on Earth

The lighted clock on the pedestal on the courthouse grounds delighted us. There has been an issue of timing and waiting here. People have been hopeful and diligent in their early morning watch or prayer times. It's been like maidens waiting with oil in their lamps…waiting to see the future (Matt. 25:1-13). The Lord is about to map it out for you! An Issachar anointing is available for those in this county. (1 Chron.12:32).

An acceleration of God's purposes are coming to this county. Proverbs 23:18, *"Surely there is a future, and your hope will not be cut off."*

Wait for the Lord! Psalm 37:18-19, 34 as well as Jeremiah 33:3 were proclaimed. A shout of praise and worship will arise. The trees will clap their hands! (Isa. 55:12; Ps. 1:3).

This is a **Garden Place!** A place to rest, relax. Learn to enter into Sabbath rest. Cease from striving. God is calling this county to learn rest so they might know a refreshing from the Lord. (Ps. 46).

This county will become very intentional with God and will have great love for Him. People here will be known for carrying the beauty of God. Where there has been coarseness, there will be kindness. Where there has been insensitivity, there will now be tenderness.

❦ eighteen ❦

SCOTT, MUSCATINE, LOUISA, DES MOINES, LEE, HENRY

"A wicked messenger falls into adversity, but a faithful envoy brings healing." —Proverbs 13:17

We felt we were leaving under a mystical cloud of God's Presence as we launched Prophetic Prayer Journey #15 on May 5th, 2007. At 7:50 AM under a shroud of fog and mist, it was a humid 63 degrees. We prayed, "Lord, keep us in Your glory cloud!"

Rolling down interstate 80 we read Psalm 80. Verse one is so beautiful, *"O give ear, Shepherd of Israel, Thou who dost lead Joseph like a flock; Thou who art enthroned above the cherubim, shine forth!"* We were just following our Divine Shepherd and we knew He would not only give ear to our prayers, but He would shine forth in the counties we would visit.

We knew it was going to be a great day! The date 5/5 with double fives was seen as a special blessing. We declared God would pour out a *double* portion of His *favor* and His *glory* upon this day and over all of Iowa. We proclaimed God's favor to soak us with His prophetic decrees across this entire land. We were still energetic at the end of the day after traveling 487.5 miles because of these very declarations!

SCOTT COUNTY
Davenport

Arriving here, we knew we had to depend totally on the Holy Spirit for guidance. We felt an oppressiveness of law. People here

Scott County Courthouse

have been overburdened with rules...burdened by civil government and also by a religious spirit. "And grant freedom here, Lord! Take off any unnecessary burdens and oppression. Bring proper administration of Your righteousness."

Amos 9:11 and 15 were proclaimed for this county:

> *"'In that day I will raise up the fallen booth of David, and wall up its breaches; I will also raise up its ruins, and rebuild it as in the days of old.... I will also plant them on their land, and they will not again be rooted out from their land which I gave given them,' says the Lord."*

"Lord, take care of the vine in this county" (Ps. 80:14). Psalm 64 was declared. We prayed Isaiah 9:4-7 for Scott County. "Release Your zeal here, Lord. Shatter yokes that have shouldered many weights."

History says the city was **5** miles wide when it was founded. We're here on 5-5-07. How interesting to see another tie-in of the number five! We declared the Lord's grace and favor throughout Scott County. "Lord, You shall rule here." Heaven rules! (Dan. 4:26d).

Declared Psalm 2, especially verse 7, "*I will surely tell of the decree of the Lord: He said to me, 'Thou art My Son, today I have begotten thee....'*" Verse 8–Let the prayers here affect the nations!

This city shall be a place of refuge and peace. Ease the heavy burdens of Your people, Lord.

Psalm 89 was proclaimed. We prayed a godly, governmental anointing to come forth and for righteousness and justice to prevail. By Your favor Oh Lord, extend Your scepter over the river. Bring forth a "Crossing Over" County; crossing over from oppression to freedom and proper justice. We proclaim that elected and appointed government officials will move in proper justice and righteousness. This place shall be a place of refuge.

We declare the day is coming when the plowman will overtake the reaper. (Amos 9:13).

Speed the cause of righteousness (Isa. 16:5). And from Isaiah 28:16-17 are the scriptures on the stones we are leaving at each courthouse, but it's a Rhema word for this county!

Linda Across Street From Courthouse.
Bonds Are Broken Through
Worshipful Dancing Like King David!

Flood them with Your Spirit, Oh God. Immerse them in You.

Bring forth "a dancing" before the Lord like King David! (2 Sam. 6). (See photo). How interesting and gracious of our Lord to use the physical realm to show forth His purposes in the spiritual realm. This old *Dance Land* sign on the side of a building across the street from the courthouse was very confirming. May the joy of the Lord be

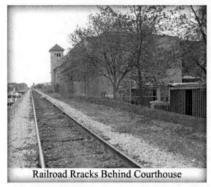

Railroad Rracks Behind Courthouse

restored to Scott County and let no one be *railroaded* by the enemy any longer! (See photo). As we walked along this railroad for a short distance, I (Linda) picked up some rusty, old railroad spikes. I brought them home and washed them off. It spoke to me of the bloody nails in Jesus hands and feet. May Calvary's Cross wash and cleanse this county. Cleanse this county Oh God, from the lusts of the flesh. Bring Your transforming power Lord!

We prayed against generational bondages and curses.

Taste and see, Oh Scott County, that the Lord is good! Have a "Come to Jesus" meeting! (Ps. 34:8).

MUSCATINE COUNTY
Muscatine

Mike was born here, so this was a significant county to visit!

The history of Muscatine, which is the seat of Muscatine County, says it is located on the west bank of the Mississippi, at the apex of the greatest *bend* found in the river. "Apex" means "highest point" or "tip or pointed end." May this county reach higher and higher into the

Mike By Muscatine County Courthouse, Where His Birth is Recorded

heart of God! "Come up higher!" says the Lord. (Rev. 4:1).

We saw mud flaps on a semi truck coming into the county that read: "Jesus is Lord. Transport for Christ." We felt this was a good SIGN that we were to declare Jesus is Lord over this county! May God's people here be transported into the heavens with dreams and visions.

Monument to Local Native Americans

As we crossed over the county line, the sun began to break through. Thank you, Lord!

Another aspect of the history we read, (WPA Guide, pg. 290), says the Native Americans in this area were called, "People of the Place of Fire." This was because the site where they lived was under brushes, and prairie fires would occur. That particular location was called, "Burning Island!" We then declared Holy Spirit fire to come in this county! Pour out Your fire Lord!

The "apex" or "turning in the river" was prophesied to spiritually cause hearts to turn to God.

At one point I looked at the clock and it was now 11:36 AM and 72 degrees. It was beginning to warm up nicely. Bring the warmth of Your fire Lord! Warm the hearts of the people of Muscatine County.

We declared this to be a place of eagles and for revelation to come forth. We prayed for a release of wisdom and the spirit of prophecy to come forth.

We heard in the spirit: "Unless the Lord builds the house, they labor in vain who build it" (Ps.127:1). Build the House of God here!

The fruits of the Holy Spirit will spring up. Bring forth fruitful vines in Christ, new fruit and fruitfulness.

Raise up the watchman.

We asked the Lord for a harvest of souls in this county. Bring new hope, healing and new births in Christ. Bring development of good character. Hope does not disappoint. (Rom. 5:4-5).

We had lunch by the Mississippi River and discovered a large statue that noted Muscatine as the: "Pearl button capital of the world." (See photo). We proclaimed the pearl of great price will come here, which is the kingdom of God. *"The kingdom of heaven is like a merchant seeking fine pearls, and upon finding one pearl of*

Statue of River Clam Pearl Harvesting

great value, he went and sold all that he had and bought it" (Matt. 13:45). A declaration was made for that kind of attitude to come forth and that it has now been released into this area.

Ironically, just a day or two before this journey I had told my

Mississippi Harvest!

husband Michael I'd like to have pearls someday. I'd never really wanted them before. But we had just been to a semi-formal event and I thought how neat they might look on a simple black dress. It was not happenstance that for the first time in my life, I had a desire for this precious jewel. The Lord has a way of intertwining His purposes into our lives and I once again found it amazing that it was actually a *prophetic statement* for the very county my husband was born in, and - which we would tour on our very next prayer journey!

Muscatine County, you must now seek the pearl of great price! Don't settle for the utility of the pearls but for the treasure of your relationship with Christ.

LOUISA COUNTY
Wapello

We crossed over the county line at 12:54 PM with sunshine all around. The heat index was climbing nicely and was now at 77 degrees. A pair of sevens! Seven is God's number of completion and perfection. We declared His perfect will to be done here. Bring completion and conclusion to the prayers uttered in this county.

Mike Anoints Door, Louisa County Courthouse

This county is named for Louisa Massey, who gained fame because she avenged the murder of her brother by shooting the man responsible. This area was founded on a vengeful spirit. The Lord says to this county: "Vengeance is mine!" (Deut. 32:35, Heb. 10:30).

We declared this to be a supple land spiritually, ready to receive the Word of God to a more fruitful degree.

We felt a "binding" here...like Lazarus, who was bound up in grave clothes. *"Unbind him and let him go"* (John 11:44). The

249

Lord says to Louisa County, "Come forth! Come forth into your divine birth rights." Likewise, the unusual awnings on the side of the building, spoke to us of a "yawning spirit." God says, *"Arise and shine for your glory is come*!" Isaiah 60 is for this county.

There were many dandelions on the lawn. Dusty winds blow across dead flowers and they are no more! This translated into physical and spiritual lives having been cut short. Divine destinies have been cut short in this area. People here have been overlooked. "Wake up! Stretch! Grow! Move forward! Come out of your sleepiness!"

Some people here came to a crossroads in their lives and may have taken the wrong path. Therefore, the Holy Spirit caused us to declared they now be shown "the way, truth, light and life" in Jesus Christ. (John 14:6).

Show teachers and pastors the way, Lord.

Shuttered Windows on Side of Courthouse

People here have felt low and lost. Lift them up, Lord! We decree the *winner's wreath/the laurel* for this county. A victory wreath! Philippians 3:10-14 in part says, *"...but one thing I do: forgetting what lies behind and reaching forward to what lies ahead..."* The victor's crown is proclaimed here. We proclaimed life and its purpose is for victory in Jesus.

This was the first county on our prayer tour where <u>God gave us a color for the county</u>! The Spirit of the Lord had us declare the color: white. This is for purity and holiness. It is the bright light of the Lord Jesus repelling the darkness. We declared the armor of God's Light.

Decreed this county has passed from death to life. It will have a new legacy, and not one born out of murder as in its name (1 John 3:14-15). The Lord is going to bestow a new spiritual name! *"And you will be called by a new name, which the mouth of the Lord will designate. You will also be a crown of beauty in the hand of the Lord...."* (Isa. 62:2-3).

We decreed this county will be known for its love. (1 John 4:7-21; 5:1-4).

DES MOINES COUNTY
Burlington

As we began to drive into this county the Spirit of the Lord began to fall on us and He said, "I have sent you My prophets and they have touched My heart for you! Therefore arise! Be alive in Me! Breathe new life in Me!" *"And as they were bury-*

Des Moines County Courthouse

ing a man, behold, they saw a marauding band; and they cast the man into the grave of Elisha. And when the man touched the bones of Elisha, he revived and stood up on his feet." (2 Kings 13:21).

We saw a sign en route into the city of Burlington which read: "Adoption. I can live with it." This of course refers to choosing life verses abortion. We declared new life in this county, both in

251

the natural and in the spiritual. The spirit of adoption into the family of God was decreed. (Eph.1:5-6).

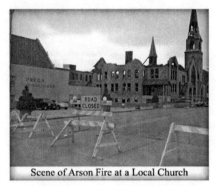
Scene of Arson Fire at a Local Church

The history of the courthouse revealed that one of the earlier structures had: "an outward charm, but the interior was a dungeon." Whereas some of the people here have been as whitewashed tombs, we declared this county will now come under the Blood of Jesus! Des Moines County is being cleansed and washed in His Blood and set free from all sinful stains. (Matt. 23:25-39, Eph. 1:7).

Witchcraft was apparent as we saw a blatant sign in a store front that made reference to this. We rebuked this ungodly influence over this county, rebuking all satanic activity in this area. Lord, lift the dark, heavy clouds!

Just about a week before our visit, an old, landmark Methodist church burned down. Arson was the cause. (See photo). This county needs a resurrection! It needs a rescue. About one block from the courthouse, we heard drum sounds near the river as a drum corps was practicing. To us it sounded like the drums of war! We raised up the war cry and prayed, "Lord, position Your people for battle and grant them victory! We come against the Leviathan spirit in the Name of the Lord Jesus!" (Ps. 74:14; Isa. 27:1).

High water mark

As we observed the bridge that went into Illinois, we declared the Lord is their bridge over troubled waters. Let people here cross over into life, life more abundantly in You Oh God.   John chapters 7 and 9 and 10:10. There was a <u>high water mark</u> on this bridge for the floods of 1993. (See photo). It was at 55 feet. The

High Water Mark on Foot of Bridge

day we were here was **5/5.** We released grace and favor over Des Moines County. This county is about to go higher in the Lord!

It was proclaimed for the people here that they come into the tent or dwelling of God so they may abide in His shadow. Let them say to the Lord, "My refuge!" Psalm 91 was proclaimed and we knew verses 10-15 were very significant in light of the fact there's a winding, stone pathway called Snake Alley located next

Snake Alley is Adjacent to a Church

to several churches. Near this *alley* is where the church recently burned down! Lord, raise up your spiritual warriors to tread upon the lion and the cobra!

Those who set a table for fun and games are about to know the fear of God! Wisdom will call forth from the corners here.

Strengthen, renew, rebuild, restore!

253

We called forth the Light of Jesus to penetrate the darkness. May God's angels do battle here. Close the evil gates of this county, Oh God. Let Your light expose the darkness. We declared a Gate of Life to be opened up according to Psalm 100. Enter the Lord's gates with praise and thanksgiving.

We prayed the lightning rod of God, His holy scepter, would poke through, penetrate, and pierce through dark clouds over this county. Break in with Your holy light of authority, Oh Lord. Rule and reign in Des Moines County!

LEE COUNTY
Fort Madison

Oldest Courthouse in Continuous Use in Iowa!

Upon entering into this county we quickly began to rebuke rebellion, self-abuse, and suicide. We declared a spirit of repentance to come forth. Bring peace to this county, Oh Lord.

Psalm 18 was proclaimed over Lee County.

People here must also lay hold of Psalm 91: 2-3 *"I will say to the Lord, 'My refuge and my fortress. My God, in whom I trust!' For it is He who delivers you from the snare of the trapper, and from deadly pestilence."*

The address of the court-house was: the corner of 7th Street and Avenue F. We took the seven and decreed that this county would come into perfect alignment with the Lord of lords and King of kings.

We sat in rays of soothing sunshine on the front steps of the courthouse on this afternoon in May. Soaking up the beautiful spring weather was so delightful! We were enjoying our visit to Lee County.

Four-Pillar Façade of Lee County Courthouse

We made a declaration that we stand in unity with the people of God who watch and stand guard in this county. Let them break through into the heavenly realm. Let the watchman see the movement of the enemy and expose it. Let the people here repent.

Righteousness was proclaimed for this county's government. Send evil spirits fleeing, Oh God. We plead the blood of Jesus over this county for protection. We asked for the arch-angel Michael to be over Lee County.

Ornate Door on Old Jail

Let the people here keep all the commandments, especially the first one, which is the greatest one. Then, all the others will flow from that first commandment - to love the Lord your God with all your heart, all your soul, all your mind and with all your strength (Mark 12:28-34). If you will do this, you will not be far from the kingdom of God!

We decreed people coming into the county courthouse will seek true justice. Mercy triumphs over judgment. Let mercy reign in this place. (James 2:13).

Cleanse this land of its sins. Cleanse this county from not trusting in the Lord.

Three different times we saw a bride and bridegroom riding in a horse drawn carriage around town. We felt the Lord was showing us something in this. We decreed the purity of holy covenants to be established here. Protect marriages, Lord! This county just may be the determining factor in the future for <u>Iowa's battles in the courts over true covenant marriage</u> between a man and a woman. This is a <u>threshold county</u>, as when a man carries his bride over the threshold. (Ruth 3; 2 Sam. 24:18-25)

An overflowing of God's love is being released!

HENRY COUNTY
Mt. Pleasant

Henry County Courthouse

This was our last county for this trip. The earlier fog and mist had turned into a hazy-like sunshine over the land. The temperature seemed to stabilize at 77 degrees most of the day much to our delight. What a mighty God we serve! Seven is such a significant number. Also noteworthy, was the fact that we drove into this county at exactly 5 PM on 5/5–three fives! Five of course represents favor, so we prayed, "More favor, Lord!" Time after time, divine set-ups occurred by the will of God. Every journey was synchronized beautifully!

Approaching Henry County, the Spirit of the Lord said, "Ascend My hill! Ascend! Go higher! Do not stay where you are!" May praise and worship ascend continually here. Psalm 128 is the Song of Ascents. (See also Psalm 24 and Ephesians 4:10).

We began by proclaiming Psalm 133. How pleasant it is for the brethren to dwell in unity. How pleasant to praise the Lord! Psalm 147 is also for this county.

We prayed Psalm 16:6 that *"The lines have fallen to me in pleasant places; indeed my heritage is beautiful to me."*

This courthouse will bring forth just decisions by the will of the Lord.

The grass on the grounds was lush and green. We prophesied a release of extravagant growth in the fruits and gifts of the Holy Spirit.

War Monuments

We decreed this to be a "<u>Delicious County</u>!" They have a desire to please God. Therefore, let the people taste and see that You are good, Oh Lord, and that Your words are worth savoring and most pleasant. (Ps. 34; Ps. 119:103; 1 Pet. 2:1-3; Ps. 84:1-2, 4).

Cheerful hearts will be good medicine for the people of this county. *"But a cheerful heart has a continual feast"* (Prov. 15:13, 15-16). We prayed those who have a cheerful heart will indeed have a continual feast. We declared the joy of the Lord to fall in this area in greater degrees.

This is a <u>dancing county</u>! The joy of the Lord will set your feet to dancing. (Ps. 149:3-6).

We declared people to be reconciled to Christ. (Col. 1:19-23).

Linda heard the word, "bouquet." We declared this to be the sweet fragrance of the Lord that's falling on this county (Song of Songs 4:15-16, 2 Cor. 2:14-16). The Lord says, "Spread My fragrance!"

According to 2 Corinthians 2:12, we decreed a door is opening here. There is a door open to preach the Word and for the aroma of Christ to come forth and cover Henry County.

❦ nineteen ❦

JEFFERSON, VAN BUREN, DAVIS, APPANOOSE, MONROE, WAPELLO

"A voice is calling, clear the way for the Lord in the wilderness; make smooth in the desert a highway for our God."
—Isaiah 40:3

Our prophetic touring of Iowa began this day at 8:04 AM. It was beautifully mild with 63 degrees gracing our departure. We returned home by **7:47** PM that evening. The "747" reminded us of the 747 airplanes. It had been a nice flight on this 16th journey to Iowa's counties and we were fully aware we'd been carried on eagles' wings! Driving 379 miles we were able to take in six counties.

The calendar was revealing Iowa's beauty in the spring months. This day's journey was May 12, 2007. Twelve represents governmental authority. We knew it was going to be a great day! As we began the Prophetic Prayer Journey for that day, I read and declared 1 Peter 2. Verse 25 was for this particular day as we declared over Iowa, *"For you were continually straying like sheep, but now you have returned to the Shepherd and Guardian of your souls."* Amen!

JEFFERSON COUNTY
Fairfield

Jefferson County Courthouse

Approaching this county we began to declare freedom. In Jesus Name, set captives free! Cleanse the land. Close the gates of hell of the Eastern religious idolatry. *"For they exchanged the truth of God for a lie, and worshipped and served the creature rather than the Creator, who is blessed forever. Amen."* (Rom. 1:25).

Thomas Jefferson, one of the founding fathers of our nation, was reputed to have cut up the Word of God and took only what he liked and wanted. This county is named for him. We rebuked the legacy of selecting certain portions of God's Word and not taking it in its entirety. Although it seems he simply put the "red letters" of what Jesus said into a book, nonetheless, the *entirety* of what Jesus said was taken out of context. We must be very careful in doing such things (See Revelations 22:18-19). We proclaimed godly, holy righteousness will flow from the Most High God into the lives of people of Jefferson County.

A sign of Iowa's Transcendental Meditation Community Presence

Where "Peace Palaces" are being built, we declare there is no peace without the True Prince of Peace, Jesus. Lord, bring revelation and discernment to people's minds and hearts unto holy truth from God's kingdom. Open eyes to that which is false and lacks hope.

We proclaimed Luke 17:21, *"...nor will they say, 'Look here it is!' Or, 'There it is!' For behold the kingdom of God is in your midst."* People caught up in this Vedic City are those looking for truth, but in the wrong places (Ezek. 12:2). Pontius Pilate asked the Son of God, "What is truth?" when it was standing right in front of him (John. 18:38)! We prophesied people will begin to say, "Now I see!" Let there be no deception! We proclaimed they will now be looking to the true kingdom of God.

Clashing swords

We heard the clashing of swords. The Lord is preparing to slaughter the enemy, the principalities in this place and in this county. (Ezek. 21:8-32).

Courthouse Depicts Justice, Mercy

Lord, bring Your commissioning swords and knight Your warrior intercessors with authority and power to slay the principalities and powers, all the falsehoods.

We declared the Spirit of Truth and the truth shall set the people of this county free! (John 8:32).

We saw the clashing swords which have a light accompanied by them. Give the people in this county the holy Light of true revelation, insight and epiphanies of God! (Eph. 6:10-20).

We decreed a restoration of the former holy dominion of the Most High God for Jefferson County. (Micah 4:2-3, 8,10). When we went to this portion of scripture, Mike saw where he had written the date 10/27/03 in the margin of his Bible. This was one of the scriptures that Chuck Pierce and Dutch Sheets declared over Iowa on their 50 State Tour. How gracious and timely is our God! "Establish Your dominion, Oh Lord!" Let people say, "Let us go to the mountain of the Lord!" We proclaimed all of Micah 4.

Settle disputes, Lord!

As for the intercessors, kingship will come! Travail in prayer. We agree with Chuck Pierce's prophecy and declare it to now be fulfilled. There is power in agreement.

Give eyes to see Your kingdom, Oh Lord. Just a day or so before we came here, Mike heard the Holy Spirit say to him, "Welcome to the kingdom!"

Rise and thresh, oh people of Jehovah God. (Micah 4:13).

Let all ill-gotten goods be given to the Lord.

We declared Isaiah 28:16-17, as we do over every county, but particularly here!

VAN BUREN COUNTY
Keosauqua

There were lots of beautiful oak trees on the lawn of the courthouse. We declared this county to be *oaks of righteousness* according to Isaiah 61:3.

This is another Gateway County for the heritage of Iowa to come forth in goodness and wholeness…the heritage of the saints,

servants and slaves. In righteousness this will be established.
Compassion fills every part of
this county–<u>deep compassion</u> for
the slaves of old, for widows and
barren women. God's heart, too,
is a compassionate heart.

Oldest Courthouse by Date in Iowa

Many years ago this area was
a part of the Underground Rail Road where slaves were being
transported. We declared those who are "slaves to sin" are now
free to walk in purity and righteousness. 1 Corinthians 7:22-23
says in part that you are now called the *"Lord's freedman"*!

The shutters on the windows of the courthouse gave it
somewhat of a homey, welcoming family spirit. We heard the
word: "hearth." Keep the "home fires burning" Lord! Build up
families in this county according to Your faithfulness as people
seek Your face (Ps. 84:1-4). Enlarge the cords of Your tent in this
area, Oh God!

This Courthouse had a "Homey" Feel

Linda saw "sure footings" and
foundations which translated into
Luke 6:46-48, but also Luke 7:44-50
where Mary washed the feet of Jesus.
We decreed God's love to be the "sure
footings" for this county.

We rebuked rebellion. Declared
that God's Word is the true foundation
and people here are called to preach it
and proclaim it!

Romans 6:15-23 was declared for Van Buren County.

We heard, "Proclaim the *good life*" (John 10:10)! The good life is found in Jesus. We prayed the fullness of the Holy Spirit to flow in this area. Remove all obstructions to the flow of Living Waters.

There was a Child Care facility across the street. We proclaimed Isaiah 54, especially verse one, that barren women would now shout for joy! We declared God is raising up strong families here. Verse 14 -17 of this same chapter is part of the release, restoration and divine covering that was decreed for what happened with the URR and the slaves.

No weapon formed against this county will prosper.

Keosauqua was the scene of Iowa's first legal hanging in nearby Hangman's Hollow. We decreed Deuteronomy 32:35 that vengeance belongs to the Lord. We declared vindication under the banner of God's love.

We drove out of Van Buren County at 1:35 PM with a warm spring temperature of **77** degrees. How divine! We found the perfect spot along the Des Moines River for a little picnic lunch. I'd have to say it was just what Dr. Jesus ordered! It was so relaxing and peaceful.

DAVIS COUNTY
Bloomfield

Linda picked up a stick on the front lawn of the courthouse. The old adage from childhood was remembered, "Sticks and stones may break my bones, but words can never hurt me." Yes they can! Words can indeed hurt. Heal and restore, Oh Lord, those who have been hurt by cruel words. God's word declares, "Do not touch My anointed!" (1 Chron. 16:21-30; 1 Sam. 24:5-6).

This stick up also brought us to Ezekiel 37:15-23. It was revealed through these verses that we were to declare that what God has joined together, let not man put asunder (Matt. 19:4-6). God is bringing unity in marriages. The stick also represented beatings or perhaps abuse, domestic abuse to women and children. There's been unfair beatings and punishment in

Davis County's Victorian Courthouse

this county. But God has brought deliverance through Jesus' Blood. Calvary saves! Psalm 34 17-18, *"The righteous cry and the Lord hears, and delivers them out of all their troubles. The Lord is near to the brokenhearted, and saves those who are crushed in spirit."* The Lord says, "You are free!" We declared the *Righteous Branch* will heal and save that which was lost. (Isa. 11).

Linda Inside the "Gates"

Psalm 19 and Psalm 29 are for this county! Pray them and live them!

Reveal hidden sins, Oh God.

There was a wrought iron, gate-like fence around a portion of the courthouse. Lord, open up the gates according to Psalm 24:7-10. (See photo).

265

Saw on a theatre sign across the street the movie showing was: "Blades of glory." We prayed for God's glory to "show" and be made manifest soon in Davis County! By virtue of 1 Chronicles 16:24 the Lord is calling this county to declare His glory.

Raise up champions to run the course of God. Raise up more champions, Lord! (Ps. 19:1-5).

Blades of Glory are "Showing" in Iowa!

Divisions have taken place here. "Heal those, Lord." We prayed against divisions between church and state which was brought in by the Anabaptists. They were the first ones to make this declaration from this county in Iowa about the separation of church and state. We declared *no separation*! We declared unity and holiness. *"But your iniquities have made a separation between you and your God."* Isaiah 59:2a, and verse 19 from this same chapter was also decreed over this county. The divisions between Catholics, protestants, Anabaptists…wherever separation began, we go to that point and declare God's righteousness, justice and His glory! And now, it shall continue onward by the Name of Jesus.

We declared a baptism of life in Jesus.

A prayer for the power of the Holy Spirit to fall was offered over Davis County. We proclaimed the Sword of the Lord will now begin to divide the soul from the spirit upon the people of this area. (Heb. 4:12).

Bring the church into justice, mercy and grace. We proclaimed no separation from God's holiness. Let no one be unfairly judged or punished.

APPANOOSE COUNTY
Centerville

We arrived in Appanoose County at a rather significant time. It was 3:21 PM! 3-2-1 is especially meaningful to Mike because God has quickened to him Revelation 3:21 and he had been seeing those numbers in various ways for quite some time. It's the releasing of the overcoming spirit for this county! The Lord also spoke to Mike of "3-2-1" resonating with the words, "ignition" or "blast off" as when a rocket ship launches. This is a decla- ration for this county! You're going higher! Ironically, the temperature had

Appanoose County Courthouse

also risen by the time we reached Appanoose County. It was now 81 degrees. Very nice for a spring day in Iowa!

The name of the county is named after the chief of the Sac and Fox Native Americans Tribes who headed the peace party during the Black Hawk War. Appanoose means: "A Chief When a Child." We then declared God is raising up children like King Josiah (2 Kings 22). We declared Isaiah 9:6 for a governmental, spiritual authority to arise upon the children in this area.

Increase their joy, Lord! Shatter the yokes that have been here.

This county was one of the main coal mining areas in Iowa

during the first part of the 20th century. We heard the Spirit of the Lord saying, "Go mining!" This county is being called to mine the deep things of God (Job 28:1-11). Mine the treasures of heaven and the treasures of God's glory.

We also decreed Job 23:10 as we heard the Lord say, "Your testings are bringing you forth as gold." God's treasures are being released to you, where moth shall not eat it. Matthew 6:19-21 is for this county.

Job 22:21-28 was proclaimed. Verse 28 says that we must "decree" a thing in order for it to be established. This is what this prayer journey is all about!

We decreed great faith will begin falling in this county (Heb. 11). Look for your rewards! Lord, You are the architect and builder in this county.

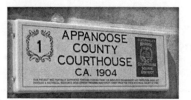

We proclaimed God's zeal for justice and mercy will reign in this place.

We proclaimed a fathering spirit, like that of Father Abraham, who left the land of the Chaldeans to go to a greater place (Gen. 12 and Gen. 15:7). A greater place is coming to this county! We decreed "something better" for this county!

MONROE COUNTY
Albia

There is grace on this county! There is readiness for discovery...discovering the deep things of God.

Someone has prepared the way!

You are seeking for those who will follow You, Lord!

There is an underground reservoir here that is ready to be tapped into. (Isa. 58:11-12).

"Spring up, O well." John 4:14 is arriving here! *But whoever drinks of the water that I shall give him shall never thirst; but the water that I shall give him shall become in him a well of water springing up to eternal life."* Gush forth with Living

Monroe County Courthouse

Waters! Drench the people here, Lord. (Isa. 49:9-10).

Monroe County, you are a repairer of broken walls and streets because you have kept up the old, old buildings from the mid 1800's. There is a sense of goodly pride. (Isa. 61:4).

We saw a young man walk across the courthouse grounds. He had on all black, wore chains, sported tattoos everywhere and had spiked up hair. We prayed that he would reach out and touch the Living Waters that we were just proclaiming. (He walked too fast for us to visit with him…as if he were trying to run away from us,

Mike Inside Gazebo by Courthouse

or avoid us). But he crossed our path for a reason and got prayed for anyway! God is after everyone in Monroe County!

We proclaimed Isaiah 35 over this county.

The Lord took us to Matthew 25:34-40 which we decreed for this area.

"Whatever you did for the least of these you did it for Me," says the Lord.

About 5 PM, we heard the song, "Holy, Holy, Holy Lord God Almighty" ringing out over the town square! The bells were proclaiming the voice of the Lord, which is going to be heard here in greater depths. Psalm 29 will come forth! This song coming through the ringing of bells was a confirmation for what God is purposing to do here and that is to bring holiness.

Children of Light are called to come forth according to the will of God. (Eph. 5:1-17).

We then proclaimed Isaiah 48:12-22 in this manner:

1) Pay attention to God's commands (vs. 18).

2) Living Waters will gush forth in this county (vs. 21).

3) Assemble yourselves for praise and worship that you may be able to drink from those hidden wells that are waiting to be tapped into.

It shall come by assembling together for prayer, praise, worship and adoration of the Lord, your God!

WAPELLO COUNTY
Ottumwa

This also was a pleasant county to visit!

A civil war monument had sculptures on each side of it. One side was of people plowing up the land, harvesting fields in the

heat of the sun. The Lord says, "Plow up your hard hearts and I will give you a heart of flesh that is moldable, shapeable, usable." We decreed people here will not have hardness of heart any longer

270

(Ezek. 11:19 and Ezek. 36:26). Another side was one of the Good Samaritan seen in the below photo. We took Luke 10:30-37 and proclaimed this kind of spirit of grace and mercy to fall like rain in Wapello County.

Another side of this beautiful monument was dedicated to heroic sons of war. Raise up heroes of faith in this area, Oh God! Then we heard the Spirit of the Lord say, "Go! And do the same as these heroes!" There was a statue of an Native

The Good Samaritan Story

American Chief on the very top of this monument as well as one at the pinnacle of the courthouse building! This "honoring" was good to see. Let it continue here, Oh Lord!

An Indian Chief Atop Courthouse

We declared right judgments to be spoken from this courthouse (Matt. 12:25). A house divided cannot stand. Let there be godly unity in the government of Wapello County.

The river here has brought division. We decreed a unity to arise that will surprise even the inhabitants of this land.

We decreed that the kingdom of God has come to this county!

We prayed for the sons and daughters according to Psalm 144:12.

We saw this county as being called to be a defender of the orphan. We proclaimed Psalm 68:5, *"A father of the fatherless and a judge for the widows, is God in His holy habitation."* Bring forth holy adoption (Eph. 1:5). Take up this mantle Wapello County and a blessing will come.

At 6:00 PM, again we heard bells ringing. This time they were chiming out the hymn "Amazing Grace!" All of this for the entire town to hear! Let the people **hear** the voice of the Lord <u>wooing</u> them into a deeper relationship with You, Oh Lord.

Let this county become one in Christ. We decreed Ephesians 4:22-24 that this county will put on the new self, which is the likeness of God. Show them the incomparable riches of Your grace, Lord.

From Luke 10: 38-42 we felt the Lord is calling this county to the <u>good part</u>! Lord, let them choose *relationship* over the *religious spirit*.

We noticed <u>five</u> churches within a few blocks of the courthouse. "Favor, Lord, favor!" Also, divine authority from on high is coming to this county. This was after all: **5/<u>12</u>**/07! Hallelujah!

At the church across the street, a wedding had just finished and a baptism was just beginning. Holy covenants are being restored in Wapello County—marriage and family in accordance with God's blessing.

❦ twenty ❦

MARION, LUCAS, WAYNE,
DECATUR, CLARKE, WARREN

"Thus says the Lord, 'Do justice and righteousness, and deliver
the one who has been robbed from the power of the oppressor.
Also, do not mistreat or do violence to the stranger, the orphan or
the widow; and do not shed innocent blood in this place.'"
Jeremiah 22:3

We set out on May 19th, 2007 and we were accompanied by Ilze Kalnins and were greatly blessed by her prophetic gifts during the course of this journey. She and I also had fun taking pictures!

Our departure time was 7:59 AM with 64 degrees hanging in the air. After traveling 210 miles and returning home at 5:35 PM, it had warmed up to a balmy 84 degrees! We had basked throughout the day in the warmth of beautiful springtime freshness. May flowers were beginning to appear everywhere. The colors are so delightful after a winter of bland whiteness.

Upon our return, Ilze declared, "The angels have carried these things in books!" And to that, we agreed, saying, "Praise the Lord! To Him be all glory and honor!" You now hold in your hands the ordained fulfillment of that prophetic statement.

> "Then those who feared the Lord spoke to one another,
> and the Lord gave attention and heard it, and a book of

remembrance was written before Him for those who fear the Lord and who esteem His name."

—Malachi 3:16

MARION COUNTY
Knoxville

Linda and Ilza Kalnins in Front of Marion County Courthouse

We were impressed by this beautiful and well kept courthouse that had a park like atmosphere.

We prayed for a heart of courage for this county. We proclaimed a patriotic spirit, a godly patriotic spirit to come here. Lord, grant them the *spark* to continue onward and upward.

We felt led to repent for this county not having a welcoming spirit to foreigners and Native Americans as well as their rejection of them (as per their history of not ever wanting to name the county after any of them). Repentance was also uttered for elitism of the rich and poor or the "status" of where people come from.

Bring a hospitable anointing, Lord. Let them feel as though they are in the arms of God.

We called forth the people of this county to live in love and friendship. May they lay their lives down for one another. Let them be known for their love. *"Greater love has no one than this that one lay down his life for his friends."* (John 15:13).

This fast track, this race in life, does not go to the fast and strong, but **speed** the cause of *righteousness*, Oh Lord. (Isa. 16:5).

The things here used for sport, we decreed it will now be used for the glory of God. What was meant for one thing, God will use it for another!

We prayed against the "dare devil" spirit. Prayed for boldness and courage in the Holy Spirit to come forth. Let the righteous roar like a lion (Prov. 28:1). Release the passion of Christ in the people of this county so that they'll fight for their families. May going to church be more exciting than going to the races!

We came against making sport of things in a sexual context, declaring people will run from it as did Joseph. (Gen. 39).

Whatever has taken away the strength of men let it now be restored. Men are seed carriers. We declared that from their innermost being, seeds of the fruit of the Holy Spirit will come forth. Let them become carriers of God's Word. We decreed a virility of the Holy Spirit so that a new generation will be born of God. The men will not be neutered or be as eunuchs. Let them be strong seed carriers of God's Word! In the natural, love births. It is likewise in the Spirit.

Defeat the spirit of abortion.

Hope deferred makes the heart sick. (Prov. 13:12). Therefore, we declared a godly hope and a restoration of passion for Christ to emerge.

God's humor

Monument of The Iowa Motto

In God's own special way of humor and in confirming what He had just given us, we saw a sign on a building that had a cartoon figure of a man tipping his hat. It read: "Call Charley - The ideal man." Oh the joy of the Lord is indeed our strength! (Ps. 73:26).

We declared holy matrimony!

The legalistic doctrines in churches were rebuked and we decreed liberty in the Holy Spirit. And, whom the Son sets free is free indeed. (John 8:36; Gal. 5:1).

Raise up godly strength in the government of this county. Let it lift the people and not oppress them.

Let them know the Word of God and the US Constitution that they may not be deceived. We proclaim life, liberty and justice for all!

We broke silence, hiding and stifling spirits that are accompanied by a "shame spirit." In the Name of Jesus we broke shame and stigmas that are on some of the people of Marion County. We asked God's forgiveness of abortions in the

Stone Swords on Façade of Courthouse

natural, and in the spiritual. Lord, bring full release of Your plans and purposes in every heart of this county.

276

Expose wickedness in high places. Bring heartfelt repentance. Raise up a godly and holy people here.

There was a monument to the woman who designed the Iowa flag, Dixie Cornell Gebhardt (1866-1955). We decreed the holy designs of God will come upon the women here. We prayed the women of this county will stand up and say: "Yes! There is something worth fighting for!" Raise up your warrior intercessors, Oh Lord. As confirmation, as we drove out of town, we saw three or four colts...very young ones, who were lying in a pasture next to their mothers. Thank you Lord!

There was sunshine, blue skies and a little bit of wind, but otherwise there wasn't a cloud in the sky while we were here!

LUCAS COUNTY
Chariton

Shackled Prisoner Led Into Courthouse

The Lord wants to feed the people here with His Word. Many are about to fall in love with God's Word!

We came against any false prophecy that may have made inroads here. Let people take the path of truth and life. We prayed for a tearing down of those things which exalts itself against the knowledge of God. (2 Cor. 10:5).

Some have been taken down rabbit trails and missed their divine destinies. We proclaimed a celebration for the true destiny of this county. The enemy can disguise himself as an angel of light

(2 Cor. 11:14). Expose it Lord! We rebuked deception. Bring forth the spirit of truth and revelation (Isa. 28:17). "Sweep away the refuge of lies, and the waters shall overflow the secret place." Expose the counterfeit! Lucas County, divorce the false and embrace truth! We proclaimed this county is now on guard for the true light. Cause them to surrender to true light! Release Your true angels, Oh God.

The Lord is open, honest and not legalistic. He is merciful. Show the people Your glory, Lord, as Moses prayed in Exodus 33. Manifest Your truth and glory, Oh God.

A Marquee Across From Courthouse

We shout grace! Grace! Bring forth loud shouts of grace! (Zech. 4:7).

Who are you, oh mountain of false doctrine (2 Pet. 2:15, 20-21)! Some prophesy falsely and the Lord says to them, "I never knew you" (Matt. 7:22-23, 26)! Let the Light of Jesus come. Let an epiphany come as people begin to cry out, "Now I know You Lord! Now I see You!"

Let not ears be tickled here. (2 Tim. 4:3).

Prepare the Bride of Christ in Lucas County! Properly dress the people for the banquet. Let them not be led down wrong trails. (We actually saw a store front that had a Bridal dress in it!)

Rebuked false and unholy surrendering as the Native Americans had to do with their own lands. It was a forced surrender. We prayed for "heart surrendering," unto the Lord.

278

From emergency to emerging

An interesting find was a clock that had been set in stone as a sidewalk in a circular fashion around the courthouse. (See photo). Also, both hands on the clock tower were on eleven, (5 minutes to 11 AM). This is a county in transition! It is transitioning from anything that's counterfeit into a path of life and truth. We heard church bells ringing as we proclaimed these things! A big rock on the front lawn had the date: 1911. We read it as the last 3 numbers: 911! This county is going from emergency to a place of emerging. (The Lord seemed

Ilza and Linda Ponder Clock-like Sidewalk Around the Courthouse

to confirm this by our seeing an ambulance racing ahead of us as we were leaving town.)

We were here in the spring of the year so we released Zechariah 10:1 over Lucas County.

In reading the plaque on the courthouse lawn regarding the trails of the Mormons, one story was of a woman whose cart got stuck in the "mud and muck," and the oxen bolted with the result that they ran over her. We were reminded of Uzziah who tried to steady the ark of God that was being pulled by oxen and how he was struck down because he touched it (2 Sam. 6:6). We decreed Zechariah 4:6, *"Not by might, nor by power, but by My Spirit, says the Lord of hosts."* We proclaimed God would make it easy for people to come into the true faith of Abraham, Isaac and Jacob and into the Lord Jesus.

We called forth the Joseph anointing. We declared the five-fold blessing of Benjamin, Joseph's younger brother. There was even a restaurant across the street called: Benjamin's (Gen. 43:34). Grace! Grace! It was Joseph who blessed Benjamin! Release the storehouses of God. Bring forth divine provision for Lucas County. The Lord had us declare a "store house" for this area. We likened it to when Joseph was taken away from his family roots and then taken to Egypt to establish seeds or roots of food for his family. This is a word for this county! It's a storehouse!

*We declared seven years of abundance over **Iowa**!*

A transition was decreed for this county. Their true journey in Christ will bear much fruit!

Bring forth a "missionary spirit" breaking all false doctrines.

People in darkness will see a great light! Linda saw lightning bolts coming into pulpits!

Amazingly, while sitting in our car preparing to leave the courthouse, we saw a police officer bringing in a prisoner in orange garb with handcuffs and shackles on his feet (see first photo for this county). As they approached the courthouse doors, they discovered they were locked. The two of them stood there as if waiting for someone to come unlock them. In the mean time, Michael felt led to get out of the car and approach them. He told the officer who we were and what we were doing there. He then asked if he could pray with the young man who was shackled. Both of them gave permission and Mike said a short prayer, indicating this divine intersection in his life was of the Lord. Ilze and I watched and prayed from the car.

Mike had asked the young man if he accepted that prayer and he responded with a "yes." The prisoner's countenance went from a sour one to a soft smile as Mike walked back to the car. We felt the Lord had us there at that strategic moment in time to pray for this young man who needs to know freedom in Christ. This was one of those divine setups by the Lord where we were here at this precise moment in time to proclaim this young man's life is going to change!

We thus decreed freedom to all who are held "captive" in Lucas County. Zechariah <u>9:11</u>, *"As for you also, because of the blood of My covenant with you, I have set your prisoners free from the waterless pit."*

As we drove out of town later, we passed by the Freedom Bible Camp!

WAYNE COUNTY
Corydon

The name of the town was won over a poker game! Therefore, we rebuked a spirit of gambling in this county.

Mike Annoints Wayne County Courthouse Doors

As we were driving here we saw numerous sheep in a pasture. We declared Wayne County will know the true Shepherd of their souls and that He is leading the lost sheep. As God would have it, as soon as we drove into the town square, we saw a sign that read: Lamb Furniture! The Lord many times confirms His revelations to us in the most amazing ways. Build up the lambs here Lord! Encourage and strengthen them.

Arriving at the county seat of Corydon, it was 12:02 PM with a beautiful temperature of 70 degrees. Walking around the courthouse we glanced at a clock in the town square, it read: 12:12 PM. Twelve is the number that represents authority, so we felt led to declare God's authority will reign in this place.

The courthouse had bright blue and yellow benches around it. We spoke light and glory into Wayne County, praying for an open heaven to come.

Plaque "Honors" Jesse James Robbery

This county seat is known for its notoriety with the outlaw known as Jesse James. We declared that where there has been lawlessness, there will now be righteousness with true and holy justice. Where people have been robbed, we ask forgiveness. Lord, may the cornerstone we put at the courthouse, override the lawless cornerstone of Jesse James.

Trust has been shattered here. Restore trust, Lord, along with healing, especially for the generations. Take away the boasting that this town was robbed! Secure the kingdom of God here. We speak the true spirit of the son of Jesse in the Bible–King David! Many times the most unlikely ones are chosen. David was chosen over his brothers even though he was the youngest. Let the spirit of true judgment come and let people here not judge by what they see in the natural, (like David's brothers). (1 Sam. 16:4-13; 17:28-50).

We called forth the spirit of David. Bring forth the good sons of Jesse!

Raise up a House of Prayer here for day and night worship. Let righteous plans for their future come forth.

Creativity

The courthouse is somewhat utilitarian in design. Release a spirit of creativity, Oh Lord! Put in place people's right callings so they can operate in their true talents.

We saw a Menorah on a building across the street. We proclaimed unity and community, of Jew and Gentile.

Lord, bring forth true, righteous and godly trust. John 10:10 was pronounced. No more robbery, lying, cheating, stealing. May an abundant and full life in Christ emerge!

May the people of Wayne County live a lifestyle of overcoming by the power of the Holy Spirit. We declare they will rise up with a driving, passionate *fire* for the things of God.

CORYDON

QUIETLY PROGRESSIVE

Perhaps Too Quiet?

There was a water tower picture with the name of the town on it. (See photo). But it seemed to us like a rocket ship ready to take off! Their collage alongside of a building read: Quietly Progressive. But a religious spirit has limited them. Release Your Resurrection power Lord and raise them to newness of life in Christ. May they be baptized anew! Raise them up in the power and authority of Christ Jesus.

On the grounds we saw an empty fountain. It had *two* spigots in it. Then we saw *two* bright red nurf balls hanging in a tree. Beside this tree there was a large evergreen that had one root but it grew with *two* tops on it! These things spoke to us of the need for the True and Righteous Branch of the Lord to be made known here. Too many things have been lofty, yet not of God. We decreed the *Blood* of Jesus will bring healing and unity, along with refreshing Living Waters!

Ilze Kalnins

Ilze had felt a "deafening" come over her ear as she planted the rock by the courthouse. The deaf and dumb spirit was declared to be broken! We prayed for open ears to hear the Word of the Lord.

This particular day in May was as beautiful as it gets in the spring time in Iowa. A picnic lunch was so much fun and very refreshing in the midst of our very focused visits to the county court-houses. We felt we could just relax a bit and enjoy the natural elements the Lord graced us with.

We found an ideal spot right next to the road. It seemed to be in the middle of nowhere and it was even

Mike and Linda

beside a little lake! How perfect was that?! It was just a small area with one little picnic table which we immediately grabbed... not that there were crowds of people looking to get it! But it was so idealistic.

These were the supposedly insignificant things along our prophetic prayer journey across our state that caused us to fall in love with Iowa - impromptu, serene, peaceful, beautiful.

DECATUR COUNTY
Leon

There's a contending for governmental authority here, a contentious spirit to authority. Lord, bring submission to Your will and to Your ways. We rebuked rebellion to authority. The Word of God says that rebellion is as the sin of witchcraft. (1 Sam. 15:23).

By Decatur County Courthouse

Driving into town, we saw an advertising sign referring to blind spots. We perceived that indeed, there have been blind spots here. The blind spot began years ago when the county was first being planted and certain county officials took/robbed documents from another town under the cover of darkness. We declared that out of darkness, the Lord will bring forth light, His light! And what the enemy meant for evil, God can turn it to good. (Gen. 50:14-21).

Lord, bring forth Your Divine Word. Farm Your Word in this land, Oh God, sow Your Word in this county.

285

This is a border county, bordering along the state of Missouri. But this area is not forgotten by the Lord!

Linda and Ilze Kalnins

In this town of Leon, Leon in French means "lion" which represents authority. Let the LION of Judah roar here (Rev. 5:5)! May the people rise up and live Proverbs 28:1, *"But the righteous are as bold as a lion."* Verse 12 says, *"When the righteous triumph, there is great glory."* Lord, bring forth the righteous ones!

We declare the covenant of death is annulled and declare new, vibrant life in Christ.

Deeds and covenants will come forth in righteousness.

We decreed the spirit of rest and Sabbath, and a renewal of the land. Bring forth the fruitfulness of Thy Spirit Oh Lord in this place.

There's been a vying for power that's taking place here. Where there had been a reluctance to relinquish documents, we ask for grace, mercy and justice. Lord, destroy "hoarding" and all works of the enemy. We decree every principality and power is defeated here.

May the Blood of Jesus cover the people and their land that cleansing and peace may come forth. "Peace. Be Still!" Mark 4:39 is for this county.

We prayed against the spirit of illegitimacy. This county was taken illegally, so we prayed for the spirit of adoption to come. (Rom. 8:23).

Put in place the fullness of Your authority, Lord. Send the "watching angels" to watch over Decatur County.

We saw that one of the courthouse cornerstones was laid by the Masons on May 23, 1907. We were here to lay the representative, foundational stone of Jesus (Isa. 28:16-17) almost 100 years later to the day with this day being May 19, 2007. Amen Lord!

Ilze discovered that Leon spelled backwards is N O E L! We declared new, holy births in Jesus Name. Lord, bring a realization of the Christ Child. Amen.

CLARKE COUNTY
Osceola

The county seat of Osceola was named for a Seminole Native American Chief.

As we were driving into town, we saw a totem pole (see photo) with a carving of an eagle on top with a poisonous snake in its mouth. This directed us to when Moses lifted up the serpent in the desert. When people repented of their sins and would look at the snake on the pole they were saved, just as when Jesus was lifted up

Carving of an Eagle With Snake on Top of Totem Pole

and saves all who look to Him (Num. 21:6-9,16-18; John 3:14-15). We declared a release of repentance. Let the pole now represent staffs and scepters according to these verses.

We heard the word, "meadow" and felt Psalm 23 was being released here. Lord, cause Clarke County to walk in the power of Psalm 23. May Your rod and Your staff bring comfort. Plant the people beside still waters.

We decreed *lushness*, fullness, and a refreshing of the Holy Spirit.

Another thing that was noted as we drove into town was that we saw a street named, "Pearl." We declared the revelation of the kingdom of God which is the pearl of great price, would arise in this area. (Matt. 13:46).

We proclaimed the "cattle on a 1,000 hills." Bless the land, the farmers and their families. Preserve their fields and may they produce abundantly. Psalm 50 was declared over Clarke County. We speak, "Becoming!" This county is becoming a new entity in God. Those graduating during the month of May will begin to find their divine destinies in God.

Clarke County Courthouse Entrance

We call this land, "Beautiful!"

Where there has been bitterness, we throw the Word/the stick, (Righteous Branch) into the waters and declare healing and wholeness. (2 Kings 6:1-7; 2 Kings 2:19-22).

Isaiah 40 was declared. Satisfy the desires of this county with good things, Oh Lord. Heal them of all their diseases. (Ps. 103).

Awaken Clarke County out of its slumber. Ignite the hearts that are hungry. Leave it not untouched by Your Spirit, Oh Lord! Cause like-minded hearts to come together. Raise up worshippers here.

We saw a U-turn sign and felt it signaled the need for a U-turn, which means repentance. Turn from your wicked ways.

Hard rock

The words, "hard rock" came to us. Some have hard hearts here. But God wants to give them a heart of flesh. They will begin to place their trust in the Rock of Ages. (Ezek. 11:19-20).

Psalm 69:30-33 and Hebrews 3:7-8, 12 was proclaimed. Let the people not be discouraged. We speak joy, faith and the "better things" of God.

It was subtly oppressive when we first arrived. We declared vision for the people of this county, for without a vision the people perish (Hab. 2:1-4; Hos. 4:6; Prov. 29:18). As we glanced around the town square we noticed a place called, "High Expectations." Yes Lord! We prayed that God would do something to cause people to *turn* their hearts. A while later we saw a hair salon called, "Turning Heads." God works in mysterious ways!

Strengthen the worshippers in this area Lord! Give them courage to come and worship at the Band Shelter! Give them creative songs that will draw people causing them to wonder and to ponder. Shake them to the core for Jesus!

Expel wickedness that has caused this place to be oppressed. Bring Your light, Oh Lord. Your light will dispel all the darkness. Bring Resurrection power and light through worship. The Lord says to Clarke County, "Worship Me in spirit and in truth and you shall come alive" (John 4:24)! We felt the Lord's tears for this county because He wants them to come to Him! This county will never be the same again!

A Beautiful Mural Depicts Osceola. Real and Painted Clouds Compete.

As we were about to leave, we received more about this county needing a vision. There was a huge mural on the side of a building in town. It was a bird's eye view of the city. We prayed for spiritual vision to arise like that of an eagle (as we saw on the totem pole). Give them eyes to see like an eagle that they may rise above their present circumstances. And just like the clouds on the mural, so too were the big, white, puffy clouds overhead. The clouds began to increase. But there were also darker clouds on the mural. We saw revival rain! We declared rain is coming to this county. Elijah rain is coming! Revive the Pastors and the churches, Oh Lord! (Isa. 40; 2 Kings 18).

WARREN COUNTY
Indianola

We saw and declared new wineskins for Warren County. The celebratory wine of Cana is coming here with new beginnings. Let the people say as Mary did, "Do whatever He tells you." (Matt. 9:17; John 2:5).

Bring the dew of the morning! Bring the *juices* of heaven here. Lord, You are the vine, we are the branches. Thank you for tailor-made wine that brings distinction, the different, and the good. Thank you for innovations, like the wines of Iowa!

Warren County Courthouse

God treasures the people here.

We declared uncommon ways to find common ground, declaring unity.

On the courthouse grounds is a statue of an elderly woman handing a bouquet of flowers to a young girl. We proclaimed a healing of the generations. Unite the young and old again, Lord. *"Posterity will serve Him; it will be told of the Lord to the coming generation. They will come and will declare His righteousness to*

Linda With Statues of Old and Young

a people who will be born, that He has performed it." (Ps. 22:30-31).

The people here need to polish things that have been tarnished! Bring back the luster of God's original intent, plans and purpose for their lives.

This area used to be known for the National Balloon Festival. Lord, lift up that which has been depressed, distressed. Lift up laughter and the joy of the Lord. Put the DNA of the Father, Son and Holy Spirit upon this county to bring balance in people's lives.

Usher in humility, Lord. Pride comes before a fall, so we declare a reward for people as they humble themselves. Extend Your scepter to Your people, Lord, in Warren County. Grant them Your, "Yes and Amen!" The effectual prayers of a righteous man, avails much. James chapter 5 is for this county.

We declared this county's air space be opened up. Open up the heavens and let the rain come!

The Lord says, "Do not whine. But drink in the wine of the vine of the Lord for My joy. Be filled and be drunk in the wine of My Holy Spirit." We declared the new wine of a new Pentecost for Warren County. Dancing in the streets was decreed because of a coming Pentecost! This new wine will cause people to dance as David did, unabashedly, unashamedly. (2 Sam. 6:14-15, 21-22).

Ilze saw as it were, a "Field of Dreams." She saw in the spirit, a grand ball game that's coming to Iowa and the name Mickey Mantle came to mind. She declared *new mantles* are coming; new, fresh anointings are being released. Each person has a part to play and each one is hitting their home runs. She declared, "Lord, let the game begin! Let Your plan and purpose begin. Let people be struck with awe to where they will say, 'Is this heaven?' No, it's Iowa!" Lord, kiss Iowa!

It was in this very area that I (Linda) had a life changing encounter with the Lord. Briefly stated...it was 8/4/96 when the Lord engulfed my car in a cloud burst of pounding rain. I began sobbing inside my car. I heard the audible voice of God say, "Ask Me for 500,000 new souls for this area" (meaning this area of the United States–in Iowa)! I've never been the same!

The Lord indeed, wants to take not only Warren County, but all of Iowa, "Up, up and away into the heavens" (Rev. 4)! The Lord is calling this county upward. Go for it by the power of the Holy Spirit!

❧ twenty-one ❧

MADISON, ADAIR, UNION,
ADAMS, TAYLOR, RINGGOLD

"The Spirit of the Lord spoke by me, and His word was on my tongue. The God of Israel said, the Rock of Israel spoke to me, He who rules over men righteously, who rules in the fear of God, is as the light of the morning when the sun rises, a morning without clouds, when the tender grass springs out of the earth, through sunshine after rain." —2 Samuel 23:3-4

It was beginning to look like we would finish this divine assignment well ahead of our projected conclusion. God had made a way where many times there seemed to be no way. Traveling across Iowa many weekends during the past year had become an incredible joy-ride, to say the least. Each journey brought us into greater and greater insight to Iowa's divine destiny in the Lord. We continually were amazed at His revelations, insights, understanding and His purposes for the heartland of the United States!

Putting the foot to the pedal, we left in our SUV on May 26th, 2007 at 8:15 AM. Since it was now late spring, we were blessed with 73 degrees as our launch temperature. It was amazing to us upon our return home at 5:35 PM the temperature again stood at 73. There is a sense here that the Lord wants us to look at Psalm 73 and glean much from that passage of scripture. It is powerful.

Read it. Eat of it. Embrace it. And know that God is the strength of your heart!

Again, we were privileged to have Ilze Kalnins with us. She is a dear friend and tender sister in the Lord. It was Memorial Day weekend and we felt our humble SUV or "mobile tabernacle" would again afford us holy travels. We had accumulated many *memories* during our landscape scouting through Iowa's counties. This trip, we tracked 265 miles. It had been another memorable day!

MADISON COUNTY
Winterset

We arrived here on a cloudy morning. It was the town's celebration of John Wayne's 100th birthday since it's his birthplace. We prayed that they would remember the Father's Son, Jesus.

Madison County Courthouse

We came against the spirit of contention and declared that past battles be forgotten. May it be replaced with a spirit of forgiveness. Today is a fresh new day!

We decree the glorification of the honoring of the movie regarding adultery (The Bridges of Madison County) be broken. We prayed against immorality declaring this county to be known more for its purity. Bring a restoration of holiness and purity to Madison County, Oh Lord, and send forth the beauty of holiness! When people come here, we declare they will see the beauty of the Lord. Ilze heard, "There is a *rest* in the beauty of the Lord." We professed Isaiah 6:1-8.

This county will make God smile!

Open the heavens, Lord, and release Your holiness from Your altar. Open people's eyes. Circumcise their hearts. Bring a circumcision/covenant out of restoration and softness of heart.

There were window-like shutters on the top of the courthouse. They had the appearance of being shut. We prayed for the windows of heaven to be opened over this county. It began to rain as we declared Amos 5:24, *"But let justice roll down like an everflowing stream."* We declared God's Living streams to be released in this area.

People here have been caught in the past. Lord, take them into Your future! Remind them of Your glory, not what's in old movies. Do an unforgettable *act* here! Show new vistas!

The Lord wants to be famous here! (Hab. 3:1-4).

We declared Isaiah 49:1-5, 8 and 15-26. Verse 23 holds a tough John Wayne-like quote about how kings and princesses will "lick the dust of our feet!" God is birthing servants of the Most High God in Madison County.

The Lord says to this county, "I will not forget you!" (Isa. 49:14-16).

Nurturing qualities

The first few years of a baby's life are the weaning years. This is a "Mother's Breast County." God calls this county to never forget His nurturing qualities. God never forgets His people! Many will become comfortable in God's arms.

Bring miracle births here, Lord. We've come to dedicate this county to the Lord, just as Samuel's mother did (1 Sam. 1:28). Hannah nurtured Samuel's divine destiny. (John Wayne was here for his first 3 years of life).

We break off any stigma of illegitimacy. We called forth the spirit of adoption (Rom. 8:23). People here will begin to adopt even in the natural. We stand against infertility in the natural and in the spiritual realms.

Let new spiritual heroes be born here!

Ilze said the name of God–El Shaddai–means "Many-Breasted One"...nurturing by the Abundant One! We pronounced an abundance of fruit and harvest.

Destroy death at its foundation, Oh Lord and bring forth the Tree of Life!

Proclaimed people here will fulfill their divine destinies.

Declared formation of godly values and the formative years of spiritual nurturing will occur. We declared God will raise up the formative growth of children and fashion it into a movement–moving many forward into the kingdom of God.

Don't look to what you can earn and learn, but to the call of life in Jesus.

Isaiah 54 is yours! You shall not be forsaken.

An old song came to Ilze and she began to sing: "Jesus in the family makes me happy!" God is smiling on this county!

Adair County
Greenfield

Significantly, we drove into this county seat at 10:10 AM. We declared John 10:10 for Adair County.

Adair County Courthouse

We decreed the splendor of God for this area.

Let the people here not be tossed and turned between opinions. (1 Kings 18:21). May they now begin to discover the secrets of God. (Dan. 12).

We prayed for the "head"–for the leadership here. Let a shifting in people's minds and hearts occur for righteousness and justice. Bring godly knowledge, Oh Lord. Position caring people. Raise up public officials who care and are enthusiastic.

We prayed Matthew 5:14 that this is a city set on a hill. Let it shine Lord. Let this county shine!

God wants to herald this county. We declared a holy reveille (reveille means: military wakeup call) and revelry (extravagantly festive) in praise and worship!

Awaken them to the God of the Bible. Give them a love affair with the Word of God.

Adair, "A–dare." When the decision for the county seat was being contested many years ago, the people took that battle as far as they could, to the US Supreme Court. Now, God is urging them to take their battles to the Supreme and holy courts of heaven. Let them hear the challenge of the Lord to enter into His Presence.

A Sign of "Rebuilding"

We called forth the foundational things that were at the first when the county courthouse was built. In one of its cornerstones they put corn, oil, wine and a Bible! Return to your First Love! (Rev. 2:4-5).

May there be a release of the holy wine of the Holy Spirit. Release a love for God's Word.

James 4:1-7 was declared. God is asking them to submit to Him. Draw near to Him! Humble yourselves before God.

Ephesians 5:14-21 was proclaimed. Let there be a submission to God and to one another. Release humility, kindness, gentleness. We declared a dependence upon the Holy Spirit.

Awake!

We felt there was a "sleepiness" over this county as we approached it and began to proclaim that it would now awake, rise and shine (Isa. 60). Lord, remove the source of slumber (Rom. 13:11-12)! Understand the present hour! Awake! Put on the armor of Light.

We saw what appeared to be a coat of armor on the front of the courthouse building. But it was plain and not very attractive. God wants to change that armor into one of revelation and light!

Snares and traps that have been spoken here and leadership that was taken away, caused us to call forth good and godly leadership.

We prayed curses be removed. Bring Your signet ring of authority here, Oh Lord. Adair County, do not give sleep to your eyes until you free yourselves like a gazelle. Bring forth child-like faith and joy. The joy of the Lord will be your new strength! (Prov. 6:2-4).

Bring clean spiritual air! Called for the intercessors to arise.

Highway 92 brings us to the county seat. We prayed Psalm 92, but especially verse 10, *"...I have been anointed with fresh oil."*

Paths of righteousness have been lost, so we prayed Psalm 23 asking the Lord to bring the people into green pastures.

An awakening was decreed for Adair County. Give them a horn of power. Release the song of the Lord. Bring a fire and fervency

Ilze and Linda By Unusual Sculptures

where they say, "It's all or nothing!" Go the distance! Let them declare: "We *dare* you to show up, Oh God! We *dare* You to do the impossible!"

Let the people here fight for Your purposes, Oh Lord.

Let all blueprints and strategies of the enemy be broken, null, void and bear no fruit.

God's "castle light" is coming! A city in darkness will become a great light. (Isa. 60).

Juliana G. Dukes, a dear sister in the Lord who lives in Adair County, e-mailed us in early January 2007 to share a few things with us right after she had attended our Eye of God Conference held earlier that month. She spoke of a dream she'd had regarding the Greenfield town square. In the dream she saw a big serpent and felt it was the spirit of anti-Christ, but she reached up and shut its mouth! (It was as though she'd used holy reveille to thwart the enemy and had used that "horn of power" we had prophesied!)

She also said after the conference, she felt led to enter into a seven day fast. Earlier that week her brother suffered a brain aneurysm, having had open brain surgery. Amazingly, he left the hospital much earlier than anticipated with no speech problems or paralysis. We believe the fresh oil prophesied brought forth healing. Certainly, this is prophetic for what God is doing and what He has planned for Adair County!

UNION COUNTY
Creston

It had been raining intermittingly but stopped as we arrived. The clouds were swirling around seemingly in every direction. However, we caught sight of a vortex in the sky, a place where it seemed to form a "V" with a bit of sunshine coming through the grey clouds. We picked up on the "V," declaring victory, as though the Lord wrote it in the skies as a *sign* for Union County!

Union County Courthouse

Driving into town we saw on a church's marquee that the sermon for Sunday was going to be: "Speaking in tongues." We did not know if this pastor was aligned Biblically with this Holy Spirit gift. However, with the next day being Pentecost Sunday, we prayed the truth of scripture would be made known to him and his congregation. We prayed for all the churches in this area to have this gift and that according to Ephesians 4:30 they would not grieve the Holy Spirit.

People here are more intellectually inclined than Holy Spirit inclined. Take away density of thinking, Oh God, and bring them into their divine destiny in You. Let them receive visions and know the divine purposes of God.

Mural in Town Square

We were here on Memorial Day weekend and we prayed for memorable times in the Lord to come. Let Holy Spirit fire fall! Send shock waves through this area. Awaken and shaken the people with the prayer language and more!

Bring fresh, Living Bread to this county. (John 6:32-48).

We declared Isaiah 44:3-6.

We saw the words, "unlimited trains" on a mural in town. We declared Isaiah 6 and that the train of the Lord's robe would fill the temple. May the Lord's Presence fill the houses of God and the people of this area.

Raise up the intercessors and watchers that will effect the Union–all of the USA! Open up the heavens Lord! Bring forth the rumblings of God and His mighty thunder. We proclaimed the people of this county would hear and feel the holy, reverential *fear of the Lord.*

Ilze saw a sign that said something about "Welsh ponies," so we declared a Welsh-like revival to come here.

"Lay aside your old self" (Eph. 4:22-24). We rebuked the enemy having his way. (Eph. 4:27).

Two banners

Balloon Emblem

There were two different kinds of street banners: 1) Old trains, 2) Hot air balloons. Therefore we declared that God desires to take the people from their yesterdays (trains) into their future (balloons) and into His heavens. Linda heard the Lord say, "Fly high!" We declared the old has passed away and the new fresh manna of God is falling. Feed them Lord! Awaken the pastors here to unity with God and with one another. Put off the old, let go of the past and put on the new man (Eph. 4:4). We decreed unity in Union County. One Lord, one baptism. We called forth unity in the Body of Christ. Let there not be a divided heart. Give people here a love for unity and with one another (Ps. 133). Let this unity be like *dew*, like the rain that began to sprinkle on us as we were about to leave the courthouse.

Known For Its Trains

In the past, the railroad browbeat the people. They've been railroaded by the enemy! At this precise moment in time we heard the sirens blowing! It was high noon. It's time for a movement of God here. It's His time! God's timing is now! Come up (Rev. 4:1)! Lord, bring Your trumpet sound!

ADAMS COUNTY
Corning

Corning is the birthplace of Johnny Carson who hosted the Tonight Show for many years. There's been a worldly distinction because of this. We called forth a new and uncommon distinction for the things of God!

This was one of the first courthouses used to hide fugitive slaves many years ago. They helped the slaves find their way to freedom. The history of this county also reveals 40 young men of this area who fought in the Civil War and who became

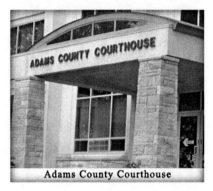

Adams County Courthouse

famous for their bravery. Bring spiritual bravery here Lord! Bring forth Your warrior witnesses! Psalm 110 was declared, especially verse 3. We prayed for God's people to volunteer for His holy army. May they march forward and take ground for the kingdom of God! Advance!

A sign along the road said: Integrity Certified. We prayed for honesty and integrity to be in this place.

We noted another sign: "Ask about points." It was regarding frequent flyer miles, but it caused us to prophetically declare, "Lord, bring this county into frequency of going higher and higher into Your will and into Your ways!" (Rev. 4).

We felt a homey spirit, a welcoming home kind of thing. There was a canopy or porch like entrance to the courthouse that reflected this kind of spirit. We felt at home as we approached the front door to anoint it with oil.

Mural Across From Courthouse

A word for this county is: honor. We declared an "honoring" here. Lord, honor these people as they honor You. We declared honor for parents. Honor your father and your mother! We decreed a double honor for the elderly in this area.

Proverbs 15:33 was pronounced, *"The fear of the Lord is the instruction for wisdom, and before honor comes humility."* Bring forth humility and the holy reverential fear of the Lord! Proverbs 20:3 as well, *"Keeping away from strife is an honor for a man, but any fool will quarrel."*

This is a storehouse county. This is a city of refuge in a time yet to come. There is a sense of comfort here.

We proclaimed no defilement will come into this county. No corruption will come here like gambling, etc.

Isaiah 40:31 is a proclamation for Adams County.

TAYLOR COUNTY
Bedford

This county has a lake area called: Lake of 3 Fires. We declared the power of the Holy Trinity to come here so that people are not thrown into the lake of fire! Revelation 20:15, *"And if anyone's name was not found written in the book of life, he was thrown into the lake of fire."* Make Yourself known Lord. (Ps. 9:16).

We rebuked misguidance. (Isa. 9:16).

Driving into this county there was a silo with these words painted on it: "Learning to love." We prayed, "Lord, bring Your holy love to Taylor County!"

Taylor County Courthouse

There was a sign set in stone beside the courthouse that read how many feet above sea level this particular spot was. (See photo below). Ezekiel 47 was declared that Living Waters begin to rise and flow in this county.

Build up the people here in the power of the Holy Spirit. We speak life, truth and righteousness to this county.

Give this area a unique character in Christ. May they reflect their heavenly Father.

This is an equipping county. They will equip others. Let there

The Only Sea Level Sign We Saw

be a shift that is felt and understood, Oh Lord, so they understand their calling. Activate an *equipping* center here. Activate the churches to equip the Body of Christ. Sharpen your spiritual tools of praise, worship, prayer, intercession, etc. (Eph. 6).

Lord, position the Body of Christ correctly. Do Your divine chiropractic here. Heal hurt bones and hurting hearts. Bring divine adjustments and justice! Proverbs 3:7-18 was proclaimed, especially verses 7-8, *"Do not be wise in your own eyes; fear the Lord and turn away from evil. It will be healing to your body, and refreshment to your bones."*

Wind-Blown Linda and Ilze

There was an old hotel that was very well kept. It was the Hotel Garland. We proclaimed Isaiah 61:3.

Taylor county, you are "tailor made" by God. He has a specialty He wants to bestow upon you. Linda saw as it were, "specialty cakes" as when people have specially designed ones for weddings, graduations, etc. The Lord says to Taylor county, "Taste and see that I am good" (Ps. 34:8; Jer. 15:16; Ps. 119:103). Let the people of this county *rise* to the occasion of special assignments God has for them. May they do this for the sake of Jesus Name and not for their own glory.

Tailors fit things and sew them together. We saw this as unity for this county. Even the cobblestone streets around the court house had to be fitted together in order for it to be smooth enough to drive on. God wants to bring the right fit!

Take the people from the common to the uncommon, Oh Lord. Separate the holy from the common (Lev.10:10). Let them walk in Your glory, Lord. Clothe them with righteousness. (Isa. 61:10).

We rebuked the Masonic corner stone on the courthouse and its adverse effects upon this county. We laid our stone beside it canceling those things with the scripture from Isaiah 28:16-17.

Bring cross cultural things, Lord, shifting people's focus and understanding of who they are. Many don't have the right fit. Let them find where they belong. Come to Jesus for a proper fit! God wants people to be fit for His tailor made purposes. We declared fulfillment of His plans! Establish a "finishing work" here, Lord.

Let angels stand guard on this southern border county. Let them guard this area and all of Iowa! Release your messengers of fire. (Heb. 1:7).

Let the people know the fire of Your eyes, Oh Lord. (Rev. 1:14).

RINGGOLD COUNTY
Mt. Ayr

Historical records tell of how 6 loads of wood had been brought in as part of the first supplies for the new government seat at the county courthouse in 1856. Along with that load of wood, they brought in 40 pounds of candles! We decreed God's people here would keep the fire burning on the altar with praise and worship! (Lev. 6:12-13).

Ringgold County Courthouse

We declared Psalm 119:105 that God's Word is a lamp unto their feet. We proclaimed that people in this county would be enlightened by the delving into the Word of God. The

Holy Spirit is wooing them to find their way through the Light of His Word.

Let Your majestic Presence fill the *air* in Mt. Ayr, Oh God, and all across this county! (Linda had just prayed this before realizing the name of the town!)

Marry this county to Yourself, Oh Lord (Isa. 54:5). Reveal to the people You are their heavenly Bridegroom and You are preparing them for Your soon return. Let them prepare the way of the Lord!

Let reality change here. We declare victory and freedom for Ringgold County.

Standing By Tree Trunk Carving

There was one lone tree on the lawn that was the only one decorated with a string of lights. It had been dedicated by Hospice. We prayed God would cause health and healing to fall like rain, like dew on Mt. Hermon for Mt. Ayr and all over this county and beyond! We rebuked disease and health issues that have robbed people of full life. We rebuked the destroyer. (John 10:10).

We felt angels around us while we were here. Michael said he saw…angels on a staircase. They were ascending and descending as people go into eternal life. There is great comfort here. Hospice will no longer be needed as there will be no more straining at the time of death.

You were dead in your trespasses and sins…according to the prince of power of the "air".… But God, being rich in mercy, because of His great love…made us alive together with Christ. Yes and Amen! (Eph. 2:1-9).

God's signet ring

We declared clean, pure air over this county. Bring forth Your signet **ring** Lord. Bring forth sons and daughters of royalty of the Most High God (Hag. 2:23). We declare a new day. And when people look to You, Oh Lord, You will extend Your royal scepter to them! (Ps. 45:6; Gen. 49:10).

We saw the words, "majestic" and "princess" around the court square. God is calling the people here to a royal priesthood. (Rev. 1:6).

Mike had to realign the way he had parked the car. It had to be readjusted because it was parked the wrong way on the street. We prayed that people be aligned with God's perfect will. Let truth be the measuring line. Cause an understanding of justice and mercy. Protect Your people, Oh Lord. We declared this county to get on the right course with God.

Reverse the curse of sin, sickness and disease. The Lord pronounced over this county: "It is finished! Remember Me on Memorial weekend!"

We declared abundant, full, vibrant life physically and spiritually over Ringgold County.

Linda on Cell Phone Pretending

We took pictures of an old phone booth on the courthouse property. We decreed the people of this county will now begin to call on Jesus. Ring up God!

There was a little ice cream shop nearby called Peggy Sue and it reminded us of the movie by that name. In a scene from this film, the girl reminisces about a conversation she'd had with her grandmother who was now deceased. It was a touching moment of remembrance. We thus felt led to declare a *remembrance/return* to a time and place where the Name of the Lord was upon this county. A spirit of forgiveness for past mistakes was proclaimed.

✦ twenty-two ✦

POTTAWATTAMIE, MILLS, FREMONT, PAGE, MONTGOMERY, CASS

"Drip down, O heavens, from above and let the clouds pour down righteousness; let the earth open up and salvation bear fruit, and righteousness spring up with it. I, the Lord have created it." —Isaiah 45:8

This was to be our last journey to the counties with the exception of the very last one, Polk, which we were leaving for the following week. We had the honor and privilege of having one of my closest friends on this last tour, Karen Holte. She has been my *armor bearer* for a long time and knows me all too well! She and I have traveled together not only on this last journey to the counties, but also to Israel.

It was a wonderful blessing as we saw in the evening sky the night before, a beautiful double rainbow. It was as if the Lord was saying, "I'm giving you a grand send off for this last journey!"

We began at 7:40 AM the next morning. It was June 2nd 2007 with a starting temperature of 63. It was to be a full and productive day. Coming full circle to the Des Moines area, we had covered 378.6 miles by 8:10 PM. Even at that evening hour, it was a warm and wonderful 70 degrees. We rejoiced that even the temperature seemed to perfect this prophetic prayer journey that was concluding in 2007 with a "seven" in atmospheric conditions! His rainbow of promises are being launched and fulfilled!

POTTAWATTAMIE COUNTY
Council Bluffs

We arrived here at 9:30 AM on a beautiful, sunny morning!

Pottawattamie County Courthouse

This county was named after a Native American term which happens to mean: "Blowers of Fire," "Keepers of the Council Fires," or "Makers of Fire." Lord, fan the flame of desire for You in Pottawattamie County. Linda heard the Lord say, "Keep the 'home fires' burning!" Build holy families here, Lord. Bring forth kingdom couples for Your glory.

Counsel the leaders here.

We decreed the wind of the Holy Spirit to descend. Infuse the winds here with godly counsel.

We proclaimed a double blessing here on this June 2nd.

God says, "Look at my people! I love them!" Touch every area with the Breath of Your Spirit! Isaiah 11 was proclaimed regarding the seven fold spirit of God, especially verse 2 for "the spirit of counsel" here in Council Bluffs.

We saw a license plate on a car that said, "Fisherman." We declared that as "fishers of men," this county will become as such.

This area is a center of commerce and distribution. We prayed the Spirit of the Lord be distributed here and that He would use the air, train and river traffic areas for His divine purposes. Raise up Your standard, Oh Lord!

Around the area of the courthouse, Karen noted 5 lions and an eagle. May the Lion of Judah roar and be heard in this county! May people mount up as with eagles' wings! (Rev. 5:5-6; Isa. 40:31).

Karen planted our stone by a marker stone that had been dedicated to those who'd given their lives to law enforcement. We prayed for God's authority, justice and righteousness for the past, present and future, declaring, "Upon this rock I will build My church" (Matt. 16:17-19)! We bind and loose according to the keys given to Peter and then to us.

The courthouse was next to a funeral home and as we approached the area, there was a casket being carried out. We declared resurrection life, new life, abundant life, full life in Christ for this Pottawattamie County! Ephesians 2:4-8, "…being raised up with Him."

Mike saw in his spirit the word: Paraliel, (a semblance to parallel)….We claimed there is no parallel to God. Nothing can compare to Him! He reigns! We proclaim His incomparable power and authority.

A Kairos Moment

At 10:17 AM, our friend Craig Leaming called us on our cell phone. His own divine assignment from the Lord was nearing an end as he now entered the last state (Texas), and the last leg of his physical walk *across America repenting for the sins of the nation. He wanted to encourage us, as we did him as well. Then we prayed together. What a powerful kairos moment! We were once again made aware how God connects His people together "for a time such as this" to accomplish His purposes. What responsibility we all carry to be alive at this moment in history!*

Karen and Linda Display the Stone

We felt led of the Holy Spirit to declare this a "gateway county" and Psalm 24 was proclaimed over it. We declared this area to be one of holy fire, not one with unholy fires of gossip, slander, etc. (James 3:5-17). Our prayer was for holy tongues of fire to fall that passionate desire for the Holy Spirit would come upon this county. Let the Breath of Your Spirit be upon this area, Oh Lord.

The sunshine was very bright while we were here. We prayed for the brightness of the Son of God to come forth. Lord, lay a canopy of Your fire glory and passion over Pottawattamie County. Heat it up Lord! (Rev. 3:16-18).

According to John 11:40, if you believe, you will see the glory of God. Use your mustard seed of faith and watch mountains be moved.

Back door

We speak justice and righteousness to the judges, lawyers and the people of authority in the court system.

Adjacent to the courthouse property was an old jail that had been restored. We sensed a "bondage issue"…people being locked up, bound in their hearts. Mike spoke against confusion and chaotic, ungodly things and called forth God's perfect will to be done. Clean the heavens over this county.

Karen felt there was something regarding our mistakenly anointing the back door of the courthouse before we had discovered the front entrance. The enemy has tried to bring deceit and deception. We rebuked the enemy's *back door* tactics…as we sensed there had been sneak attacks upon the people of this county (Ps. 51:6,15,17; Isa. 51). Awake! God will be your rear guard! We declared a back door gate for the Holy Spirit according to Isaiah 52:12, *"But you will not go out in haste, nor will you go as fugitives; for the Lord will go before you, and the God of Israel will be your rear guard."*

Prayed Micah 2:13 for this county.

We saw a man walking by and Mike saw him as a man full of folly. Thus we proclaimed a "crown of the wise" to come here instead of foolishness according to Proverbs 14:24. We decreed no more folly! No more loss at the back door. No more loss of resources, children, families and life. We declared the crown of wisdom in Jesus Name.

MILLS COUNTY
Glenwood

The four streets surrounding the courthouse were: Vine, Sharp, 1st and Walnut. Each spoke prophetically to us. Let the people here enter into the True Vine (John 15:1). Sharpen the people to have their eyes and ears open to what the Spirit is saying to the churches (Rev. 2:7). May they make the Lord first in their lives according to the First Commandment and may they bear much fruit.

We saw street banners declaring Glenwood to be the: "Best of both worlds." (See photo on next page). We declared heaven and earth converging here. We decreed the people to be citizens of heaven! Drive darkness away.

Street Banners

Saw a monument with two water spouts. (See the photo below). It had been dedicated to a prominent married couple. Bless marriages in this county, Lord! Release the power of the wells of God! Let the "gushing" begin, Lord! Deep calls to deep (Ps. 42:7). Let Your divine destiny begin. Bring forth unity in marriages and families. We also decreed a Pool of Bethesda in this area (John 5:1-9). Freedom in the Spirit for healings to occur was proclaimed in the name of Jesus.

Water Spouts On Memorial

In light of the two water spouts, we declared Genesis 24:42-60 where Abraham's servant was sent to seek out a wife for Isaac; it says in part: *"So I came today to the **spring,** and said, 'O Lord, the God of my master Abraham, if now Thou wilt make my journey on which I go successful...'."* Lord, we ask You to bring forth the Isaacs and the Rebekahs! There was a flower, fruit, or wheat-like emblem on this fountain. However, only one side of the drinking fountain worked. It seemed to us like Esau and Jacob. We were struck with the aura around it. We had the strong sense it was associated with a blessing. It was at a well where Jacob's wife was found. There is blessing here for godly marriages!

Amazingly, across the street we saw a stained glass window of a maiden with a water pot! (See photo). Pour out Your Living Waters here, Lord, that people of Mills County will drink deeper of You.

A Stained Glass Window Nearby

We decreed the churches will tap into new wells of fresh waters. May they be like David, who longed for the waters of Bethlehem. (2 Sam. 23:15).

Change

The temperature and the winds changed when we got here. The temp had dropped and the winds came up, the clouds stirred and swirled within the blue skies. There were big, cumulus clouds along with dark, grey ones. It signified the warfare here. We also saw it as representing "change" that's coming to this county.

We proclaimed Mills County to have a pioneer spirit upon it. The clock tower had the dates of 1876 and 1974. May they glean the best of the past and the best of the future - the best of both worlds! Song of Songs 7:13, *"...And over our doors are all choice fruits, both new and old, which I have saved up for you, my beloved."*

This was declared to be a gateway county. Shut the gates of the enemy and let the children of God possess the gates.

There has been slavery in mental illness. We declared freedom in Jesus Name. May justice and a "flourishing spirit" begin to flow.

The Lord wants to release a bouquet here…the fragrance of Christ (2 Cor. 2:15). May the Lord's will be done.

Mills County Courthouse

As this county once harbored slaves on the run, we declare slaved sinners are being set free! We also declared a double blessing for this county.

Lord, we pray for circumcised hearts. Make and mold people here into what You want them to be. Take away stony hearts and give them hearts of flesh. (Ezek. 36:25-27).

We saw a building with the word "oasis" on it. It confirmed what we saw regarding the Jacob and Rebekah word we had just given this area.

Mills County, you are called to drink deeply of the Living Waters of the Lord!

FREMONT COUNTY
Sidney

Sidney is known as "Rodeo town USA."

Like a rodeo rider, we bind people to the Word of God.

There is a spirit of adventure here. Lord, draw it into the right direction, not of the world, but of God. We decree godly adventures and ventures. The maverick spirit will not be one of lawlessness. Tame the wild, Lord!

We prayed for the sons, daughters and parents, asking that mercy would fall like rain. Draw them all into their proper authority. Mercy triumphs over judgment (James 2:13). We next prayed against oppressive applications of justice.

Fremont County Courthouse

Demonic, spiritual giants in this area are being defeated. We have been deployed "for a time such as this" in spiritual warfare. Fremont county, arise to your divine destiny! A significant stake is being driven here today.

Karen Holte By
Honor Roll of Veterans

We prophesied that proper judgements made will bring clarity and truth.

On a Vietnam War Monument it read: "Take time to rest and reflect on those who have gone before you." This county must also reflect and consider those who have gone before and plowed in the Spirit. Hebrews 4:1-2 was proclaimed. We prayed a holy rest for this county.

We came against hardened hearts. Let the people be bound together in love.

It seemed hard and dry here. We cried out, "Where is the God of Elijah" (2 Kings 2:14)?! We decreed the God of Elijah is coming! Cry out to Him, Fremont County, and you shall see!

Come Holy Spirit with Your fire! Bring thundering horses, open up the heavens!

A single drop from Calvary cleanses and empowers this county.

Lift this area up into more visibility in the things of God. Take it to the highest level. Fremont County, freely climb the mountain of the Lord!

We proclaimed Psalm 147:8,10-11,13-14, "*...He does not delight in the strength of horses...He makes peace in your borders....*" Lord, let Your Word run swiftly here. Let the people put their hope in You. Satisfy Your people Lord.

Isaiah 35:3,6 and 10 was declared. We speak to the skies and call forth moisture for that which is good. We speak to the sky gates, "Open up and rain down!" Heard in the spirit: "Take your Saturday night bath in God!"

We saw a blue jay on the lawn; this little bird represents **joy** which we decreed over this county.

Protection was also prayed over Fremont County.

Footprints

Karen's Feet Show "Turn Around" Footprint

As we were about to leave, Karen saw foot prints that had been made while the cement was wet. (See photo). This sidewalk led to the front of the courthouse. We had all three walked over it upon our arrival, but God made sure we saw it when we left! Karen saw how it appeared that someone accidentally had walked on it without

322

realizing it was wet and upon their discovery of this fact, they'd turned around and walked off. We knew the Holy Spirit had given us a powerful prophetic sign for Fremont County! We decreed it to be a TURN AROUND COUNTY! People, like this person who left foot prints in the wet cement, will see the error of their ways and turn around. People will begin to repent and come to the Lord.

Just moments before this happened we were all sitting on a little bench in front of the courthouse saying our concluding prayers. A butterfly lighted on my (Linda's) hand. Thinking at first it was a bug of some sort, I had quickly brushed it off. But when we saw the "turn around" footprints in the cement, we recalled the butterfly! Butterflies represent change. There is something new emerging in Fremont County!

Lunch time

Before heading to our next county, Karen knew of a great place to have our picnic lunch. Since she grew up in this area, she knew it well. This partic-ular area was just outside of Sidney in Fremont County. You should go there! From this high

Karen Holte and Linda

perspective, you can see three states: Iowa of course, Missouri and Nebraska. What a beautiful view! Iowa, so richly blessed!

PAGE COUNTY
Clarinda

Our friend, Karen Holte, was born here, so her name is found in the records of this county. We prayed, "Lord, You are now recording people's names in the Lamb's Book of Life!"

Page County Courthouse

The town of Clarinda is named for Clarinda Buck, who carried water to the town's initial surveyors. She was popular among the settlers for this reason. We thanked the Lord for His nourishing character upon this county and proclaimed it had been prophetically conveyed through this woman. She had indeed given a "cup of cold water," to those who were thirsty. (Matt. 10:42).

Multiply Your wonders here, Lord. Pour out Your Spirit to the offspring. We declared this county will not lose its reward. Let them not continue in the error of their ways.

Lord, remember those who come to the well like the Samaritan woman in John 4. We proclaimed verses 7-30 of that chapter and also John 7:38. We prophesied a holy rescue! Holy Spirit come!

The courthouse was dedicated on June **5,** 1994. The Lion of Judah has roared and a new song is coming! When we arrived it was 77 degrees, therefore we declared the "7 seals" of Revelation **5.** We are in a time of seals being broken by the Lion of Judah. New revelation, insight and understanding are coming. (Dan. 12:4).

We declared freedom from oppression and for people to seek and find You Lord!

Records, seals of adoption, and secrecy will now be revealed for the heritage of those living here, their heritage in the Lord.

This is the home of Glen Miller and his band. Let new songs come forth for Your glory, Lord! Let there be a trumpet blast of God. May it add incense upon Your altar as Page County offers praise and worship unto You.

Open door

We found an open door leading into the courthouse, which was a rare occurrence on a Saturday. As we entered, we noticed a green-like, globe light above the entrance and one at the back entrance as well. Since green represents growth, we decreed this for Page County. Spiritual growth is coming (Isa. 44:1-5)! Karen also saw the globes as "global" and that this county has some tie in to Iraq and other global areas. Iowa is considered the breadbasket of the world. We proclaimed that which has been hidden will now be brought into light.

Karen Places Stone by Monument to One of Seven African-Americans to Receive the Medal of Honor

We then discovered a Lion Exhibit on the 3rd floor. There was quite a display of bobcats in Iowa along with confirmed sightings. I've (Linda) actually seen them because they've been in our yard at least three times that I'm aware of. This was confirmation from the Lord as we remembered when we first arrived in this county we began to declare the roar of the Lion of Judah to come here!

We declared heavenly, open doors for this area, but also prayed that some doors need to be closed on the past…things that have brought harm. Isaiah 45:1-3, 8 was proclaimed. Verse one says, *"Thus says the Lord to Cyrus His anointed, whom I have taken by the right hand, to subdue nations before him, and to loose the loins of kings; to open doors before him so that gates will not be shut…."*

There was a monument to Vernon J. Baker who was one of seven African-Americans given the Medal of Honor during World War II. We decreed a bringing forth of a great spiritual movement by spiritual heroes!

Raise up rulers and leaders (in government) who know how to use authority, Oh Lord.

Bless Page County with the spirit of Deborah, who was a judge, a leader, a prophetess. Bless this county with the spirit of Jael, who prepared "more than" (more than just water, but milk!) which resulted in over-powering the enemy! This is a "more than" county! It's a leadership county. (Judg. 4).

There was a portal-like arch on the grounds. Open up the heavens Lord! Karen also saw it as a prophetic banner. Lord, let the banner over this county be love. (Song of Songs 2:4).

Page County, God is writing a new page of history for you. It's one of revival!

MONTGOMERY COUNTY
Red Oak

We had driven through a stormy, pounding rain to get to this county. As we approached the county seat of Red Oak, we sensed there was some heavy spiritual warfare going on in this area.

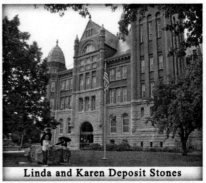

Linda and Karen Deposit Stones

We proclaimed refreshment for tired souls in Montgomery County. (Matt. 11:28-30).

A house or *city* divided against itself cannot stand. We saw something was bringing division. The 10 Commandments were broken resulting in disunity. It was rebuked and we declared unity in Jesus Name.

We decreed *vision* in place of division! *"After these things the word of the Lord came to Abraham in a vision, saying, 'Do not fear, Abram, I am a shield to you; your reward shall be very great'"* (Gen. 15:1). We say to the people of this county, "Do not fear!" We ask for a shield, Lord. Genesis 15:17-18 speaks of the rewards of keeping covenant with God. Give them a great reward. Red Oak, we declare the covenant Blood of Jesus now cleanses and caresses you, heals and restores you!

The top half of the courthouse was finished in red brick while the bottom half was in grey brick. Karen saw the top half as the Blood of Jesus covering this county and the bottom half as though they were feet representing the work of God. She also saw, as it were, "keys." The Lord quickened to her Matthew 16.

Montgomery County, "Who do you say Jesus is?!" Declare as Peter, "You are the Christ, the Son of the Living God." Then you shall receive the keys to the kingdom of God. The keys are for the gates. You shall receive authority in the earthly and heavenly realms! We decreed Isaiah 22:22.

Fatigued!

We saw the most unusual sign on a building adjacent to the courthouse. It had almost faded away. (See photo). It spoke

"Fatigue" Sign Caught Our Attention

prophetic volumes. It wasn't just about this county, but the entire state of Iowa! It read: Fatigue. This place is fatigued! We prayed for renewed hope. We called forth divine destiny in the Lord! We proclaimed the power of agreement in this county so that the house of God may stand strong, and families and marriages will also be strong. Bring strength. Break the spirit of fatigue, distress, discouragement! Loose harmony, unity and cause people here to walk in victory, Oh Lord.

The clock tower on the courthouse rang out at 4:30 PM at the ½ hour mark....again speaking to us about division and how the hour was noted at the half way mark. We declared harmony, unity and open heavens! (Ps. 1:1-3).

The forefathers had stood for liberty and had dedicated the foundation of the courthouse. Refresh! Restore! Fan into flame the good work You've begun, Lord. We proclaimed Isaiah 61:3-4 that they will become as oaks of righteousness.

1 Samuel 30:10 and 21 (re: those who were exhausted) was read. We decreed verse 26 over Montgomery County. This area has been exhausted. We proclaimed the spirit of David will bring forth a blessing and that which has been taken from you, will be restored. The Amalekite spirit that came against this county is being defeated! (Exod. 17:8-14; 1 Sam. 15:2).

Let the weak say, I am strong! (Joel 3:10).

Give them victory and restoration, Oh Lord. Those beaten down by losses will be restored and renewed. This county has fought its last battle. It is now being led into victory after victory after victory!

Natural armies wear "fatigues." But in God's army, we are equipped with Light and armor! (Eph. 6).

Montgomery County, this is your final greeting as we leave your area: "Make the most of every opportunity!" (Eph. 5:14-21).

Make music!

Submit to one another in love.

Just after we had decreed Isaiah 40:29-31, the sun came out! We had come into this county under sprinkles of rain after having driven through **hard** rain. But now–here was the sun! How comforting!

CASS COUNTY
Atlantic

Coming up on our last county of the last journey of this divine assignment, we prophesied restitution! What the enemy meant for evil God is turning it to good, both in this county and all over Iowa! (Gen. 50:17-21).

We declared Psalm 30! Amen!

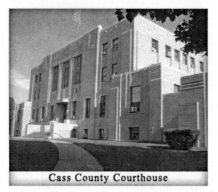

Cass County Courthouse

We praised and thanked the Lord He had commissioned us as runners or heralds, pronouncing good news. Blessed are all those who bring good news in this county. (Isa. 52:7).

Proverbs 4:18 is for Cass county: *"But the path of the righteous is like the light of dawn, that shines brighter and brighter until the full day."* Bring the full day anointing! Light! Revelation! *"Bright eyes gladden the heart."* (Prov. 15:30).

Prepare this county with liberty, truth and Your mantle, Oh God. We bind deceit. Where there has been corrupt authority, bring Your authority, Lord.

We thanked the Lord for cleaning and cleansing Cass County. Bring forth a spirit of forgiveness.

The clouds were constantly swirling and changing while we were here. Therefore, we declared change is coming—transformation! God has a *"designer message"* for this area, and since this was our 98th county on this Prophetic Prayer Journey, we decreed Psalm 98. The intense action of the clouds all day long, spoke to us of how the Lord will appear in the clouds at His Second Coming (Luke 21:27)! Prepare ye the way of the Lord, Cass County!

Holy Spirit, drive out anything that's less than true and proper. Any hidden thing, bring it to light, expose it.

According to Psalm 98, we declared a prophetic song of praise for the Lord's victory and His salvation will now arise. It's now being fulfilled by spiritual proclamations of the Gospel of Jesus Christ.

Touch hearts that are closed and let them know You love them, Oh Lord. Let people here know that You are willing to go after that *one* who is missing. (Luke 15:4-7).

Cass County, this is *kingdom time* here! Unite your Bride! We are here during the month of June, which is typically called the Bridal month. Ready Your Bride, Lord. We decreed the love and holiness of Song of Songs for this area. Be overwhelmed with the beauty of Your Bride, Lord, the Body of Christ–Your believers. (Song of Songs 2).

Your Name, Jesus, is being poured out like perfume upon Your Bride (Song of Songs 4:15-16). Let Cass County hear Your voice, Oh Lord!

There was a statue of a woman on top of a tall pillar in the park nearby. (See photo). She held a shield and a sword. There was also what appeared to be a dove on top of her head. Song

Nearby Monument

of Songs 6:9, *"But my dove, my perfect one, is unique...."* Thus the *"designer message"* God wants to bring to this county was confirmed.

Jewish people believe Song of Songs to be the holiest book in the Bible. We also declared a revelation of God's exquisite love for our Jewish brethren will begin to arise here.

We declared Isaiah 35:8 as we observed the main road going through town. When we turned to this passage, I (Linda) discovered this is the verse we began with one year ago as we began this Prophetic Prayer Journey. I'd written the date in the margin: 6/24/06. It was now one year later to the month that we were concluding these divine travels. I marked today's date of 6/2/07 right beside it. Praise the Lord!

Also regarding the main street in Atlantic, it led to the train station. We then prayed Isaiah 6:1, "Lord, let Your Presence, the train of Your robe, fill this county. Take the people here deeper, higher, richer and purer."

We also declared Psalm 68.

Departing at 6:32 PM with partly sunny, partly cloudy skies hovering overhead and a temperature of 70 degrees, we felt enormously blessed. We were driving away from the last courthouse on 7th Street! God's number of perfection! We were confident He who began a good work will indeed perfect it and complete it (Phil. 1:6). Hallelujah!

A MIGHTY CONCLUSION!
The 2nd of June, 2007

We arrived back in the Des Moines area, took Karen home and headed for ours, looking forward to getting a bite to eat, relax and rejoice in all God had been doing. As the sun was setting that evening, Karen gave us a call from her home, asking if we could see the sunset. Unfortunately, the trees around our property shield us from the west. (We do have a beautiful view of sunrises, however.) Karen began to describe for us the spectacular sunset.

She said it was like a *banner of red fire...like ribbons strewn* across the sky! She described red, orange and dark clouds within it. She recalled how I kept speaking of the strange cloud formations as we drove home that day. One in particular looked like a mushroom resembling an atom bomb swelling up. It had the appearance of a heavenly explosion! Karen felt this was the rear guard of the Lord, protecting the "ending" of our Prophetic Prayer Journey!

We concluded that indeed it was a sign, a signature if you will, a grand finale of the Lord, as if to say to all who have participated in this calling: "Well done, good and faithful servant." (Matt. 25:21).

All glory and honor unto our Most High Jehovah God!

❧ twenty-three ❧

POLK COUNTY AND THE STATE CAPITAL

*"Remember the former things long past, for I am God, and there is
no other; I am God, and there is no one like Me, declaring the end
from the beginning and from ancient times things which have not
been done, saying, 'My purpose will be established, and I will
accomplish all My good pleasure; calling a bird of prey from the
east, the man of My purpose from a far country. Truly I have
spoken; truly I will bring it to pass. I have planned it, surely I will
do it.'"* —Isaiah 46:9-11

POLK COUNTY
Des Moines

The Lord arranged many significant things on this last journey to Iowa's 99 county courthouses, ending with Polk County, segregated from all the rest because of its location in the center of the state and being the location of the state capital. Our journey could not have concluded any better than it did! God was gracious to us in so many ways.

This final county reminded us of Dutch Sheets and Chuck Pierces' prophesy over Iowa in 2003, that this state was to glean from the four corners so the dark clouds in the center would lift!

We completed this divine assignment in 12 months, much sooner than we had anticipated. We began on June 20th of 2006. And on this ninth day of June 2007, we were wonderfully blessed

335

with a perfection-plus, clear blue sky over the Des Moines, Iowa area. There was not one cloud in the sky for almost the entire day! We declared all obstructions removed and for an open heavens over this county and the entire state!

Amazingly, our prayer time on this warm June day was noted as beginning at 12:00 PM high noon. How significant the Lord arranged for us to conclude this divine excursion with the authoritative number twelve. Additionally, Mike and I had not been aware of the KHOP (Kingdom House of Prayer, Des Moines) sponsoring a prophetic workshop for that day and that the class would have as one of its "exercises" a time of prophetic prayer at the Polk County Courthouse with IWG Ministries. What perfect timing!

Our Group Prays Next to the Courthouse

Consequently, thirteen of us gathered under a tree on the front lawn. Someone asked what 13 meant. It means, "the baker's dozen." It means "more than." It signifies abundance! This was decreed for Polk County!

Significantly, Polk County's number alphabetically in Iowa's counties is #77 and used to be printed on car license plates years ago. Several noted while driving over to the courthouse to join us, the temperature was 77 degrees. I noticed it as well on the gauge of my own car. "Thank you Lord, for these outward signs confirming Your divine plans for Polk County. Bring your completion, Your perfection, Your divine purposes, for this capital county."

Even the date of June 9th blessed us! Upon looking up in my Numbers Book what <u>nine</u> represented, the page number for this chapter was **77**. This was a divinely designed coincidence! Everything in this prophetic prayer journey flowed together like a divinely woven fabric of many colors, not unlike Joseph's coat made by his father. Joseph's coat was a rainbow of colors representing covenantal promises (Gen. 37:3). This prophetic fabric that's been woven over Iowa is like a puzzle giving us–piece by piece–a greater enlargement of all God is about to do in this strategic state. Nothing is by accident in His kingdom! One of the most significant meanings of the number *nine* is that it represents the nine **fruits** and the nine **gifts** of the Holy Spirit, which we proceeded to declare over Polk County (Gal. 5:22; 1 Cor. 12:8-10). Let it begin to flow!

The address

The official address for the Polk County Courthouse is <u>500</u> **Mulberry** St. When I (Linda) heard that, I felt the power of the Holy Spirit surge through me! Others felt it as well! Someone then declared the vision I'd had on 8/4/96 regarding the 500,000 new souls I saw for Iowa and that it is about to come forth because prophetically speaking, the "500" was seen as representative of multiplication for those very souls! Those gathered began to proclaim the "harvest" would be a result of this prophetic prayer journey! Not so ironic, just the night before, Janice Sceney (a prophetically gifted woman of God) was the guest speaker at KHOP and called Mike and I forward for a prophetic word. One of the things she proclaimed over me personally was that God was going to "multiply" what I set my hands to do for His kingdom.

We were all amazed and praised God for all He is doing and what He is about to do!

The other part of the address of the street name "Mulberry," brought revelation to Karen Holte. She read Luke 17:6 and we decreed it over this county: *"And the Lord said, 'If you have faith like a mustard seed, you would say to this mulberry tree, "Be uprooted and be planted in the sea;" and it would obey you'."* Let faith and authority arise in this county!

One of the street corners on another side of the courthouse is "6th and Court." We proclaimed man's government will now begin to be administered with godly justice and righteousness. May the courts of heaven rule in this place. Michael planted our stone, with Isaiah 28:16-17 written on it, right next to the foundation of the building. We'd left a stone at all the Iowa county courthouses as a physical sign of what was prophesied.

Randy Bixby, Director of the Des Moines House of Prayer (KHOP), brought our attention to the fact that another corner surrounding the courthouse was 5th and 6th Streets. We declared Isaiah 56 particularly verse 7, where it says God's house will be called a house of prayer for all the nations! Randy began to prophesy that God would advance the HOP, and nations will come here to be blessed. Yes and Amen, Lord! We prophesied Polk County to <u>be</u> a House of Prayer.

Prophecies began to flow

As has been our custom throughout this journey, we would scout out the land first by physically walking around each courthouse taking in the natural surroundings. 1 Corinthians 15:46

tells us the natural proceeds the spiritual. When we concluded our circling the building, prophecies began to flow like a river!

Jayne Tuttle said the scripture that came to her while she approached one of the stair steps was, *"The steps of a good man are ordered by the Lord and he delights in his way"* (Ps. 37:23). "Lord, order the footsteps of people in this county. Let them walk in Your ways and not in their own." Jayne then anointed the steps leading into the courthouse. Mike had anointed the door just as had been done at all the other courthouses in Iowa, but this was perhaps the first time the steps were anointed! Let people begin to sense something different when they enter this place.

Karen Holte found a coin on the steps. She declared the deep treasures of God will come forth upon this county and across Iowa. (Job 23:10; Col. 2:1-3; Matt. 13:44).

Downtown Des Moines has a farmers market on Saturdays during the summer months. One of the significant prophetic proclamations made had to do with the Joseph anointing and that Iowa is being called to "store up" during seven years of plenty. We called for the Josephs to prepare the land and that they would give fruit to the world. Our friend Adam proclaimed God would raise up instruments to nurture the crops both in the natural and in the spiritual. We decreed the market place anointing like that of Joseph, to arise in this hour. (Gen. 41).

Adam also said that as he walked around the courthouse, he was led, as were several others, to look outward and not inward. Some noticed the jail across the street. Joseph was also jailed at one point in his life. But God brought him out. "Lord, release prisoners to live godly lives in this county and across the state" (Gen. 37-50). Mike declared this to be a county of Josephs!

Our Group Walks Perimeter of
Polk County Courthouse

Someone said that people here had been told they can't do certain things just as Joseph's brothers said to him. Mike began to prophesy this to be a county of holy dreamers and that God is giving it the signet ring. We declared as Joseph, that God has made people in this county forget their troubles and has made them fruitful.

Mike also spoke that we have entered into God's authority. We proclaimed godly and righteous decisions for this area. A new day was decreed! "Set up stones for your glory, Lord." We declared the seal and signet ring of covenantal promises of provision. Your sons and daughters have authority as never before.

Bridal

Rebecca Couchman had seen a vision of a dainty woman's hand with a diamond ring on it. She declared Polk County as a hidden diamond and that "she" is safe. A confirmation of this came through Victoria Worthington who had picked up an article on the grounds that spoke of a wedding that had taken place at the Botanical Center. June is known as the Bridal month and we were here on this particular June day at the conclusion of this prayer journey, to declare Iowa's "wedding day!"

> "It will no longer be said of you, 'Forsaken,' nor to
> your land will it any longer be said, 'Desolate;' but you
> will be called, 'My delight is in her,' and your land,

'Married;' for the Lord delights in you, and to Him your land will be married."

—Isaiah 62:4

Many remarked about the contrasts they saw around the area: trash and litter, green grass and trees, heavenly prophetic adornments such as eagles, but there were also gargoyles. There were beautiful flowers along with wilted ones. Across

Ungodly Gargoyle Sculptures

from the courthouse was the jail. All these resonated with conflicts and contrasts of life and death. In the jail itself, many souls are held captive. "Release them into their divine destinies Lord!" We saw engravings of statues of men blindfolded and some not blindfolded. "Release spiritual insight, Oh God, that people who have been blind may now see, gain understanding, and set free from any darkness."

We saw a monument or marker for a gentleman who was known for his gentle spirit. We declared that our Most High God would raise up spiritual markers in this place, that a line of demarcation for the power of God would be known here.

The clock

Someone else remarked about the clock tower and prophesied that "time is no more" in the sense that this county is no longer on man's time as we know it. But it's now on God's time!

Another took note of the American flag and the colors of red, white and blue and prayed the "red" for the blood of Jesus over this county, "white" for purity, and "blue" for heavenly revelations. Blue is also the color of Israel's flag in the Holy Land. And just as Israel is known as the "Beautiful Land" or Beulah Land, so is Iowa! (Isa. 62:4).

Roger Armstrong was drawn prophetically to the "reserved"

An Interesting Parking Sign

signs around the courthouse. He decreed that *reservations* with God are now being made and fulfilled. He declared the oppression that Dutch Sheets and Chuck Pierce saw in the middle of the state is now lifted and the heavens are opened over Polk County and Iowa. There is a whole new atmosphere here!

In regard to those reservations, Jayne saw a parking spot that read: "Reserved. G." (See photo). To us it prophetically read: "Reserved for God." He is about to show up here!

2nd Floor

Randy also noted the gargoyles were placed on the 2nd floor of the courthouse. This represents the spiritual warfare that takes place in the second heavens. We declared a breakthrough in the mid-heavens (Eph. 1:17-23; Col. 2:8-15). "Lord, make a public display of Yourself once again!"

There was a statue of a little girl reading a book. It appeared to be a Dr. Seuss book that ended with the words, "I am." We decreed the holy I AM God to rule and reign in this county and in this state. (Exod. 3:14).

As we began to conclude our time at the courthouse and move on to the state Capitol, someone prayed this was the *beginning* of this journey, not the end! We decreed healing has been released for Polk County and the Blood of Jesus has cleansed it. "Draw people up into your Throne Room, Oh Lord. Let people's eyes be opened. Blind no more! Let Your glory fall, Oh God!"

A declaration was made that every place the sole of our foot was set forth on this journey, now belongs to the people of God in the Name of the Lord (Josh. 1:3)! "Thank you Lord for godly wisdom, Your goodness and mercy. Provide spiritual food and harvest with the double portion according to the number revealed today, 77!"

THE STATE CAPITOL

The 13 people dispersed from the Polk County Courthouse, some returning to Victoria's pro- phetic conference for the afternoon session and a few of us went further down the street to the State Capitol. Michael had felt very strongly that this was the actual place the Lord wanted us to symbolically end this Prophetic Prayer Journey. There was an

Jayne Tuttle, Linda and Anita Doughty Stand Before State Capitol on New Concrete Map of Iowa's 99 Counties

overload of revelations here and we were glad we listened and obeyed the voice of the Lord for this finale!

The things recorded within these pages do not do this justice. But we shall make a worthy attempt.

We arrived here about 1:15 PM. I remember when I wrote down the time, I thought to myself, "Why did I do that? 1:15 doesn't speak to me at all!" But I'd already recorded it so I left it

Linda and Mike Schreurs

alone. It wasn't until I actually began transcribing the notes from that day, that I realized its significance. As a prophetic people, we are to be on alert for things in the natural realm that speak to us of things in the spiritual (1 Cor. 15:46). Con-sequently, taking all those numbers together: 1 + 1 + 5 = SEVEN! Again, the number of completion! This was yet another way of God confirming this holy assignment on this absolutely, picture-perfect June afternoon. Oh, the glory and power of our Jehovah God who is abundantly gracious to His children!

Likewise, as with the 13 precious saints at the courthouse, we felt the **five** of us who were now at this last chapter were also significant. Five is the number of grace and favor! It also tied in with the Joseph anointing we saw over Polk County. Joseph's younger brother, Benjamin, was given five portions (Gen. 43: 34; 45:22)! Apparently Iowa is only one of seven courthouses in the nation with <u>five</u> domes affixed to its top. Praise God from whom all blessings flow!

The Bridal aspect spoken at the courthouse was also brought out here as I (Linda) saw the three of us ladies were all wearing white. Anita Doughty even had on bright red shoes! We declared the blood of Jesus to be over the Bride of Christ in this state. *"Come here, I shall show you the bride, the wife of the Lamb"* (Rev. 21:9; Rev. 19). The Blood is aligning Iowa for a release of all its bondages and a release into the heavenly realms with the wonders and awe of God!

We decided to put several more stones with the inscription from Isaiah 28:16-17 around the capitol building. We found it interesting that one of the cornerstones had the date **AD** 1873 carved into it, which of course, acknowledges the Lord Jesus Christ. It delighted us greatly because far too often on our prophetic prayer journey, we saw many government buildings with ungodly cornerstones. This was refreshing to see.

Anita found an interesting place in which to place one of our stones - in an ash tray! We prayed Isaiah 61:3 that God would give Iowa a crown of beauty instead of ashes, the oil of gladness instead of mourning, a garment of praise instead of a spirit of despair.

We asked the Lord to bring FRESH BREATH!

We rebuked the religious spirit over Iowa.

A mothering state

Mike has felt for some time, after we'd gone to about half of the counties on this prayer journey, that God has designated Iowa to be a "mothering state." We saw an unusual statue that confirmed this: A woman who was holding up her bare "nurturing" breasts! Most unusual to say the least! But Isaiah 66:11 says this:

> "…That you may nurse and be satisfied with her comforting breasts, that you may suck and be delighted with her bountiful bosom. For thus says the Lord, 'Behold I extend peace to her like a river, and the glory of the nations like and overflowing stream; and you shall be nursed, you shall be carried on the hip and

345

dandled on the knees. As one whom his mother comforts, so I will comfort you; and you shall be comforted in Jerusalem.'"

We recalled the flag prophesies made at the Polk County courthouse regarding Iowa and Israel. Iowa, you will feed the nations!

Mike also saw the sons and daughters of Iowa are in the heart of God. There is going to be new birthing...new strategies for the church...strategies to feed nations.

One Side of a Monument

Mike also decreed this to be a place of angels. Angels everywhere! We saw this prophetically through a dramatic statue on the capitol grounds. (See photo). On one side of this stature there were two angels going before and behind a woman holding a child and a man carrying a book of knowledge. On the opposite side was a man carrying sheaves of what looked like wheat; another had a torch, while yet another, a cornucopia. Iowa, you are destined by the Lord to be bountiful in the natural and in the spiritual! Seize your destiny in the Lord now while it is still called "today"! (Heb. 3:7,15; 4:7).

The Opposite Side of Same Monument

Spiritual agriculture!

We decreed Iowa as bountiful and fruitful. The Lord our God is the Master Gardener. It all began in a Garden. Iowa is assigned to spiritual agricultural! The Lord is plowing up cold hearts and making them supple (Ezek. 11:19-20). Our inheritance in the kingdom of God is coming forth.

At this point, I said something about being very thirsty, it had warmed up considerably and it just served to remind us that Iowa is becoming thirsty for God. Psalm 63:1-8; but verse one says, *"O God, Thou art my God; I shall seek Thee earnestly; My soul thirsts for Thee, my flesh yearns for Thee, in a dry and weary land where there is no water."*

Lord, advance the cause of righteousness here. Break off all obstacles to justice.

Light up every aspect of Iowa. We decreed snares to be broken. Destinies fulfilled. "Make Iowa what You intend it to be, Lord. Release a higher authority to Your children. Release the pioneer spirit. Release a forerunners spirit. Pour it into our children; let them not go the way of the world."

We proclaimed a release of healing into the Body of Christ.

We were made aware of how the Good Shepherd will leave the 99 to go after just one sheep (Matt. 18:12-14). "Go after **each one of the 99 counties** Lord! Go after every man, woman and child!"

"Teach us to be good stewards of the abundance You've bestowed, Lord."

We then thanked Him for how blessed we are in this state. From sea to shining sea, Iowa is sandwiched in the middle of the

United States as ordained by God, to become the heartbeat of His plans and purposes for this nation. All glory, honor and praise be unto Him forevermore!

♦ twenty-four ♦

IOWA SUPREME COURT

"This command I entrust to you, Timothy, my son, in accordance with the prophecies previously made concerning you, that by them you may fight the good fight, keeping faith and a good conscience, which some have rejected and suffered shipwreck in regard to their faith." —1 Timothy 1:18-19

"A river of fire was flowing, and coming out from before Him; thousands upon thousands were attending Him, and myriads upon myriads were standing before Him; the court sat, and the books were opened." —Daniel 7:10

O nly the Lord God Almighty can weave a fabric of glory by the splendor of His Hands to create the beauty of His holy will. Obedience carries a reverential fear of the Lord with the astounding fragrance of His Presence lingering in our lives through the garments of praise and worship that's been woven before Him all across Iowa's 99 counties. *"All Thy garments are fragrant with myrrh and aloes and cassia; out of ivory palaces stringed instruments have made Thee glad. Kings' daughters are among Thy noble ladies"* (Ps. 45:8-9a). I stand amazed! This assignment was sheer obedience to God's will and was beyond our own capability.

Always sensing the Lord's anointing as I'd compile the history of this prophetic prayer journey, I decided to check the date as I began the last few pages of this book. It was October **25**th, 2007. Combining the two numbers of the date, 2 and 5, it equals **seven** which is the Lord's holy number of completion and perfection. 1 Corinthians 15:46 says the natural proceeds the spiritual. God's divine and perfect purposes are forthcoming in this state! It is only unto Him that all glory and honor for this project must be given. He initiated it, He worked it, and blessed it. May Iowa glorify Him with extravagant love and thanksgiving until its people take hold of their heavenly mansions!

THE IOWA SUPREME COURT

Iowa Supreme Court

Since prayer had been conducted at all 99 Iowa County Courthouses, we felt it was imperative to actually end this strategic prayer assignment at the Iowa Supreme Court! This took place on June 30th, 2007 and we were wonderfully blessed to have with us great warriors in the faith, Craig and Diane Leaming, along with Roger Armstrong. As you can see from the photos, it was another picture perfect, spectacular day.

We began to pray that we would be taken into the councils of heaven where the Lord knows the end from the beginning.

We see and speak renewal for Iowa.

We decreed peace! Peace! Peace, be still! *"The Lord bless you, and keep you; the Lord make His face shine on you, and be gracious to you; the Lord lift up His countenance on you, and give you peace."* (Num. 6:24-26; Mark 4:39).

Set captives free! (Col. 2:8; Isa. 61).

There were jets crisscrossing in the skies overhead. Iowa is "marked" for peace and renewal! *"Peace I leave with you; My peace I give to you; not as the world gives, do I give to you. Let not your heart be troubled, nor let it be fearful."* (John 14:27).

We declared that angels are pushing back the darkness.

Looking out over the city landscape from on top of the hill where the Supreme Court building sets, there is a red bridge. Craig said it has been mentioned in a number of prophecies given to him as well as other intercessors he's acquainted with. He said it's a gate of authority. It is a governmental gateway and we prayed it would now be opened. We declared Isaiah 22:22.

Craig Leaming and Roger Armstrong

We decreed that what is not possible with man is possible with God (Matt. 19:26). Let every law be inspired by and aligned to the Lord.

Interesting discovery–the gate!

The guys discovered an area behind the building, along a ledge or cliff, where there were things left from previous construction projects. (See photos). Many of these items had been strewn in

351

Craig and Roger Stand Behind Stone Gate

various places giving it the appearance of a salvage yard. There was even a wooden, cross-like beam. They found something else, something very significant–an old stone gate. First of all, we saw this pro- phetically as many souls who've been lost, will now begin to find saving grace in Jesus Christ. They are now being salvaged, redeemed, saved and made whole! They once were lost, but now are found, as the old song says; were blind, but now they see! Hallelujah! *"For the Son of Man has come to seek and to save that which was lost."* (Luke 19:10).

Secondly, Psalm 24, especially verse 7 is important regarding those old, stone gates: *"Lift up your heads, O gates, and be lifted up, O ancient doors, that the King of glory may come in!"* And Psalm 118:19-24:

> "Open to me the gates of righteousness; I shall enter through them, I shall give thanks to the Lord. This is the gate of the Lord; the righteous will enter through it. I shall give thanks to Thee, for Thou hast answered me; and Thou hast become my salvation. The stone which the builders rejected has become the chief corner stone. This is the Lord's doing; it is marvelous in our eyes. This is the day the Lord has made; let us rejoice and be glad in it."

Then we decreed Psalm 100 and John 10. The man who enters by the gate is the true shepherd. We declared people not follow

352

strangers, but the One True Shepherd. Too many have gone by way of the "cattle gate," which is what the stone gate looked like in the back of the Supreme Court building. The Lord Jesus is the Good Shepherd and we asked that He lead us through His holy gates.

Gates full of the abundance of God are now opened!

For the shepherds in Iowa, the pastors, teachers, leaders in the churches...we speak upon their shoulders, a greater godly authority to impact Iowa!

"O Lord, speak now to Iowa!"

We prayed that justice and righteousness would always be applied here.

Mike saw by the spirit, someone who was studying. He saw this person as a law clerk before becoming a judge. He said this man will be significant in establishing good laws and will see to it that present and future decisions will be made righteously.

Note Wooden Cross Beam and Cannon

Mike went on to declare that this person will walk in truth, holiness and wisdom. He also prayed this person would not be wise by man's ways, but by God's ways.

It was noted that in the Old Testament, God gave judges before He gave kings. We repented for lack of prayer over our judges. In the past, we have abdicated our judges to the enemy. "Open our eyes, Lord!" We then prayed for godly men to arise from here. Let us turn our prayers to the judges! Isaiah 11:1-3 was pronounced in regard to this particular branch of government and we decreed Jesus is the Righteous Branch!

Our ROCK Next to Stone Gate

We prayed the spiritual realm here would change forever. It was proclaimed that people in authority would not operate out of their own wills, but the will of God; that they would be unable to do anything *but the will of God*! We proclaimed a "build up" of new people for godly justice.

"Awaken Iowa to its divine destiny in You, Oh God! Let this state not miss what You have for its people. Let us not be sleepy anymore!"

Conclusion

As we were about to leave, the clock tower read 10:17 AM. Combining all those numbers equals nine. Nine is strategically significant for this prophetic prayer journey! Thank you Lord! Praise you Lord! This number is the last of single digit numerals

Diane Leaming and Linda

beyond which there are merely combinations of the previous digits. Therefore it marks the **end.** It signifies **finality or judgment.** Iowa, awake! Let us recall that when Jesus was crucified for the sins of the world, it was the ninth hour when He cried out, "My God, my God, why have You forsaken me?" (Mark 15:34).

354

We need to take note of Acts 3:1 where at the ninth hour - the hour of prayer - Peter and John made their way to the Temple. Cornelius also was in prayer at the "ninth hour" when he encountered a heavenly vision (Acts 10:30)! Pray, Iowa, pray!

Wonderfully, the number nine also represents the nine fruits and nine gifts of the Holy Spirit (1 Cor. 12:8-10; Gal. 5:22-23). Fruitfulness and abundance has been ordained for Iowa!

We proclaimed, "Bring forth **that day** Lord! Bring holy ordination of Your purposes and plans. We stand in our **godly heritage** according to Isaiah 54 that these prayers will indeed bring epic changes, bearing much fruit for Thy kingdom! Hallelujah!"

God bless Iowa and God bless the USA!

TO CONTACT THE AUTHOR

Intimacy With God Ministries
P.O. Box 1294
Johnston, Iowa 50131-1294

Web site: www.intimacy-with-God.com
E-mail: LindaSchreurs@intimacy-with-God.com

OTHER BOOKS BY THIS AUTHOR:

ARMAGEDDON BRIDE
An Urgent Message to Mankind Before the End Times

Published by Creation House

Available at: www.intimacy-with-God.com

Printed in the United States
153469LV00002B/2/P